Dr. Monica-Maria Stapelberg has been employed at various universities for many years as a lecturer in history of literature, as well as medieval languages, medieval history and cultural studies. Since retiring from academia, she has had two books published, both aimed at the popular market. Monica lives on the east coast of Australia with her family.

STRANGE BUT TRUE

A historical background to popular
beliefs and traditions

MONICA-MARIA STAPELBERG

CRUX
PUBLISHING

To Fred,

My wonderful husband, lover, and best friend

CONTENTS

INTRODUCTION

Throughout history, humans have interpreted their surrounding world and its mysteries relative to their level of understanding. From ancient times to the Middle Ages and beyond, most of the population, from the humblest peasant to the most learned scholar, embraced a somewhat ignorant, sometimes preposterous and absurd viewpoint, when seen from a modern perspective. Because scientific explanations were unavailable, irrational fear and superstition of unexplained phenomena prevailed. Blind terror and sublime awe struck in the heart of the populace at the experiences of thunder, lightning, earthquakes, floods, droughts, mysterious sicknesses, and plagues. All such occurrences were attributed to the displeasure of higher powers, or the workings of demons, evil spirits, and witches.

The general populace often lived in dire circumstances and depended on the success of their crops and nature's continuing influence on their daily lives. Fuelled by illiteracy and ignorance, strange notions and beliefs thrived amongst humanity, where the poorer classes made up most of the population, and the distinction between rich and poor was enormous. An implicit belief in the power of witches, devils, fairies, dangerous mythological beasts, and various demons officially sanctioned and categorised by the Church, instilled horror and fear.

All these factors compounded to form the unquestioning assumption of supernatural forces external to humans, regarded as tyrannical, capricious, and highly dangerous, and hence, to be appeased or driven away at all costs. This led to the development of an intricate system of elaborate safeguards against unknown powers, thereby laying the foundation for many beliefs and traditions still observed.

Often, we are unaware that certain actions, gestures, and codes of etiquette, which we observe and perform on a day-to-day basis, are actually based on relics of long forgotten ancient beliefs, anchored in archaic ritual magic, past sacrificial observances, or simply fearful superstition. When someone sneezes, we immediately respond with a 'bless you', or we cover our mouths when yawning and coughing. We consider it ill mannered to point at someone and take pains not to leave our knives and forks crossed on our plates when having finished a meal. We believe these actions to be 'good manners' and do not realise they are originally born of superstitious dread. Why do we dress baby boys in true blue, trick or treat on Halloween, kiss under the mistletoe, wear the wedding ring on our ring finger, or show someone 'the finger' in contempt?

There is only a difference in degree between worshipping a tree – as our distant ancestors did – and touching wood, in the vague belief that to do so will ward off some calamity. We still christen a ship by breaking a champagne bottle against its bow, refer to ships and sailing vessels as 'she', throw coins in a fountain while making a wish, ceremoniously lay a building's foundation stone, and wet a newly built house's roof – reminiscent of a time when all these were considered magic acts to appease higher forces.

Relics from the past are buried like forgotten treasures in our figures of speech. We use these frequently, unaware of how ancient, profound, and loaded with symbolic and precise meaning many are. For example, we say everyone has a 'skeleton in the cupboard', not realising this once had a literal meaning. We say 'if looks could kill', which relates to the belief in the evil eye, still widely prevalent in many European countries, the Middle East, Asia, and Africa. Similarly, we refer to a 'lily-livered coward', an expression harking back to ancient divination practices; or we speak of 'walking in someone's shadow', once a universal taboo; or being 'spellbound', dating from a time when spells or words were thought to have the power to bind and root someone to the spot.

The material for this book was collected and researched over many years and pertains predominantly to Western culture. However, wherever beliefs and traditions have been found to be in common with those of cultures in other parts of the world, references to their similarities have been made. The myriads of facts presented highlight the historic origins of many beliefs and traditions, as well as their fascinating and often 'strange' but 'true' origins.

Monica-Maria Stapelberg

I

MAGIC PRACTICES

A belief in various forms of magic was once common in most communities and still exists in many societies. For example, in Aug 2014 newspapers in the United Kingdom widely reported the discovery of a young Nigerian boy's dismembered body floating in the River Thames near Tower Bridge in London. Experts testified that the wounds on the boy were consistent with those of ritual killings practiced in western and southern parts of Africa where human sacrifices are still often used to tap supernatural powers for magic purposes. Every year hundreds of Africans lose their lives in ritual murders by tribal members who go in search of human body parts at the behest of witchdoctors or traditional medicine men. These human body parts are used in magic rituals or potions, to ensure the witchdoctors' 'clients' have success in finance, business, politics or other ventures. Similar news reports are still found in many developing countries, where traditions in magic continue.

Magic, as a protective and procuring agent, has existed universally in all cultures since ancient times. It can be described as a ritual activity that aims to produce an affect on the physical world by using supernatural powers. Ritual magic also attempts to control powerful supernatural forces such as a spirit, a god, a demon, or a cosmic force through elaborate ceremonies. Magic's ultimate goal is supreme authority over all things, but a distinction must be made between black and white magic. Whereas black magic aims to destroy and harm, white magic aims to affect the community and individuals beneficially.

In traditional tribal societies, the magician or sorcerer is seen as all-powerful and is never questioned. For example, during the Zulu uprising in South Africa in 1906, the witchdoctor applied war medicine, believed to immunize the Zulu warriors against bullets, to all battle-ready men. Believing in the witchdoctor's power and his medicine or magic, hundreds of Zulus, armed only with assegais, hurled themselves at the British batteries of rifles and guns. They were mowed down almost to a man. Yet, no one would have thought to question the medicine man's efficacy – the loss of life simply meant the enemy's medicine was stronger. Generally magic has always been seen as immune to failure – if it does not work, the procedure followed is deemed incorrect or the counter-magic applied is seen as superior.

Magic practices range from rituals involving the entire community, such as those for successful hunting or a plentiful harvest, to peripheral or minor magic acts concerned with individual community members. Simple magic, often called sorcery, involves practices such as tying or untying knots; rituals involving human or animal blood, hair, and nails to cast spells; and sticking pins or sharpened splinters in waxen images, small dolls, or poppets. There are two main types of magic: contagious magic and sympathetic magic.

Contagious magic is based on the belief that someone can be hurt by damaging or inflicting harm on anything that has been in contact with that person. Therefore, Australian Aborigines put glass, sharp crystals, or bone splinters in an enemy's footprints, believing this lamed the man. An interesting parallel to this notion is found in India, where it was believed that an enemy could be vanquished by tying the dust of his footprints in a leaf and burning it. Similarly, it was thought that a thorn placed in the footprints of a runaway thief would make him grind to a halt.

The idea that special influences are inherent in particular objects is universal. A magic connection is believed to exist not only between a person and any severed body parts, such as hair or nails, or footprints and handprints, but also with every item with which the person has had physical contact. Therefore, many cultures took great care to dispose of bodily refuse. Whoever managed to get possession of these items could work his or her will from a distance on the hapless owner. The same association of ideas is shown in the meticulous care many people formerly took not to let anything they owned or used fall into their adversaries' hands. To this day, abandoned gypsy encampments are always left cleaned of all their possessions whether still useful or useless, except for the fire ashes and sometimes a stick left standing upright in the ground to indicate their having been there. The same principle applies to the Australian Aborigines who have always taken great care not to let anything belonging to their tribe fall into the hands of another.

In sympathetic magic, however, the effective principle is that 'like cures like', or 'like influences like' and that any effect may be produced by simply imitating it. Therefore, anything regarded as evil may be used to repel evil. During the Middle Ages, in times of plague, it was firmly believed that any poisonous substance such as arsenic carried on one's person, would draw to it the 'contagious air' of the plague. Another more current example can be found in a CNN report of 9 June 2014 titled: 'Albino activist fights witchcraft murders'. The news item relates that in Tanzania and other African countries, where little is known about the genetic disorder affecting albinos, atrocities committed against them are still prevalent. In Tanzania alone, dozens of albinos have been mutilated and slaughtered in recent years, their limbs hacked off and used in potions or magic rituals to bring 'good luck'. The news item further states that traditionally, albinos in African societies are viewed with great superstition, regarded as demons, ghostlike evil beings, or spirits. It is most likely that because albinos are regarded as fundamentally 'evil' by these societies, witchdoctors use their body parts to repel evil – hence inviting good fortune or 'luck'.

Sympathetic magic is found worldwide amongst all societies at some or other stage in their history. A belief in sympathetic magic is evident in cannibalism, in that by eating a brave enemy warrior's flesh, his many virtues might be absorbed. The Tupi Indians of the Amazon Basin especially prized dead prisoners' genitals, indicating that their sexual prowess was highly esteemed and thought transferable. The notion that by eating the flesh or drinking the blood of another human, one could absorb that person's nature into one's own is one that appears among various tribal peoples in many forms. It lies at the root of drinking enemies' fresh blood and the habit many early huntsmen practised of eating some part, such as the liver, of dangerous carnivores so that the animal's courage might pass into them.

Many tribal peoples once customarily ingested brave men's flesh and blood to inspire courage. The Australian Aborigines rubbed themselves with a killed enemy's belly fat so that all his qualities, mental and physical, might be communicated to the vanquisher. Deep within the jungle of Indonesia's Papua Province, the Kombai and Korowai tribes still practise ritual cannibalism of their enemies, thereby ingesting their specific attributes. On 13 July 2012, The Daily Telegraph, a British newspaper, reported the arrest of 29 alleged cannibals in Papua New Guinea's jungle interior. The perpetrators were charged with the murders of seven suspected witchdoctors. Cult members had purportedly eaten the witchdoctors' brains and penises to attain supernatural powers and sexual prowess.

Apart from sympathetic magic being evident in cannibalism, it is found in countless other everyday cultural activities – always reflecting the principle that 'like influences like' and that 'any effect may be produced by simply representing it'. Sympathetic magic is the reason women sowing rice in Sumatra would let their hair hang loose behind their backs – the hair blowing in the breeze was seen to mimic a luxuriant growth of rice. In the same way, buffalo dances by Apache warriors, were performed to lure buffalo herds for the hunters – the warriors ceremoniously clad in head-dresses made from buffalo heads, miming the herd movements.

Similarly, to induce the growth of breasts, young girls in various Australian regions fashioned mud breasts and wore these while holding 'mud babies' in paper-bark carriers. A traditional form of love magic in western Arnhem Land, Australia, consisted of men drawing the likeness of a desired female on the wall of a rock shelter. If the chosen woman was, however, not enamoured of the man trying to court her, he could 'magically' forge an attraction by simply drawing her having sexual relations with himself. In the same context, Australian Aborigines used sympathetic magic to try to induce pregnancy by repeatedly drawing a woman with a foetus, or breastfeeding a child, in the sand.

Sympathetic magic was similarly also believed to influence the elements – through imitating a desired effect, it was believed that that aspect of the weather would be produced. Therefore, to persuade the setting sun to rise again, the ancient Europeans lit bonfires. Especially at times of solar changes such as equinoxes or solstices, these bonfires were believed to encourage and strengthen the weakening sun in its renewal. Thus, by making a fire, the sun would be compelled to shine, and by sprinkling water on the ground with a bunch of twigs, rain would be made to fall. In this context, rituals used around the globe in appeasing and coercing the rain-gods were many and varied. For example, Australian Aborigines and West African tribes squirted water from the mouth to imitate a fine drizzle of rain and, in so doing, induce it. Ancient Mexican magic ceremonies included pouring water from pitchers to induce the gods to pour forth rain, while the black smoke from sacrifices was believed to generate clouds. Similarly, the fringed trimmings and tassels of Red Indian tribal dress were intended to evoke rain, the fringes' lively movement simulating rainfall.

In Europe, the spread of Christianity in no way halted the once pagan rituals. The focus simply shifted, and rainmaking processions and ceremonies then centred on such acts as dipping a cross or any relic in holy water or dipping the statues of saints or holy personages in rivers and lakes during times of drought. In Navarre, France, it was customary to pray to St. Peter for rain, and it is reputed that on one occasion, when there was no rain, one village's inhabitants carried the saint's statue to the river, and despite the irate priest's outrage, submersed it in the water. In the Outer Hebrides, on the Island of Uist, the locals had a cross set up, specifically called the Water Cross. When rain was needed, this cross was raised, and when enough rain had fallen, the cross was laid flat on the ground. Similarly, if popular legend is to be believed, the monks of Iona in Ireland shook their patron St. Columba's tunic in the wind to procure rain.

All harvest customs, including Maypoles, the marriage of trees, the presence of the King and Queen of May, and all the emblems of animal and vegetable fertility, could be said to fall into the category of sympathetic magic. These rites were intended to stimulate nature, to procure the desired effects of fertility, and to ensure an abundant harvest. Analogous harvest customs have been found in places as far apart as Sweden, India, Borneo, Africa, and North and South America.

A subsection of sympathetic magic is called image magic, which also aims to produce a specific effect by simply imitating it.

Image Magic

Image magic is based on the idea that if an image made of a person is harmed or destroyed, then that person physically feels the injuries done to the image because of the physical sympathy existing between the person and his or her image. The custom of sticking pins into a person's effigy in order to harm him is by no means only linked with voodoo and not confined to the Indies. In the 1950s, it was still common practice in scattered backwoods of the United States to stab doll-figures with pins and other sharp objects to harm the person whose likeness was reflected in the doll.

This form of magic was known in Egypt, Mesopotamia, India, Greece, amongst the Romans, and in many other countries throughout the world from ancient to modern times. The practice is referred to in the Old Testament: '... for handfuls of barley and for pieces of bread, to slay souls.'[1] This relates to the making of a figurine, representing one's enemy, out of dough and repeatedly stabbing it, thereby in effect killing the represented person. Whereas crafting the statue of a person from wood or stone required skill, making one from dough was easy and cheap.

The ancient Egyptians revealed their belief in this type of magic by placing many little figures made of stone, pottery, or wood, called ushebtiu, in the tombs of their dead. These figurines were representations believed to provide the dead with servants, attendants, and combatants in the hereafter.

Curiously, during the Middle Ages, image magic was frequently used as a method of attempted murder. European history is filled with many failed political assassinations of this kind, and although this seems absurd to us today, they were criminal by intent, as the objective was to deprive the victim of his or her life. For example, Caroline of Brunswick (1764–1821), unhappy and neglected wife of the prince regent,[2] apparently spent her lonely evenings making waxen images of her husband. She would stick these with pins and then slowly melt them over the fire, hoping to rid herself of the man.[3] Similarly, in 1591, Richard Batte, a surgeon from Burton-on-Trent, was accused in a court of law of using the same technique to try to murder his mother-in-law.

In England and Italy it was still customary during the last century to stick a pig's heart full of pins and thorns. This object was then hidden in someone's house, either for protection or for harm. It was believed that the inflicted shrivelled pig's heart caused suffering and eventual death to a targeted victim's heart. In Europe, such pig hearts were hidden in chimneys and house walls and have often been found in old homes during renovations or when the houses were demolished to make way for modern buildings.

It is interesting to note that the same parallel is found on the Australian continent. The Yolngu Aborigines of Arnhem Land drew their opponent's image on a certain type of tree and then rubbed poison on this image to kill or poison the opponent. Alternately, the opponent's image could be drawn on a so-called poison tree, a tree that should not generally be touched or its fruit eaten. The enemy's likeness placed on the tree was then thought to cause bone disease in the person targeted.[4] The belief in image magic persists in a notion still found in many Asian, African, and Middle Eastern countries that it is dangerous to have one's photo taken, believing that if harm came to the photograph, this could physically affect the person in the picture.

The Healing Touch of Class

In the past, the touch of a reigning monarch's hand was thought imbued with healing powers, and for centuries, this widely held conviction persisted.

The implicit belief in the supernatural healing powers of sovereigns is a relic of the ancient doctrine of the divinity of kingship. The ancient Sumerians first developed the concept of divinely ordained kings, descended from heaven as primary intermediaries between God and humankind. It was believed in ancient cultures that kings and rulers were sons of the Holy Sun. Therefore, in line with priestly tradition, the first Egyptian king, a certain Menes, meaning 'the sole light', and all subsequent ruling sovereigns were seen as the living image of the sun-god Ra. Similarly, the early Babylonian and Mesopotamian monarchs were worshipped as gods in their lifetime. The emperor of China was regarded as the 'Son of Heaven' and the chief priest of his people. The same notions also existed about Mayan, Aztec, and Incan rulers. Even in modern times, vestiges of this ancient belief remain in many cultures. For example, the word king in Thai means 'god of the land.' In the same context, the Japanese emperor has been viewed as a god throughout history, and in the twenty-first century, Emperor Akihito continues to bless land and crops.

The exalted status of monarchs and rulers was believed to impart distinctive excellence on them. Hence, they were credited with healing powers, which their subjects thought they could pass on by their touch. The priest-kings of ancient Egypt and Babylon; the Roman Emperors Constantine, Vespasian, and Hadrian; and the Norwegian King Olaf were known to heal by touch.

In England, Edward the Confessor was the first monarch credited with such powers, before the Norman Conquest in 1066. Throughout the reign of the Tudors, the touch of the king's hand for healing seems to have been regularly performed. King Charles II (1630–1685) is reputed to have touched up to 600 people at one sitting and up to 92,100 during his reign.

The touch of kings was believed especially to heal scrofula, a tubercular disease of the lymph glands, which on this account came to be called The King's Evil. On Easter Sunday in 1686, King Louis XIV of France is said to have touched 1,600 scrofula sufferers. Queen Anne in 1712 was the last English monarch credited with the healing touch. During that year, she is reputed to have touched 200 sufferers, among them, the then infant Samuel Johnson who later became one of England's great literary figures.[5] French kings continued the custom until 1825.

A factor, which, of course, must be mentioned, is that scrofula was only rarely fatal, and the disease was naturally prone to lengthy periods of remission or spontaneous cures. But the superstitious believed all miraculous cures of the disease came from the divine touch of kings, and consequently, all failures were simply put down to a lack of faith.

Curative Powers Associated with the Dead

A report in the well-known German magazine Peter Moosleitner's Interessantes Magazin,[6] describes how, after a public execution in Berlin in 1864, the executioners' helpers dipped strips of cloth in the running blood still gushing from the two criminals' neck stumps. These dripping little bits of material could not sell fast enough, even at exorbitant prices, among the throng of people milling around the execution platform.

Throughout the ages, certain preconceptions have dominated the practice of healing. For example, it was firmly believed that anything related to death had healing ability and that sanctity had curative powers. This is why immediately after the beheading of Charles I in 1649, every small fragment of the execution block, the bloodstained sand, and even strands of his hair were sold for their believed healing properties.

In olden times, when little was known about the causes of illness and disease, it was generally believed in Europe and on other continents that evil spirits were the source of all maladies. Only the well to do could afford conventional medicines and medical treatments of the time, despite often involving very painful and unpleasant procedures and treatments without painkillers or anaesthetics. Dependent on largely ineffectual methods such as bloodletting and purging, medical success rate was low. Therefore, the public turned to alternative healing methods, many of which, of course, originated in superstitious beliefs.

Until 1868, when public hangings in England ceased, offenders were left hanging indefinitely and often coated with tar to delay decay, making it quite clear to all passers-by that crime did not pay. Many deliberate indignities happened with these exposed corpses of convicted criminals. It was thought that because such perpetrators were evil, illnesses – all believed to originate through evil forces – could therefore be repelled and cured by using the various body parts of the unfortunates. Often their teeth were pulled out and kept as charms against toothache. The association, following the principle of sympathetic magic, was that like cures like. Body parts, especially hands and thumbs, were simply cut off and used for varying nefarious needs.

Throughout the ages, powdered fragments of a corpse's skull were administered to cure fits, or if illicitly removed altogether, the skull was used as a drinking cup for epileptics. In 77 CE, Pliny the Elder recommended water drunk from the skull of anyone who had suffered a violent death as a cure for epilepsy.[7] The custom was prevalent as recent as only a few decades ago when it was still believed in certain areas of the Scottish highlands that well water drunk from an ancestor's skull was a certain cure for epilepsy.[8]

Splinters of a human skull, grated and ingested or made into a poultice, were believed to be a certain cure for rabies and arthritis. This remedy was also considered effective against epilepsy and other serious conditions. When King Charles II of England faced the final curtain, doctors administered all manner of cures and potions. When these failed to work, he was given the guaranteed cure of forty drops of extract made from a man's skull. However, even this proved unsuccessful in saving the king's life, and he died five days later.

Moss growing in a dead person's skull was used as a cure for ailments as varied as the plague and toothache. Moss taken particularly from a dead man's skull – dried, powdered, and used as snuff – was thought to cure headaches. Swiss physician, Paracelsus (1493–1541), first introduced chemistry to medicine and was famous throughout Europe for his cures and remedies. Some of his treatments were, however, bizarre to say the least. To treat wounds, he recommended mixing red wine and earthworms with powdered fragments from the skull of a man recently killed or hanged.[9] Besides the skull, Paracelsus recommended the powdered remains of executed criminals as a cure-all for everything from asthma to poisoning. A more gruesome remedy advocated by Pliny the Elder was to scrape sore gums with the tooth of a man who had recently been executed.[10] In connection with skulls, it is important to note that oracular powers were thought to issue especially from the skulls of departed chieftains and kings, a concept based on the belief that the head was the centre of spiritual power. The Celts preserved the heads of important personages in cedar wood oil, and many are the tales in Teutonic and Nordic mythology describing the gold-trimmed skulls of the enemy used as drinking cups – perhaps to imbibe inspiration with intoxication.

Many healing powers were also attributed to a dead man's hand, especially if that person had died violently. A notable example is the right hand of St. Edmond Arrowsmith. The hand, preserved with great care and wrapped in white silk, is still kept in St Oswald's Roman Catholic Church in Ashton-in-Makerfield.[11] At a time when England was largely Protestant, Father Edmond was convicted of trying to convert Protestants to the Roman Catholic faith and was later executed at Lancaster in 1628 for this 'heinous' crime. After death, his right hand was severed, a custom frequently observed following executions. This holy hand was regarded with great veneration for centuries, and pilgrims came from all parts of the countryside to be cured from various ailments by touching it. The Catholic Church finally officially approved the hand for public veneration in 1934.

The hand of someone who had died violently was considered to have the power to dispel most diseases, especially skin diseases, birthmarks, and growths or swellings of various kinds. It was still customary in England during the late nineteenth century for sufferers of various ailments to crowd around a gibbet hoping to receive the 'dead stroke' on execution days, paying the presiding hangman handsomely for his services.

High on the popularity poll were also chips or cuttings from the gallows or a gibbet, where one or more persons had been executed. Such pieces were worn close to the skin and believed to cure all ailments. Wood splinters from the gallows were especially effective against toothache, and in Sussex, a popular cure for ague, a recurrent fever marked by chills and sweating, was to wear a necklace made of wood chips from the gallows.[12]

Equally cherished for various cures was the hangman's rope. Pliny the Elder in his Natural History advocated binding the temples with a recently used hangman's rope as a sure way of curing headaches.[13] Naturally, hangmen throughout the ages made a tidy profit on the side by selling bits of recently used rope, and until the middle of the nineteenth century, when public hangings ceased in England and other European countries, such pieces of rope were readily available for sale.

Death was so shrouded in superstition that parts or pieces of coffins were still pilfered to cure illnesses around Europe in the late nineteenth century. Linen used to wrap the corpse before its burial was considered lucky and prized for its curative powers and, consequently, usually did not remain with the dead for very long. Similarly, rings made of decayed coffin handles were worn as amulets against cramp, rheumatism, and epilepsy. Henry VIII reputedly wore a cure-all ring made from the metal of coffin hinges,[14] and as the following example goes to prove, belief in the healing powers of the dead was still evident in England during Victorian times, when a woman in Manchester requested a pinch of clay from a priest's grave to protect her children from epilepsy.[15]

Similarly, we find associated beliefs in Australia amongst the Aborigines. Tribes of the Murray River believed that a rope or band made from a dead person's hair, tied around the head or loins cured and prevented all illness. Amongst some tribes, it was customary when arriving at a burial site, for the women to take handfuls of grave sand and to sniff and inhale its smell and rub it over their bodies, especially their legs. The smell of grave sand was thought to make them strong and healthy, and rubbing it on their legs was believed to keep them from getting tired on their long journeys.

The Scapegoat

Every year on January 13, a curious festival, the Konomiya Naked Festival, which started in 767 CE, occurs in modern Japan. A week before the festival, a 'man of god' is chosen from among the citizens. Once chosen, he takes up abode at the Shrine of Konomiya, where he will stay until the festival, purifying himself by shaving all his body hair and ingesting nothing but water and dry rice. On the day of the male-only festival, the shrine throngs with hundreds of men wrapped in bleached cotton but naked from the waist up. When the man of god appears, everyone desperately tries to touch him. Because of the milling crowd, getting close enough is difficult, but anyone who succeeds in touching the 'scapegoat' is guaranteed to have transferred all misfortune for the coming twelve months.

The notion that misfortune and sin can be transferred onto another being is ancient and universal. The expression to 'make someone a scapegoat', meaning to blame someone else for one's own wrongdoing, has become a metaphor but refers to what was once a very real occurrence.

The term scapegoat was first coined in 1530 when the English religious reformer, William Tyndale, translated the Hebrew Bible into English. He wrongly translated azázél, a proper name of uncertain derivation, as 'the goote on which the lotte fell to scape', that is, as 'scapegoat'.[16]

According to the Book of Leviticus,[17] each year on the Day of Atonement, the holiest festival on the Jewish calendar, the Israelites sacrificed two he-goats. One animal was offered up to God, that He might absolve the Jews of their sins, and the priest placed his hands on the other goat's head and confessed all the Children of Israel's iniquities and transgressions over it. The goat 'laden with sins' was then chased into the wilderness. This goat was conceived as embodying the spirit of Azazel, the fallen angel perpetually bound and chained in the wilderness. By its escape, it could carry away the Children of Israel's sins. The traditional role of the scapegoat linked with sin and impurity might have been a contributing factor to its becoming an animal of Satan in early Christianity – a connection it retains.

Not very different in principle is a sacred practice amongst the ancient Egyptian priesthood, described by the Greek historian, Herodotus (circa 490–420 BCE), of conferring all disasters threatening the community on the heads of sacrificial bulls: '...they take the beast to the appropriate altar and light a fire; then after pouring a libation of wine and invoking the god by name, they slaughter it, cut off its head and flay the carcass. The head is loaded with curses and taken away [...]. The curses they pronounce take the form of a prayer that any disaster which threatens either themselves or their country may be diverted and fall upon the severed head of the beast'.[18]

The custom of killing an animal, or even a human, on whom a certain evil has been transferred, in order to banish that evil, is widely diffused. In most societies it was customary to have a general expulsion of sins once a year. As nations became civilised, they did not abstain from human sacrifice altogether, but used criminals who were to be executed to absorb the sins of a society. During the sixth century BCE, the Greeks sacrificed a deformed or particularly ugly person as a scapegoat when any calamity befell them. The ancient Greeks also carried out a ritual called 'the expulsion of hunger' once a year by beating a slave while chasing him outdoors with the words: 'Out with hunger, in with wealth and health'.[19] Similar customs are found in India, Japan, and various African countries. The Ga people of Ghana still celebrate the festival of homowo, 'jeering at hunger', by feasting for days on specifically rich foods, prepared to defy hunger.[20]

The so-called Wicker Man is still part of neo-pagan festivals in Scotland, England and Seratoga Springs in the USA in modern times. Julius Caesar first described this gigantic human figure, looming in the skyline, made of sticks and branches, consumed by crackling flames. The Wicker Man was filled with livestock as well as screaming men, usually criminals or prisoners of war, and set alight by the ancient Celts, as offerings to appease the angry pagan gods. Similarly it was still customary in European countries at the end of the nineteenth century to light bonfires outside churches, to burn the Judas Man, a straw effigy representing the communities' accumulated sins, a Christianised version of the scapegoat.

In the same context, it was customary once in European countries to hire so-called sin-eaters for small amounts of money to attend funerals and to take on the sins of the deceased. The dead person's relatives prepared a meal for the sin-eater, which he had to eat on the coffin of the deceased, symbolically ingesting the sins this person committed and making the journey to the afterlife easier. The custom of sin-eating was also believed to stop the dead from walking or haunting the neighbourhood. Because of the life he had chosen, all villagers abhorred the sin-eater as unclean, given to witchcraft and unholy practices, and regarded as unfit for any social intercourse with his fellow creatures. Therefore, he generally lived isolated from everyone else, avoided like a leper, and was only sought when a death had occurred, and his services were needed. Once he had eaten the food placed on the corpse or coffin for his consumption, the utensils were immediately burned. Sin-eating was popular in Wales and Scotland and in many other parts of England and Europe during the Middle Ages and right up to the beginning of the nineteenth century.

To this day, orthodox Jews transfer transgressions to a fowl, the Kapporah Huenchen, as it is known in Yiddish phraseology, on the eve of Yom Kippur, also called The Day of Judgement, characterised by prayer and fasting. A live chicken is grabbed by the legs and swung around the head of a man, woman, or child with a prayer that the chicken absorb the person's sins. The chicken is offered as atonement, and by its death, symbolically shields the person from punishment.

The Transference of Disease

Universally, animals have been used as a vehicle for carrying away or transferring disease. In Morocco, the highland folk customarily transfer a headache to a lamb or goat, and then beat the animal until it falls to the ground, believing that the headache will thus be passed on. In Sumatra, women who remain childless perform a ceremony of making the curse fly away. After sacrificing three grasshoppers, which, for this ceremony, represent a buffalo, a horse, and a cow, a swallow is set free with the prayer that the curse might fall on its head and be carried away by the bird.

In many African countries, it was and still is customary for witchdoctors to conjure up the demons of disease when curing a very ill patient, and then ritually take the illness into their own bodies. The witchdoctor then reclines on a bier, shaming death for some time, and eventually jumps up to claim his reward.

In Peru, twenty-first century folkloric medical practices to extract illness and disease include 'passing the egg' or 'passing the guinea pig'. The curative procedure entails rubbing an egg or a guinea pig over the patient's affected body area, thereby absorbing the malady. The patient either buries or ingests the egg, now thought to contain the sickness, to then pass the sickness out of the body naturally. Similarly, the guinea pig is chased away or killed.

In England, an advocated cure for whooping cough was to pass the patient under a donkey's belly, contending that the donkey absorbed the cough. This cure was especially popular in Scarborough, where many donkeys were for hire, specifically for such a purpose.[21] Similarly, it was customary in seventeenth century Ireland to place a live trout near the mouth of a child with whooping cough. Immediately after inhaling the cough, the trout had to be thrown in a fast flowing stream, carrying off the disease. Alternately, a hair was plucked from a sufferer's head and then fed to a dog. If the dog coughed up the hair, as it got stuck in its throat, this was seen as a sign that the whooping cough had been successfully transferred to the animal.[22]

In European countries, it was customary in the past to preserve a sick person's nail clippings in wax, and by sticking this mixture on someone's door, thereby transferring the illness to a different person. A popular superstition contended that to cure the fever, one should take the sufferer's nail parings and hair clippings, place them in a bag, and put this under the threshold of a neighbour's door. So much for 'love thy neighbour'. Hundreds of years earlier, the ancient Romans similarly used nail parings embedded in wax, from fever-suffering patients and symbolically transferred the disease by sticking the wax onto an unsuspecting stranger's door.

In the seventeenth and eighteenth century, it was also quite common in Europe to transfer sickness and disease that resisted conventional treatment to the family cat by dousing the poor animal with the patient's washing water and then driving it from the house.

In the early parts of the twentieth century, farmers in England and on the Continent customarily kept one or two goats with their other livestock, believing that the goats absorbed all physical ills that would otherwise affect the livestock.[23] It was thought that the stronger the smell emanating from the billy goat, the less likelihood of any cows, horses, or other livestock falling ill. Responding to such beliefs, owners usually lovingly cared for their goats. If a goat was unaffordable, a goat's horns, a hoof, or simply some hair nailed over the barn door, had the same magic effect in warding off evil.

Like a Hole in the Head

At one time or another, we have all heard it said: 'I need this like I need a hole in the head', which is not as unusual as it seems.

Trepanning (from Greek trypanon, meaning 'borer') is probably the oldest surgery known to humankind and refers to boring, drilling, cutting, sawing, or scraping a hole in the human skull. The Dutch doctor, Bart Hughes, started the modern trepanning movement in Europe in the 1960s. He advocated that the increased volume of blood flow in the brain's capillaries, caused by 'a hole in the head' achieved higher levels of consciousness and increased function in certain brain parts, in effect restoring the cranium to infancy, when the skull is unsealed. How prevalent the practice has become is evidenced by an article published on March 4, 2000, in the British Medical Journal that explicitly warns about the dangers of trepanning after many websites advocated do-it-yourself trepanation to treat depression and other illnesses.

Trepanning, although for different reasons, was practised as early as 10,000 BCE in Europe, South America, Asia, Polynesia, Melanesia, the Pacific Islands, and some parts of Africa. This cranial operation is of interest and importance to archaeology, to anthropology, and to medicine, and seems to have been widespread in certain areas. For example, out of 120 prehistoric skulls found at a burial site in France dated to about 6500 BCE, some 40 skulls had undergone trepanation. Similarly, amongst the exhibits at the New Grange Visitor Centre in Ireland is an example of a prehistoric trepanned skull. Hippocrates, the Father of Medicine (460-370 BCE), gave specific directions on trepanning in his classic medical text on Injuries of the Head and the Greek physician, Galen (c.130-210 CE), later elaborated further on the operation.

Anthropologists believe that the purpose behind this painful surgery related to extracting practically all head ailments. These included demons and evil spirits of the possessed and the removal of foreign bodies, real or imagined – so-called 'stones of insanity' – fractures, inflammations, headaches, vertigo, and deafness. Often, a patient demanded the operation, spurred on by the belief that black magic or an evil-working sorcerer had projected specific material objects into his head. Amazingly, in ancient times, most people seem to have survived the procedure.

Trepanation was performed while the patient was fully awake, often sandwiched between two planks or frames, held down and kept immobile by relatives and helpers. The cranium usually healed after a period, forming new bone. There is, however, disconcertingly abundant evidence of people undergoing the procedure several times!

During the Middle Ages and the Renaissance Period, trepanation was frequently practiced. Barber surgeons often trepanned those suffering from 'falling sickness' and to relieve chronic headaches. Those patients dying after the procedure usually died of sepsis, and not the procedure itself.

Bone pieces cut from the skull were usually kept as protective charms or ground up to cure various ailments. In Mesoamerica, there is archaeological evidence of trepanation, but also of skull mutilation and modification carried out after the death of captives and enemies. Pre-Columbian art depicts rulers adorned with their enemies' modified skulls and skull racks displaying rows and rows of sacrificial victims' skulls.

Curative, Sacred Waters

A drive on the A832 to the famous Clootie Well near the village of Munlochy, Scotland, reveals a curious location. As the road enters a forested area, passing motorists are treated to a strange sight of hundreds of bits of rags and cloths hanging from the trees and bushes. These cloths have all been in contact with a sick person. Such clooties, still placed here near the well are the remnants of a tradition dating back thousands of years.

Archaeological evidence dating to c. 1500 BCE has shown that wells, ponds, springs, rivers, and especially thermal water sources were places of pilgrimage throughout Europe. These were regarded as sacred sites, piercing deep into the Earth's bowels and hence seen as linking the world of the living with the underworld.

Water from such sources was believed to have great curative powers, and tales of miraculous healing waters are common in the folklore of most nations. In fairy tales, such waters are usually described as the Well of True Water, the Well of the World, Cordial Balsam, or Living Waters. The quest for such Water of Life, which was thought to have the power to cure the sick, revive the dead, cure blindness, and impart strength, youth, and loveliness, forms the nucleus of a large group of fairy tales worldwide.

Around Europe, thousands of votive offerings, dedicated to the water spirits or gods thought to dwell within, have been found in wells, ponds, lakes, and other water sources. High on the popularity poll of offerings were wooden and stone figurines. Often, the figurines represent only a certain body part, such as a leg, an arm, or a head, implying that people suffering afflictions in certain parts of their body, would throw a representation of only that particular body-part in the curative waters, in the hope that the powers of the water spirits or the gods would cure them.

Representations of specific body parts as votive offerings are very common. A fitting example is the Isola Tiberina on the Tiber River in Rome, where a large temple was built to Aesculapius, the god of healing. Archaeological remains have been found indicating that votive offerings were made to the god here. Such votive offerings included countless representations of arms, legs, heads, and other body parts.

Similar rituals are still found in modern times at Fatima, Portugal, and Lourdes, France. At the many small shops outside the shrines of Fatima and Lourdes, wax casts representing countless body parts and organs are for sale to devout pilgrims seeking a cure. The devout buy and ceremoniously burn the appropriate wax cast as a votive offering in a specially enclosed area, in effect, psychologically dispelling the malady through the offering.

The hot spring in Bath, England, is another example of votive offerings made to cause healing and good fortune. In Celtic times, the spring was renowned as a gateway to the underworld. Until the present time, hot water at the rate of more than a million litres a day rises to the surface here and has been doing so for thousands of years. The Romans built a temple dedicated to the goddess Sulis Minerva, a deity with healing powers, next to the spring. The mineral-rich water supplied the ornately decorated bathing complex, which attracted pilgrims from across the Roman Empire. Many votive offerings, including more than twelve thousand coins, were thrown in the sacred spring, where the spirit of the goddess of healing was thought to dwell in ancient times. Similarly, in Switzerland, Germany, France, and Denmark, such votive offerings have been found in almost every lake and pond.

In later times, such offerings were often replaced with pieces of cloth, tied to the surrounding vegetation overhanging various healing springs, lakes, ponds, and wishing wells, as is still the case at Munlochy, Scotland. Everyone afflicted with disease who came to these healing waters hung a piece of cloth torn from their clothes on a bush nearby, in this way symbolically transferring the disease or ailment to the vegetation. As the piece of cloth rotted away, the illness was also believed to slowly recede. All who ventured here took great care never to touch or remove any pieces of cloth – otherwise, the sickness or disease would simply transfer to that person.

During Christian times, such wells, ponds, and springs were given the names of local saints to divert the faithful from the pagan customs linked to these water sources. By Christianising the springs, they were, in effect, put under the protection of the local saint, who then simply took over the healing powers originally related to water spirits. All superstition attached to holy wells in Britain and Europe date to ancient times when the belief in water spirits prevailed, and this has sometimes resulted in a curious synthesis of Christian and pagan practice. At St-Jean-du-Doit, in France, for instance, the parish priest leads a procession yearly to renew the spring's healing qualities by dipping a relic, St. John the Baptist's finger, into the water.

On the other side of the globe in Australia, it was similarly customary amongst the Aborigines to apply water's healing powers. In Healers of Arnhem Land, John Cawte describes various healing practices amongst the Aborigines, and how a healing well is excavated by hand in a dune near a billabong.[24] The supplicant is a man who has lost his vitality. The medicine man ministers to him and lowers him into the healing well, while chosen onlookers sing to the Earth's spirits to dispel the bad spirits causing the sickness. Then, the 'cured' man is raised from the well – an account that once could have come from any country in Europe.

What's in a Name?

In the distant past, the first name was not only regarded as a means of identification and differentiation, but also was believed to be endowed with magical properties containing the person's soul essence. A name was seen as an integral part of the person who bore it. Therefore, the choice of a name was not only important, but most of all, it was essential not to reveal it to anyone. To know the name of someone rendered the hapless person into one's power. The same principle also applied to gods, angels, and demons. To have known someone or something's true name and its pronunciation and use was to be able to tap its power.

Around the world, amongst most societies, the fear of keeping one's real name secret can be traced to some or other period in that society's history. Amongst the American Indian tribes from the shores of the Atlantic to the Pacific, a person's real name was always concealed. Famous American Indians such as Hiawatha of the Mohawk and Pocahontas of the Powhatan are only known to us by their assumed names. Taboos on speaking one's name still exist amongst some North and South American Indians. Such taboos are also found as far as the Philippines and New Guinea.

All Australian Aborigines have a secret and personal name given by the elders at birth, known only to the initiated, because a stranger knowing the secret name otherwise would have power over the individual. In Aboriginal society, there were secret names, personal names, nicknames, kin names, age-status terms, terms of social status, and terms for membership of social divisions. Naming an Aboriginal child was by no means a matter for the parents alone, and near and distant kin were consulted. The name chosen was regarded as a gift, bestowed as if it were a valuable object. As in other parts of the world, the name was regarded as part of the child's personality, not to be treated lightly. The tie between the child and someone else carrying the same name always remained a special one, and when one of them died the name went out of use, and the other was called by a different name.

To this day, a child's real name is concealed in Abyssinian society and a nickname used instead so that the maleficent spirit called Bouda cannot do harm to one whose name he does not know.[25]

In ancient Egypt, the naming ceremony was conducted in secret, as power could be exercised over an individual by uttering his personal name. Thus, the ancient Egyptians considered it necessary to have two names: a 'great name' and a 'little name'. The great, true name was kept secret, as it was a part of the person's spiritual being, and the little name was used instead. The great name was uttered with magical spells to open the way and secure the spirit's welfare to the land of the dead. To neutralise the powers of demons assailing the spirit on its way to the land of the dead, one needed to know and pronounce their names. In the Egyptian Book of the Dead, the names of demons, which might come on the spirit in its passage through the underworld, are explicitly given. Hence, the soul of the deceased says: 'Not let be done evil to me in [this] land, [...] because I, I know the name of these gods who are in it [...]'.[26]

We find the same belief in medieval Europe, where it was believed that in cases of possession, a demon could only be driven out by calling it by its specific name, according to the ancient principle that to know the name of a being is to have power over it.

As indicated, the belief in a secret name that had universal power was widespread in ancient times. This also applied in a religious context. Extreme reverence for a principal god's name is reflected in ancient Egyptian religion. For instance, the Egyptian sun-god's secret name is only revealed once to his daughter Isis.[27]

The deity of the Hebrews was referred to by various terms such as Adonai or Elohim, but the personal name was considered so sacred that it was rarely pronounced aloud. It was called the Tetragrammaton, or word of four letters, 'YHVH', which was considered to mean, 'I am that I am'.[28] Because there are no printed vowels in Hebrew, and because the name was so rarely spoken, only the high priests were entitled to use it in the Temple's innermost sanctuary once a year on the most sacred of days, the Day of Atonement. No traditional pronunciation could be followed, and to this day, the word's pronunciation remains unclear.

In the mystical discipline of the Indian Tantric tradition, where not Hebrew, but Sanskrit, is regarded as the primal language of the universe, pronouncing the name of god was thought to make him appear and his force to operate, because the name was the audible form of the god.

Similarly, the early Celts, Greeks, and Romans did not divulge their gods' names. Here, it must be remembered that the classical gods and goddesses were honoured by a variety of local names. One main reason for the secrecy surrounding the names of protective deities was the ever-present fear that if the enemy knew a local deity's name, the enemy could then invoke that deity and reverse its loyalties. In this context, the

Roman scholar, historian, and naturalist, Pliny the Elder, explains: 'It was the practice before laying siege to a town, for Roman priests to call forth the place's patron deity and promise him the same or more lavish worship under the Romans. And it is agreed that this is why the patron deity of Rome has been kept secret, for fear that any enemy should act in a similar manner'.[29] The Romans even went so far as to memorise the names of enemy gods, conducting ceremonies known as elicio, where power from the enemy's god was drawn out and directed as a negative flow at the people they were attacking.

The power of names is, of course, a popular theme in traditional literature, and we are all familiar with Jacob Grimm's tale of Rumpelstiltskin. As in all folk and fairy tales, when the enchanter's name becomes known, he loses his power.

During the witch-craze era in Europe, it was popularly believed that all cats turned into witches after seven years. Therefore, in days gone by, many people would show reluctance to discuss family matters in the presence of a cat, just in case it happened to be a witch in disguise. Often, cats were marked with crosses to prevent them from turning into witches. But, the most effective solution was to simply give one's cat another name, a name only known to select family members, in the belief that a witch could not take on the cat's body if she did not know its name.

A Jewish custom of bygone days, sometimes observed in the event of a serious life-threatening illness, was to change the name of the person close to death. It was thought that by changing the name, the person's fate would also be changed. Because the 'angel of death' did not know the person's new name, he or she could not be taken away.

In the early 1900s, calling a child by its name before baptism, or even letting the name be known to anyone except the parents was still considered unlucky in European countries. Often, only the father chose the child's name and kept it secret from everyone, even the child's mother, until whispering it to the nominated godmother at the baptismal font, believing that public knowledge of the child's name exposed the hapless child to great risk. Until the Christian Church had sanctified the child's name, evil forces in spells and binds could use the name.

The fear of voicing names, speaking of sickness or death, and referring to catastrophes, is probably responsible for the birth of euphemisms in all languages. The chief objective of euphemisms was to protect one from evil influences by not speaking of these influences directly, which invited their presence. To mention a name was believed to summon the owner. The evocative power of speech was much feared, especially concerning occult forces. We still say jokingly: 'Talk of the devil and tread on its tail!' as it was once believed that by the mere mention of him, the devil appeared. Derived from the Greek, the term 'euphemism' means to 'speak favourably' of a person, object, or situation. For instance, in the days when fairies were feared, they were referred to as the 'little people' or 'the kindly ones'. The ancient Greeks called the spirits of vengeance by the name Eumenides, meaning 'the kindly ones'. By not mentioning the real name of the spirits of vengeance, they were not aware of being discussed and hence kept away.

Amongst the Australian Aborigines, the use of a dead person's name is forbidden, and all knowledge of that person, except perhaps in the nearest relatives' secret reverie, disappears. When someone dies, the Aborigines refer to the relatives of the deceased as having bad luck. Because names are not mentioned, and the word 'death' is never used, it is all done indirectly. The name of the dead person is not spoken for some time following a death, as is common throughout Aboriginal Australia. Anyone with the same name as the deceased has to cease using that name. George Taplin, in The Folklore, Manners, Customs and Languages of the South Australian Aborigines, describes how, amongst the tribes of the Lower Darling, the name for 'water' was changed nine times in about five years because eight men bearing the name of 'water' had died in that period.[30] The reason the name of a departed person was never mentioned was because of the belief that should the name be mentioned, the spirit of the deceased would appear immediately. This is reminiscent of a quote from the Egyptian Book of the Dead: 'To speak the name of the dead makes them live again, brings them back to life'.[31] Similarly, in European countries, the topic of death is also avoided, and we say that a friend or relative has 'passed away', 'passed on', 'taken the road of no return', or that the 'thread of life has been severed', thereby avoiding a direct referral to the unpleasant topic of death, the evocative power of speech still lingering subconsciously as a fearful superstition.

Magic in a Word

The belief that words, spoken and written, are instruments of power is probably as old as language. Because words of command and coercion can sway and influence humans, they are thought to have the same effect on supernatural forces when used in magic ritual. Any word was thought to have a creative force, which is why the knowledge of names was so important, as it could be used to gain control over people and objects. By reciting not only the names, but also the characteristics and acts of a god, a magician could capture that god's essence and hence exert control over the deity. In ancient Egypt, mummy wrappings were inscribed with words intended to make the body imperishable – a mixture of command and prayer combined with solemn, striking language – confirming the belief that saying a thing 'is as it is', makes it so.

The ancient Egyptians also practised magical cursing of their actual or potential enemies. In the Berlin Museum are fragments of pottery proving this practice. Clay bowls had been inscribed with the names of foes and then smashed. This act was thought to break the enemy's power. In the Cairo and British Museums are figurines inscribed with curses, no doubt intended for the same ritual. Various ancient Near Eastern texts describe magic rituals, designed to ward off evil spells, to protect from demons, to avoid the consequences of omens, and to ensure success in life.

Amongst the most remarkable finds recovered from the Roman baths in Bath, England, are the many dedications, vows, and curses inscribed on pewter sheets and dedicated to the goddess, Sulis Minerva, thought to reside in the sacred spring. These dedications, vows and curses cast into the waters over the centuries by thousands of pilgrims, list stolen property, lost loves, or grievances, with an appeal to the goddess for the guilty party to meet with a foul end. Common also are spells to counter the curses of others, very often written backwards, thus thought to imbue the magic with extra potency.

Superstitious tendencies towards achieving wished-for ends continue. They appear in the form of repeating certain catch phrases, believed to produce the desired reality if repeated often enough. For example, we still intone that 'every cloud has a silver lining', 'prosperity is just around the corner', or 'everything will be all right', in the forgotten belief that voicing this will make it so.

Which Is Best — Right or Left?

We all, at some time or another, have commented: 'He definitely put his best foot forward,' or 'she got up on the wrong side of the bed today'. What in fact is the 'best foot' and what is 'the wrong side'?

In the world of superstition, the right side is generally regarded as the lucky side. As most people have always been right-handed, the left side of the body was considered the weaker side. It was therefore believed to be advantageous for evil forces to lurk on the left and to strike from this side.

This notion has left its mark on most Western languages, which explains why the Latin word sinistra, meaning 'on the left hand' became the English word 'sinister', describing all that is foreboding and ominous. In a similar context, the word 'awkward', meaning 'clumsy', originates from the Middle English word awk, which meant 'in the wrong direction'. The French word gauche, meaning 'left' has a more negative connotation when used in English. Similarly, we state that someone is 'right', meaning the person is 'correct'.

The concepts of right and left as used in a positive and negative association date to the dawn of humankind. Cultures in the Northern Hemisphere observed thousands of years ago that the sun, the symbol of life, moves through the heavens sunwise, or towards the right. Traditionally, the left side was identified with the west, the side of the setting sun and, thus, death. A euphemism for death still in use is 'going west'. Vanishing light must have been associated in earlier days with the departing of good fortune and strength, irrevocably influencing humankind's foreboding about the left side, which was therefore associated with ill luck.

Ancient augurs, when viewing the flight of birds, drifting clouds, or the layout of entrails from sacrificial animals to predict the future, invariably regarded a tendency to the left as indicating coming misfortune.

The left side is the side of illegitimate occult powers and inspires fear. The left hand is used for ceremonial magic. Black magic is still regarded as the 'left-hand' path, and to 'move to the left' in magic is to attract evil influences.

A tradition found worldwide associates male gender with the right side and female gender with the left. The differentiation of male and female into the opposites right and left was Pythagorean (570-495 BCE) in origin and written down in his Table of Opposites. First century Roman scholar and naturalist, Pliny the Elder, confirmed this belief, stating that boys are usually carried on the right side of the womb and girls on the left.[32] Medieval anatomical drawings show the womb as a mysterious organ with seven chambers. The three chambers on the left were thought to produce girls; the three on the right brought forth boys, whereas the chamber in the middle produced hermaphrodites.

In African societies, women are generally associated with the left side and men with the right, women always occupying the left side of the homestead and men sitting on the right, as seen from the entrance. In Europe, even in modern times, the bride and her relations are customarily put on the left side of the church. Formerly, there was also great superstition attached to a priest's left hand. The left hand was considered unlucky to the faithful. As the priest used both hands in blessing during communion or confirmation, the superstitious purposefully positioned themselves, not without much disruptive scuffling, so as to avoid his left hand.

Getting out of bed on the left side or with the left foot first was also considered unlucky, and this superstition similarly applied to entering a house left foot first. If one inadvertently did so, the bad luck was only averted by leaving immediately and re-entering with the right foot first. The Romans felt so strongly about entering a house with the right foot first that wealthier families employed servants to cry out 'right foot first' to ensure visitors did not visit ill luck on the house. This was the forerunner of what later became known as the footman – a servant who answers the door.

To Point the Magic Wand or Finger

Today, the phrase 'to point a finger' is used in an accusatory sense. Formerly, however, it was considered unlucky to point at someone, which is the underlying reason why etiquette today considers it uncouth or ill-mannered – customs remain even if the reasons for them have changed or have been lost in obscurity.

To point at any specific object or person has always been considered unlucky because it meant concentrating bad luck in a particular direction by drawing the attention of evil spirits. Consequently, 'pointing a finger' at someone became synonymous with seeking retribution on or harming a person. Curiously, to be pointed was a potent form of sorcery in Australian Aboriginal tradition. Whatever tool – finger, bone, or any other – was used to point and whatever spell or words were used, once the intended victim knew he had been pointed, he would sicken and die, unless a medicine man reversed the process. On the other side of the world, in Europe, witches allegedly used pointing with wands, sticks, and staffs for nefarious purposes in black magic.

Like pointing a finger, the wand was regarded in the ancient world as the agency of intense psychic energy and, therefore, a means of aiming magic power at a particular object. This made the wand an agent of transformation, and as such, it is found in countless legends worldwide. In all mythologies, wands and rods have obvious magical powers. We have only to think of all the tales involving magic wands contained in our folklore and fairy stories. The Fairy Queen is invariably shown bearing her wand and performing marvels.

A stick or staff, the simplest form of the wand, must have been one of humankind's earliest weapons against wild animals and human foes. As a phallic symbol, it is also a sign of power and virility. As symbols of authority, the wand, the crook, and the rod can be traced back to the priest-kings and magicians of antiquity. In ancient times, amongst pastoral peoples, the patriarch bore the shepherd's crook as a symbol of authority over his tribe. In ancient Egypt, the crook was an emblem of supremacy and discipline. The most famous examples of rods used for supernatural purposes were the rods of Moses and his brother Aaron, employed to divide the waters of the Red Sea, to confound the enchantment of the Pharaoh's magicians, and to cause water to gush from a rock in the desert. The rods of Moses and Aaron are believed to be the origin of the crosier or pastoral staff of Christian bishops.

Over time, the wand or crook developed into the insignia of royalty known as the sceptre. In the form of a sceptre, the wand represents temporal power. In Britain, the sceptre, symbolic of kingly authority, is customarily placed in a monarch's right hand at his or her coronation. The white staff carried by the Lord Chancellor symbolises the execution of his duties with purity and uprightness, as well as the authority invested in him by the monarch. As the king's inviolable emissary, the herald also carried a staff of office. Further examples of the wand representing power are the swagger sticks carried by army officers and the baton used by an orchestra's conductor. The modern conjurer's wand, used for pointing and so essential in performing magic tricks, is a remnant of the magician's wand of old. Any appearance on stage by the conjurer without a wand, the symbol of psychic powers, would dissipate the magician's authority and his power of command

Another close connection to the magic wand is the divining or dowsing rod, which can also only be used effectively by pointing it. The discovery of something concealed by a wand or rod has been practised since the beginning of history by most races. Dowsing, using a forked stick or bent wire, is an ancient form of divination. This technique can be used to find underground water, mineral deposits, oil, lost objects, treasure, missing persons, or murder victims. It is impossible to determine the origin of the first divining or dowsing rod, but the Hindu Vedas mention it, and it seems to have been widely used amongst the ancient Chaldeans and Egyptians. The divining rod could be regarded as an atrophied vestige of the magic once associated with sacred trees. The functions of the divining rod were not restricted to the search for water or buried treasure in ancient days. Amongst the Greeks and Romans and the Druids of Britain, France, and Ireland, the divining rod also had many magical uses.

It has not yet been explained why certain individuals, whose honour and good faith are beyond suspicion, have a specific ability to which the divining rod responds by twisting in their grasp. Many professional dowsers will be the first to admit that they do not know how or why the selected dowsing or divining rod moves in their hands, and not in the hands of someone else. The cutting and preparation of the dowsing rod, in all countries throughout the ages, had been accompanied by great ceremony, requiring the rod to be severed at a particular moment and from a particular kind of tree – varying from country to country. Whereas the Chinese favoured the peach tree, in Europe, the hazel, as well as the willow, blackthorn, and mistletoe, were especially popular.

When using a divining rod, both forks of the Y-shaped branch are held, not too firmly, with the palms of the hands turned upward, the main stem of the branch parallel to the ground. The holder then slowly advances towards the location where water or minerals are suspected to be. When the auspicious spot is reached, and there is water or a mineral deposited below, the rod turns in the diviner's hands and bends towards the ground like a magnetised pointer. In World War I, the army used dowsers to help locate unexploded mines and shells.

To Lay the Foundation Stone

The tradition of ceremoniously laying a foundation stone or of placing a coin in the foundation of a new building is still customary and is in effect the relic of an age-old protective magical act. This ancient custom derives from the belief that the Earth spirit, on whose territory a building was to be erected, needed appeasing. Originally, human sacrifices, such as children, gypsies, slaves, or outcasts, were dedicated to the Earth spirit and interred alive in the foundations of proposed constructions to influence the denizens of the deep favourably.

Unbeknown to most people, vague remnants of the fear of angering the Earth spirit, on whose territory a building is to be erected, are still evident when the first sod of earth is dug with a silver spade, the first mortar is laid with a shiny trowel, the foundation stone or the cornerstone of a building is ceremoniously laid, or ribbons – considered to bring luck – mark the start of work or the opening of a building, bridge, or shopping centre. All these traditions stem from ancient rituals and impulses to appease higher forces.

The belief in offending the Earth spirit or the Earth mother is universal. Before the disintegration of traditional customs, the men of African and Amerindian tribes would have no part in mining, tunnelling, or hoeing, lest they anger the Earth mother and, in so doing, invoke drought, disease, and other calamities.[33] Smohalla, nineteenth-century native American prophet and chief of the Wanapum tribe of the Columbia River Valley, refused to till the ground as he contended that mutilating and tearing up the Earth, the mother of all, was sinful. He said: 'You ask me to plough the ground! Shall I take a knife and tear my mother's bosom? Then when I die she will not take me to her bosom to rest'.[34]

Similarly, the Celts laid votive offerings at the bottom of shafts, whereas in India, cattle were sacrificed when a new mine was opened, to atone for the forceful penetration of the sacred Earth. Miners in South Africa were reluctant to go into the bowels of the Earth without having made special dedications of coins pushed into crevices underground as substitute offerings to the Earth spirit.

The same belief is found amongst Australian Aborigines. In Healers of Arnhem Land, John Cawte recounts the story of how a new sanitary system was installed in the Australian town, Turtle Street, in Arnhem Land: 'The big objection raised by the older men to the Turtle Street project was that their earth was sacred and that you should never dig it deeper than the length of a digging stick, as the underground world must be left undisturbed'.[35]

Contrary to popular opinion, the idea of appeasing the Earth spirit was by no means confined to paganism. Legend has it that the Irish missionary, St. Columba (521–597 CE), founder of Iona, found it necessary to bury St. Onan alive beneath the foundation of his new abbey to propitiate the spirits of the soil. The monks firmly believed that these spirits, unless suitably appeased, demolished at night what had been built during the day. Accounts of skeletons immured in old churches, buildings, bridges, and dykes, usually only discovered many decades later during restoration or demolition, are documented from around Europe. The survival of this custom in Christian times is suggested by discoveries of skeletons in the foundations of old churches. An example is at Darrington, Yorkshire, when it was found in 1895 that the church walls were resting on a human skull. If popular legend is to be believed, the bridge at Arta, Italy, kept collapsing until a human victim was immured in the foundations. This does however give a new and quite literal meaning to the saying that 'someone has a skeleton in the cupboard'. In later times, animals and precious objects replaced human sacrifices.

Deliberately Concealed Items

'Mystery of mummified cat in office basement'. The Edinburgh Evening News carried this story on February 13, 2007. The 180-year-old find in a basement in New Town, Scotland, was attributed not to feline misadventure, but to a deliberate act of witchcraft to protect the building against evil spirits. In the early 1960s, during restoration work at Lauderdale House in Highgate, London, workmen found an ornate goblet, shoes, and four mummified chickens, which had been immured in the chimney when the house was built in the late sixteenth century. Similarly, a mummified cat was found in the walls of a cottage in Cricksen, Essex, where it had been buried alive. Numerous such reports from the UK and other Western countries are extant. For example, on 15 July 2012 ABC National Radio in Australia broadcast a comprehensive lecture by historian Ian Evans on 'deliberately concealed items' in Australian heritage buildings.

The phrase 'deliberately concealed items' describes items of clothing or apparel, dried cats or other animals, witch bottles, and various artefacts, intentionally hidden or buried by builders or the occupants of buildings. Such deliberate concealment of items relates to the ancient practice of foundation sacrifice and pertains to the ritual protection of a household and its occupants. To qualify for consideration, such objects must be found hidden within a building in such a way as to preclude accidental concealment or loss. Typically, where the concealed items are garments, in order to be protective they are never new, but have been worn and used, that is, they are imbued with a protective essence from the previous wearer.

Protective ritual objects of this kind have been found in Continental Europe, the United Kingdom, North and South America, and Australia and are usually discovered when alterations and renovations are undertaken. The majority of 'deliberately concealed items' are found in buildings constructed before 1800, although such items have also been discovered in buildings dating from as late as the early 1900s. In rural Bolivia, foetuses of dogs and llamas, believed to bring protection and good luck if buried under the foundations of new buildings, are still for sale in modern times.

Shoes were especially high on the priority list, thought to have wonderful protective qualities. Therefore, shoes were amongst the most popular items deliberately concealed in buildings. Formerly, most people only owned one pair of shoes, which was repaired over and over again for many years. A shoe is the only item of clothing that retains the shape of the body part it covers. Worn over many years, shoes were thought to become charged with their owners' soul essence. Consequently, shoes were seen as imbued with protective qualities. The concealment of shoes is such a well-known folk custom that the museum at Northampton in the United Kingdom has set up a 'Concealed Shoes Index'. Usually, only a single shoe is found concealed. Hundreds of finds are made and recorded in the museum every year. Many, however, remain undocumented, in all likelihood simply thrown out by builders who are uninformed and ignorant of this protective custom of the past.

Children's clothes are often found among caches of deliberately concealed garments. Speculation has it that the purpose behind concealing children's garments might have been to promote fertility, counteract infant deaths, and generally to protect the household's children.

Amongst ritual objects frequently concealed in houses were so-called witch bottles, used specifically to counter witchcraft. Made of stoneware or glass, these were little potbellied bottles, representing a witch's bladder. To keep witches away, such a bottle was filled with urine, to which had been added bits of sharp glass, pins, thorns, and other small sharp objects. Tightly sealed and hidden, the bottles were believed to transmit terrible agony to any witch nearby.

Similarly, cats, buried after they had been killed or while they were still alive, were thought of as highly protective. Under the laws of sympathetic magic, this was because of their association with witchcraft and evil, in other words cats were thought to decoy witches away from the house's occupants. Popular locations for concealment were near chimneys, fireplaces, under the floors, above ceilings, and in sealed voids, typically places where witches and evil spirits could enter.

Interestingly, the custom of deliberately concealing garments and objects for protective purposes is not solely a historic practice, but occasionally still takes place in modern times.[36]

Sailing Vessels Referred to as 'She'

The popular ceremony of launching a new ship by breaking a large bottle of champagne across its bow has its origin in the distant past when anything new and yet unused, be it a building, a bridge, a dam, a dyke, or a ship, was perceived to be at the mercy of various gods who had to be propitiated with a live, usually human, sacrifice.

In the distant past, the rituals concerned with a new vessel's launching were of profound importance to the future safety of the ship and all who sailed on her. In those times, the propitiation of all ocean deities was taken so seriously that it was even considered unlucky to save a drowning man. It was thought that the drowning person was marked by fate and had been irrevocably claimed by the denizens of the deep. To deprive them of their prey would result in misfortune for the remaining crew. Therefore, at a time when every sea voyage was already fraught with so many unknown dangers, and very few sailors could swim, to rescue a man overboard was doubtless considered near impossible.

In ancient times, it was unheard of to commit a sailing vessel to the waves without the appropriate blood sacrifice to appease the gods of the deep and, in so doing, to bring the ship 'to life'. In keeping with the tradition of blood sacrifice, the Vikings crushed prisoners under the keels of their long ships when first launching them. In northern European countries, it became customary to enclose valuable objects in parts of the ship, once blood sacrifices were not conducted anymore, to appease the sea gods. The ship's builder often hid a gold coin for good luck in some recess of the keel, in a hiding place known only to him. Incidentally, the ship's keel was regarded as its backbone or 'foundation', hence, strictly speaking, such a coin constituted a foundation sacrifice. Alternatively, the first nail knocked into the keel was tied with red ribbons to protect the craft from evil influences.

The ancient Greeks and Romans changed the traditional sacrifice by splashing red wine instead of blood on their vessels. Therefore, the red wine, fruit of the earth, became the emblem of sacrifice. In addition, the Greeks and Romans also appeased the ocean gods by giving all their sailing vessels female names. In this way, such ships became the symbolic 'brides' of Poseidon and Neptune, which is why we still refer to all sailing vessels as 'she'. It was of course presumed that Poseidon and Neptune would not let harm come to their 'brides', which set the minds of seafarers in ancient times at rest.

Today we have replaced the red wine with 'bubbly'. Champagne, the aristocrat of wines, traditionally linked with new births, beginnings, and celebrations, came into vogue as a christening fluid for ships in the mid-nineteenth century.

Incidentally, it is considered a bad omen if the bottle does not break the first time, a superstition still believed by many, as the following headlines in the BBC News, April 24, 2007, indicate: 'Bad omen cast over ship's launch', when the champagne bottle failed to smash at a launch in the Southampton dock.

Ominous Crossroads or Trivia?

The suicide of a loved one evokes emotional turmoil, anguish, pain, loneliness, and many questions for those left behind. Today, there is increasing knowledge and tolerance of psychological conditions and disorders leading to suicide as well as counselling available to grieving relatives. In modern times, the judgemental hostility of the past towards suicides and their families seems incomprehensible and difficult to understand. In the past, ecclesiastical condemnation reinforced the horror of so seemingly unnatural a deed as taking one's own life. Suicide was formerly labelled 'self-murder', which is why the Church inflicted harsh punishment on those taking their own lives. Suicides were regarded as so heinous and opposite to God's will that people who committed suicide were refused burial in consecrated soil. It was sacrilege to bury such people in ground dedicated to the Almighty. Instead, suicides, executed criminals, and suspected vampires were interred at crossroads, regarded from ancient times as the abode of evil forces and thus debased and abandoned. To prevent the maleficent ghost from rising and perhaps harming the living, a stake was usually driven through the corpse's heart, or it was decapitated. In Hungary, it was customary to also bury all those who had allegedly died under the influence of witches or demons – those who in modern times would be described as being of unsound mind – at crossroads.

Traditionally the gallows, an ominous sight for all passers-by, were erected at such intersections. Tyburn, the famous London gallows, was once situated at a crossroad. In the United Kingdom, many archaeological finds of skeletal remains, some dating from Anglo-Saxon times, have been unearthed at such intersections. For example, in 1977, at a crossroads between Dry Drayton and Oakington in Cambridgeshire, UK, twelve skeletons were uncovered, while sixty skeletons from differing historic periods were found at the crossroads at Fowlmere, also in Cambridgeshire. Numerous other examples exist. Although such burials were abolished in the United Kingdom by an Act of Parliament in 1823, prejudice against suicides remained, and they could only be buried in graveyards in the dead of night without ceremony.

Crosses made by juncture roads were, of course, heavy with symbolic meaning, and many beliefs and portentous implications were attached to such intersections. Witches were said to gather here making pacts with the devil and performing various magic rites to summon evil spirits. Therefore, people were fearful of being delayed at crossroads, especially after dark.

Already in ancient times, Hecate, the Greek goddess of the night, linked with the moon, the underworld, and crossroads, was believed to preside at these intersections. As queen of the spirits of the dead, she was active at night and was accompanied by dogs, suicides, and all those who had died violently. In ancient times, small pillars were erected in her honour at crossroads, and food sacrifices, called Hecate's Supper placed on these pillars, were offered once a month – a custom that the Church was still trying to eradicate in Europe as late as the eleventh century.

Interestingly, the fear of such junctions is also found in other parts of the world. For example, in Japan, phallic symbols used to be set up at crossroads to frighten away evil spirits and protect passers-by. In India, offerings were made at crossroads to Rudra, the god ruling over evil powers and ghosts of the underworld. Such an overwhelming presence of evil was believed – throughout both Europe and Asia – to be present at crossroads that, from ancient times, altars have been erected at such places to protect the passer-by. Such altars, decorated with flowers and other offerings, many of which are now dedicated to Christian saints, can still be seen at crossroads in the rural areas of European countries.

In closing, some trivia: The derivation of the word trivia, meaning 'commonplace' or 'less important', comes from the Latin word for tri-via, literally meaning 'three roads'. The most common explanation for the word trivia is that such junctions or street corners were meeting places for the common, ordinary folk. Here passers-by would speak commonalities, mention matters of no importance, 'trivialities' to one another. However, given the unfavourable, sinister associations of such junctions, this is hardly likely. A more plausible explanation for the word's derivation is centred on Mercury, the Roman god of ways or roads. The statues erected at crossroads, or tri-via, to this particular god were so numerous and such a common sight that the word trivial in the English language came to denote something unimportant or commonplace.

II

CHARMS

From ancient times, the general belief existed that unseen hands directed and controlled human destiny. As humanity imagined itself surrounded by spirits of doubtful or evil intent, humankind sought various protective means from the terrors of the unseen world. Although these were convictions firmly held in the past, many traditions relating to them have survived. Despite modern thinking and attitudes, the irresistible attraction to enchantment has prevailed in all human endeavours, constantly reasserting itself throughout the ages.

In modern times, charms and charm bracelets can be purchased in countless stores and online, with literally hundreds of sites advertising such luck-bringing baubles. In Western countries, charms are for sale, not specifically as protective agents, but as fashionable trinket jewellery, their original meaning lost in the obscurity of commercialism.

In the past, charms were considered to counteract all misfortune and promote good luck. But it was also thought that they could inflict great harm. In 1558, the Church of England condemned all charms, sorcery, invocations, enchantments, and witchcraft as inventions of the devil. But, despite this vigorous ecclesiastic prohibition, most of these practices have survived.

The word charm derives from the Latin carmen meaning 'song'. Hence, originally, a charm involved only reciting a verse or chant to induce a magical effect. Later, charms were classified into numerous verbal or spellbinding charms, as well as into the various object charms, many of which are still popular today. The meaning of most verbal charms has always been rather obscure and not fully understood which, in itself, lent them an air of magical power and mystery.

A charm can be perceived as a collective expression describing a formula, a potion, a precious stone, or an emblematic object. Such a charm can repudiate ill luck or inflict misfortune. In other words, a charm can be used for good or evil intent. Any charm, be it a verbal, a spellbinding, or an object charm, was believed to derive its magical efficacy from tapping supernatural powers. In early societies, all charms had a very private character, as they were often kept secret and transmitted solely amongst relatives or close friends.

Spellbinding

A spell is a verbal charm, the incantations of which can be spoken or chanted. Surprisingly, spells are as popular today as they were in ancient times, blind belief in their efficacy seemingly persisting. A quick search on the Internet brings up money magnet spells; various types of love spells; lottery, magic and 'make me confident' spells, as well as exam spells, and a myriad of others. Nothing much seems to have changed over the millennia!

Ancient societies believed that the power of spells and incantations was without limit. In Homer's Odyssey, the bleeding wound in Ulysses' thigh is healed by a spell, and Virgil is said to have copied love spells to prevent being jinxed.[1] The enchantress, Circe, could change men into beasts with her incantations. According to Pliny the Elder, the belief that the witches of Thessaly could enchant the moon out of the sky was so strong that once, during its eclipse, a great many people, fearing the heavenly body might tumble out of the sky, set up a persistent noise of brass trumpets to prevent the moon from hearing the witches' spells.[2] Pliny also refers to the Roman belief that vestal virgins had the power to root runaway slaves to the spot with a spell.[3] It was further believed that spells had the power to blight crops, control blazing fires, make rivers flow backwards, and bring or drive away rain. Spells were intended to cure or create illness, arouse or repel affection and passion, and inhibit or promote fertility by rendering men impotent and women submissive. Words used in spells are usually characterised by their unintelligibility and strangeness – the very characteristics thought to impart power to this type of verbal charm. Spells might consist of garbled rhymes or prayers, or their efficacy relies on the repetition of sacred names. Often, spells are stereotyped, employing invocation, repetition, alliteration, and word patterns spoken in rhythmic form, as demonstrated in the following example:

> Hickup, hickup, go away,
> Come again another day.
> Hickup, hickup, when I bake,
> I'll give you a butter cake.

The weirdness of many spells was and still is due to a deliberate attempt to baffle and impress the uninitiated listener. Although the etymology of the word spell comes from the Anglo-Saxon word spel, meaning 'speech, discourse or idle talk', there is a non-verbal usage of the term as well. Thus, a spell can also refer to the paralysing power exerted on a person without the use of words, but with a look instead. An example of this type of spell is the very powerful and universally feared evil eye.

'If Looks Could Kill'

Not only was the gaze of mortal enemies feared in ancient times, but also the watchfulness of vengeful, jealous, and capricious gods. A remnant of this fear is still contained in the expression 'if looks could kill', going back to the days when it was firmly believed that a glance or look from someone thought to have the evil eye was indeed fatal.

The belief in this superstition is prevalent in many countries worldwide, and nothing has been able to root it out. In rural areas of England and the United States and the foreign populated sections of most large cities, the belief in the evil eye's effect is very much in evidence and is called 'overlooking'. In modern Greece and Turkey and countries of the Middle East, Asia and Africa, various amulets are freely available to ward off the evil eye, confirming how widespread this ancient belief still is. References to the evil eye date back thousands of years. Mention of the evil eye is made on Sumerian, Assyrian, and

Babylonian clay tablets, in the Talmud, the Bible, the writings of the ancient Greeks and Romans, and in medieval literature. Scholars often refer to the belief in the evil eye as a purely Semitic and Indo-European phenomenon, as it is unknown in countries such as China, Korea, Burma, Indonesia, Thailand, Vietnam, Cambodia, Japan, Aboriginal Australia, New Zealand, and native North and South America.

The belief in the evil eye originates from the concept of an envious and malignant mind able to project evil thoughts and cast spells through the eyes, thereby causing misfortune, illness, and even death to humans and animals. A malevolent influence is thought to flash from the eyes of envious or angry people, infecting the surrounding air and corrupting any living target or inanimate object. In the same category as this belief is the notion, held at the time of the Black Death in England, that even the glance from an afflicted person's distorted eyes was enough to communicate the infection to others. A similar belief in modern times in certain African and Asian countries is that just speaking to and looking at someone with HIV can transmit the disease.

Plutarch (46–127 CE) tells us that envy exerts a powerful evil influence through the eyes, piercing with the strength of poisoned arrows. The Romans called the workings of the evil eye fascinatio, and according to Pliny the Elder, the faculty of fascination was so well recognised in ancient Rome that special laws were instituted to protect against injury to crops by incantation or fascination.[4] In effect, fascination is probably what is nowadays called mesmerism or hypnotism, by which someone is able to exert an extraordinary influence over others. In ancient times, the gods were also believed to look enviously on humankind's good fortune and to destroy it with malicious joy. The Greek historian Herodotus warns emphatically: 'I know that the gods are jealous of our success'.[5]

Various physical defects such as crossed eyes, drooping lids, chronic red or bloodshot eyes, and heavy eyebrows meeting in the middle, even red-headed people or hunchbacks, in the past, inevitably resulted in an accusation of possessing the evil eye. During the witch-hunts in the Middle Ages, many an innocent person suffered a cruel death for having any one of these afflictions. In the Mediterranean and Aegean rural regions, there is still a tendency to view blue-eyed locals as possessing the evil eye, probably because few of the locals there have blue eyes.

From earliest times, mostly women, especially old women and suspected witches, were accused of having the evil eye. A fixed stare, particularly if accompanied by a frown or scowl, was seen as aggressively wishing someone ill. Nowadays, especially in rural areas of Europe, it is still believed by some that to stare fixedly and steadfastly into a fire indicates possessing the evil eye. Formerly, children were therefore severely rebuked if they happened to be fascinated by the flames. The ability to overlook was not only confined to humans. Certain animals, with prominent or glittering eyes, such as snakes, toads, rabbits, foxes, and wolves, were also highly suspect.

Women, especially during pregnancy or childbirth, and children were considered particularly vulnerable to the evil eye's effects. Anyone who naturally attracted envy, such as very handsome or wealthy people, the proud and the boastful, or a person receiving praise from others or even from themselves, were considered most at risk. Too much admiration of any person or object would bring about the curse of fascination. Thus, the Greek god, Narcissus, by falling in love with his own image, was thought by many to have 'fascinated' himself.

At one time it was taken for granted that any malady not easily recognised, was due to the evil eye. It was commonly thought that the evil eye could make food poisonous and rob it of all nourishment, a belief dating from biblical times and expressed in the Old Testament: 'Eat thou not the bread of him, that hath an evil eye'.[6] This is as much a maxim today as it was in ancient times, and thus, saying grace before a meal was considered in many homes a protective gesture.

Because fear of fascination or of being overlooked was, and is, so universally prevalent, countermeasures to guard and protect against the malignant rays of the evil eye are many. The custom of blackening one's eyebrows and darkening one's eyelids, especially common in the East, was originally believed to protect from the darts of those casting the evil eye. Amulets of all shapes and sizes, multi-coloured mirror charms wrapped with beads, buttons, and tassels to deflect the evil eye, as well as bracelets, brooches, and bangles are also believed to protect. Women still often wear amulets suspended between their eyes in many parts of the world to ward off evil glances.

According to the laws of sympathetic magic, evil has always been used to repel evil, which is why grotesque gargoyles in church architecture are believed to keep away negative influences. Based on the analogy that 'like cures like', or 'like influences like' in accordance with the principles of sympathetic magic, it was natural that through an association of ideas the representation of an actual eye would serve as a potent protection against the malignant influences of the feared evil eye. Many charms representing the eye were found in Egyptian tombs. Not only the Egyptians, but also the Phoenicians, Etruscans, Greeks, and Romans used depictions of the eye and the hand as powerful amulets against the evil eye's influence. All these nations observed the custom of painting a large eye on the bow of their boats and ships, not only to imitate the vigilance necessary to captain or pilot their vessel, but mainly to protect against the evil eye – a custom which continues to be observed in the backwaters of rural India and other Asian countries. Representations of the eye are still sold as amulets against fascination in all Mediterranean countries, the Middle East, and Asia.

Garlic, traditionally considered a devil repellent, was also used as a potent prophylactic. A little bread and salt, both blessed ingredients, sown into a piece of cloth and worn around one's neck or on one's person, also protected against being overlooked.

The first glance of the evil eye was regarded as fatal. It was therefore very important that any object intended to protect against the evil of fascination should attract the first, immediate, and fatal glance. As indecency or obscenity was inevitably regarded as attracting attention, these were also believed to capture the focus of the dreaded evil eye. Therefore, the most potently protective amulets have always been considered those depicting something strange, uncommon, or obscene. The most popular of these amulets was a representation of the phallus, named the fascinum by the Italians. For the ancient Egyptians, whose belief in, and dread of, the evil eye was ever-present, their efforts to avert or baffle the evil eye from the living and the dead were constant and elaborate. In one of the tombs of the kings at Thebes, a painting depicts the goddess Hathor presenting a double phallus in the shape of a horseshoe to Ramses IX.[7] In this case, two protective symbols have been combined – the representation of the phallus and the horseshoe. The idea of phallic necklaces is of great antiquity and was passed on from the ancient Egyptians to Greece and Rome. Preferred charms in Rome were those representing a phallus made of gold or silver.

Similarly, hideous and contorted faces, seen on masks and used in the rituals and festivals of many religions, are objects used to attract the evil eye and to absorb its harmful influence, thus protecting the person wearing the mask. In ancient Greece, one favoured amulet was that of Medusa's head, one of the three Gorgons of Greek mythology who had snakes for hair and whose stare could turn anyone to stone. This further bears out the universal idea that grotesque, devil-like images were considered protective against the very same beings and entities they were supposed to represent.

Another powerfully protective symbol is the human hand. Although the eyes were regarded as the chief medium of communicating evil, touch also played an important part. The personal contact through touch seemed to convey an invisible influence of heightened intensity in addition to that included in the evil eye's general effect. The most natural and commonly used appendage in touching someone is the hand, which is considered a very powerful protector in warding off evil influences of any kind. Early examples of hands used as amulets are small pieces of bronze cut into shape with eyelets for suspension, found in Etruscan and Greek tombs. In modern times, hand-shaped amulets, also depicting an eye for double protection, known in the Middle East as the 'Hamsa Hand', amongst Jews as the 'Hand of Miriam', and amongst Muslims as the 'Hand of Fatima', are still in popular use.

Given the ancient background and widespread belief in the evil eye, common phrases such as 'to give someone the evil eye' or 'if looks could kill', suddenly take on a whole new meaning.

The Preventive Amulet

An amulet is credited with the inherent power to ward off all evil influences and is still universally popular. Explanations for the etymology of the word amulet are varied. The word is derived either from the Arabic himalah, meaning 'to carry', or from the Latin verb amoliri, meaning 'to remove' or 'to drive away'.

An amulet is a preventive charm believed specifically to remove dangers or to drive them away. It is thought to protect through mere passive possession. It is also credited with providing good luck, strength, fertility, virility, success in battle and in love, and last but not least, providence in agriculture. Psychologically, the amulet gives the wearer a feeling of security and well-being. Amulets can be placed in one's surroundings or worn anywhere on one's person, such as around the wrist or ankle, but are usually suspended from the neck.

An amulet can be made of almost any substance that can be fashioned into some or other significant representation or shape. Although amulets need not be shaped in any specific way for them to be effective, they usually are given some distinctive form to convey symbolic meaning. Amulet shapes and forms are almost unlimited and might include holed stones, abnormal vegetable growths, shells, minerals, rings, inscriptions, cords and strings, representations of the eye, the hand and the phallus, and many other objects.

Throughout history, good spirits have always been perceived as willing to be propitiated and bargained with so that benefits could be obtained, whereas evil spirits were mostly seen as unwilling to be reconciled and forever remaining insatiable in their desire to inflict harm. Hence, the protective powers of amulets were sought universally amongst all peoples. Amulets, since antiquity, have been considered indispensable, especially for those who dared evoke spiritual forces from the netherworld. Without the protection given by various amulets, a magician ran the risk of being severely attacked by these spiritual entities.

Amulets were in use from the earliest times and are relics of stone worship, when they were worn as luck stones to protect from evil influences and diseases and to secure good fortune. In Europe, naturally holed pebbles were probably amongst the first amulets ever worn, the use of which goes back to prehistoric times. Their intriguing, unusual shape must have conjured promises of hidden magic powers protecting from famine, storms, peril at sea, and most of all, from evil and witchcraft. Threaded on twine or rope, they were often attached to the bows of sailing vessels to protect against sorcery. In some parts of England, they were called witch stones, or alternatively, fairy stones or holy flints, and if worn by a succession of owners, thought endowed with even greater protective magic powers. These holed stones often supplemented medieval healing methods, and they are still worn today for good luck.

The ancient Babylonians and Assyrians hung amulets modelled in clay outside their doors to keep away evil spirits. Nearly three hundred different varieties of amulets have been discovered in ancient Egyptian tombs. In fact, ritual practice of Egyptian religion and social life were so wrapped around by magic and myth and the bodily wearing of protective amulets that its followers must have been both mentally and physically weighed down. Amongst the diverse protecting amulets worn by the ancient Egyptians, the most common were the scarab and the 'Eyes of Horus'. The right eye of the Egyptian god of the underworld, Horus, represented the sun and the left eye, the moon. Therefore, to afford twenty-four hour protection, by day and by night, both eyes were habitually worn. These amulets were found in great profusion in tombs and placed on the dead to guard against evil influences in a future life. The Eyes of Horus conferred on the dead the power to see and protection from evil influences in the Tuat or netherworld.

The ancient Greeks and Romans also had great faith in using the power of amulets to protect the body from diseases, believed caused by malignant influences. Both Pliny the Elder and the renowned 2nd century physician Galen mention the beneficial properties of amulets in protecting against disease. In the early part of the 1st century, amulets were not only worn on a person's body but also used as ornaments in houses, much as we use vases and other decorations on tables and mantels. In his writings on the cyclamen plant, Pliny the Elder mentions that the plant '.... ought to be grown in every house, [....] wherever it grows, noxious smells can have no effect. This plant is what is called an amulet'.[8] In the past, noxious smells were thought to cause pestilence and other diseases.

According to sympathetic magic, an amulet's shape was thought to influence its effectiveness profoundly. All objects worn as protection against specific diseases of bodily organs or limbs represented the shape of that organ or limb. A stone shaped like a human foot was therefore carried to prevent gout, and an amulet shaped like a mole was worn as a cure for cramp because of this animal's cramped appearance. The claws and teeth of wild animals were believed to be protective agents against being attacked by savage beasts and to give courage and agility to the wearer. A piece of wood shaped like an acorn was carried in the pocket as protection from lightning during thunderstorms because the oak tree was considered a stalwart against lightning strikes. Shells and corals have also been popular amulets for hundreds of years, necklaces of shells and corals originally believed to protect against drowning at sea.

Many amulets worn in early Christian times bore heathen or heretical symbols, which is why the Christian Church registered its opposition to the practice of wearing amulets as early as 364 CE at the Council of Laodicea. Amulets were labelled 'fetters of the soul', and all who wore them were threatened to be cast out of the Church and thus forfeit any redemption for their sins. However, despite this grave threat, the insurmountable tendency in humans to wear objects believed to be endowed with protective properties simply found expression in another form. Instead of heathen or heretical symbols being worn, emblems linked with Christian belief, especially those blessed by priests, supplanted them. Examples are the Cross and medallions depicting various saints, typically Saint Christopher as the patron saint of travelling. Amongst the early Christians, pieces of the true Cross were also believed to offer effective protection and held in great reverence as amulets for their healing and shielding powers.

Frequently, amulets were inscribed, usually consisting of a few words written on a piece of skin or parchment. This type of amulet could be encased in a small metal or leather case, suspended from the neck or bound to the body. In the past, the great importance attached to these amulets was due to the awe illiterate people felt for the written word, which they could not decipher. Examples of inscriptions appearing on amulets were magic names, the names of saints, angels, holy personages, and spells, prayers, or passages from ancient holy books, such as the Torah, the Bible, or the Koran. Some Christians still customarily wear short passages from the Gospels or the Lord's Prayer concealed on their person, whereas Moslems might wear small necklace amulets containing passages from select suras of the Koran to protect them against misfortune.

In India and Tibet, the use of amulets dates to ancient times and is still widespread. Enclosed in small boxes made of copper or silver or sewn in pieces of cloth, amulets consist of pictures of deities, relics, or specific verses written on pieces of paper. Many Buddhists wear sacred symbols, relics of holy lamas, or pebbles and other materials from holy shrines as amulets, all prepared with elaborate ritual and ceremony.

A Hand of Glory

Representations of hands have always been considered very powerful protectors, used since ancient times as amulets and charms, especially in warding off the evil eye. A particularly revolting and utterly gruesome charm depicting the hand is the so-called 'Hand of Glory'. This charm was made from the hand cut from a hanged criminal, and in order for it to be effective, it had to be severed while the body was still on the gallows, then dried and pickled. This powerful charm was considered not only to have great healing powers, but also to protect felons from detection when committing a robbery.

The Hand of Glory was reputed to prevent sleepers from waking and to stupefy anyone who was awake in the middle of the night. There were two ways of using the Hand of Glory. Shortly before breaking and entering, either a candle was fixed between the hardened fingers, or the outspread fingers and thumb were set alight to burn as long as it was considered necessary, the fingers themselves thereby becoming a five-fold candle. If only the fingers of the upright hand burned, but the thumb would not catch fire, then this was a sign to the thief that someone in the house was still awake and free from the charm's effects. It was firmly believed that when the affixed candle or the hand was lit, everyone in the vicinity, except the owner of this gruesome object, fell into a deep slumber from which they could not be roused. As the following nineteenth century rhyme indicates, this charm was an invaluable aid for any thief conducting nocturnal robberies:

> Let those who rest more deeply sleep,
> Let those who wake their vigils keep,
> Oh Hand of Glory shed thy light,
> Direct us to our spoils tonight.

The underlying idea, based on sympathetic magic, was that a death-like condition could be induced in someone, if only temporarily, by using portions of a felon's corpse. The custom of leaving bodies to rot on the gibbet – a warning to passers-by that crime did not pay – made human remains readily available for creating such gruesome charms.

Thieves in England reportedly still used the Hand of Glory in the late nineteenth century. Although this revolting charm was peculiar to Europe, similar charms were used by burglars around the world, the line of thought persisting that 'like influences like', and anything related to death, such as bones, ashes, or dirt from graves, induced a death-like state in others. For instance, it was formerly thought in Germany that anyone who had silently carried off an undertaker's measure and leant it against a house door at night could rob the people inside without their waking. Jacob Grimm attests to this in his Teutonic Mythology.[9] Similarly, in Slavic countries, thieves flung a human bone over the rooftop of the house they intended to rob, and Hindu thieves scattered ashes from a funeral pyre in front of the entrance of the house they had selected, while Indonesian thieves sprinkled grave dirt around their targeted abode to ensure that everyone inside would not wake up. How widespread such notions often are!

'All Tied up in a Knot'

Throughout the ages, great emphasis has been placed on the magical power of knots. This is reflected in the traditions of many cultures. The ancients believed in a world swarming with evil forces, continuously desirous to harm living beings. Specifically, knots were believed to entangle malignant forces, hence keep them at bay.

The custom of protecting oneself against illness and misfortune with knots, strings, and cords, worn as amulets, is widespread and ancient.

About four thousand years ago, the Babylonians believed that seven knots tied thrice on a three-fold cord and wound around the head, cured a headache. The ancient Egyptians considered an amulet depicting a human hand as effective protection for their children, and Egyptian mothers suspended this from a knotted cord around their baby's neck. A knot was required to be tied every morning and another every evening, until there were seven knots. On each occasion, a formula was repeated over the knot to ensure maximum protection from forces responsible for disease, accident, or hardship.

Amongst the Parsees in India, young initiates into the Zoroastrian religion are girded with the kushti, a knotted cord which must be untied and re-knotted several times a day to the accompaniment of prayers in order to express the devotees' determination to defeat the powers of evil as well as his dedication to God.

A common emblem of folk magic in Europe is the witch's knot, a symbolic representation of knot magic allegedly practised by witches during the Middle Ages. Under the laws of sympathetic magic, the symbol of the witch's knot, scratched above doorways and entrances, was frequently used as a charm to protect against witchcraft. As late as the early nineteen hundreds, it was still customary in many countries in Europe to wear knots tied on a long piece of string around certain affected body parts. The knots were believed to cure many ailments, from whooping cough to warts and sprains.

The tightly bound folds making up a knot were symbolic of a sealed bargain, the underlying implication being that anything with the power to bind the body could also be used to bind the spirit. Hence, we still speak of 'tying the marriage knot', a phrase which might have originated in the days when threads from the couples' clothes were used to bind together their hands, thumbs, or shoulders.

The power thought to reside in every act of binding or tying could be either positive or negative. Hence, knots were thought to cause illness, but also to cure or drive it away. Similarly, knots were used to bewitch, but also to protect against bewitchment; they were used to hinder childbirth or facilitate it; cause death or prevent it. Ambivalence of this kind is found in all magico-religious uses of knots and bonds. In Europe, knot and string magic were used in nuptial rites to protect the young couple, though at the same time, knots could be used to imperil consummation of the marriage and therefore implicate great disappointment in the nuptial bed.

Knots were also believed to hinder conception when specifically tied by an ill-wisher. To tie three knots in a handkerchief or string during the benediction of the marriage ceremony was thought to render a couple childless. The bridegroom, however, could stave off any such possible ill luck by leaving his shoelaces untied or one of his shoe buckles undone when standing before the altar. Immediately before the marriage ceremony, every knot on the bride and groom was to be carefully loosened. In parts of Scotland, it was considered sufficient for the groom's shoe to be without a buckle or latchet 'to prevent witches from depriving him of the power of loosening the virgin zone'.[10]

Universally, knots feature strongly in superstitious beliefs concerned with birth and death. A woman giving birth was to ensure that all knots in her clothing were undone. Similarly, it was also required to untie all knots in the clothing of someone in the process of dying, as this was believed to allow the soul an unencumbered passing. The belief that specifically tied knots could actually prevent death is aptly illustrated by the following account: 'When, at St. Andrew's, Scotland, in 1572, a woman was led to the stake to be burned as a witch, there was taken away from her a white cloth, on the strings of which were many knots. As it was removed she said: Now I have no hope of myself'.[11] The custom of untying knots before a birth or when death was in progress, is still observed in some parts of Africa, Asia and the Middle East.

The custom of tying a knot in one's handkerchief to remind one of something specific is the variation of a superstition going back to the Middle Ages. Any knot was believed to be a charm to ward off unwanted forces, as the knot was considered able to entangle or preoccupy these forces, and thereby keep them at bay. The intricacy of a knot was believed to totally confuse, intrigue, and beguile the evil influences, bent on distracting someone from whatever they were trying to remember – hence, the knot in a handkerchief reminded a person of something not to be forgotten.

A derogatory phrase still in use is telling someone to 'get knotted', an abusive and dismissive term meaning to 'get lost'. Another expression concerning knots stems from ancient Greek mythology and is still in modern use – 'To cut the Gordian Knot' describes solving a problem by quick, decisive action.

The Lucky Horseshoe

Anyone who has travelled to the charming little Scottish town of Gretna Greene, once famous for runaway weddings, will remember the Old Smithy's entrance arch made of multiple horseshoes. Here, under this luckiest of archways, happy newlyweds pose for their wedding photos, the horseshoe, of course, being one of the most popular good luck charms still used. It adorns wedding cakes and greeting and good luck cards and features prominently in twenty-first birthday decorations. Even confetti is often made in horseshoe shapes these days.

As the horse was domesticated thousands of years ago, humans began protecting the animal's feet to have their horses as serviceable as possible. Hence, the ancient Romans strapped leather and metal sandals to their horses' feet, and by the sixth century, horsemen began nailing the metal shoes on their animals' feet. Formerly, horseshoes as well as coins were made of iron, and there was a time when horseshoes were more valuable than coinage, which is why, during the twelfth century, horseshoes were frequently used to pay taxes. This factor, however, never distracted from the object's function as a good luck charm.

The origins of the many beliefs surrounding the horseshoe as a good luck symbol are uncertain. Such beliefs might be linked to ancient horse worship or alternatively to iron, considered the most magical of metals, from which the horseshoe is made. A further explanation for the horseshoe's assumed powers originated with the spread of Christianity in Europe, which postulated that the horseshoe resembled the letter 'C', symbolising Christ. However, the likeliest explanation for the special properties linked to this good luck charm is connected to its shape – the shape of the crescent. The crescent, symbolising pagan moon-deities, was enshrouded in superstitious awe and worn as a protective amulet in ancient cultures, long before the advent of Christianity.

Universally, the crescent was depicted as horns, specific to many deities in various mythologies. The notion that horns exercised a potent and evil-averting influence is very ancient and is evidenced in some of the earliest human societies, which seem to have revered horns as symbols of supernatural power and protection. Prehistoric cave drawings discovered in France show numerous figures of men, in all likelihood shamans, clad as stags with enormous antlers. The wearing of horned helmets might have originated from the early custom of wearing a headdress of animal skin with the animal's horns still attached.

There is a proliferation of horned gods and goddesses in the ancient world. The Sumerian gods Anu, Enlil, and Marduk are shown with horned headdresses. Similarly, Egyptian deities such as Isis, Nut, Seth, Amun, and Hathor and many deities in the Indian and Greek pantheon are depicted as wearing a headdress comprising of the crescent, elongated to assume the appearance of cow horns. The gods distinguished with the crescent and disc headdress were mostly moon-deities, although the disc might also have represented the sun. In ancient times, animals with parted hooves were dedicated to moon deities, as hoof prints were seen to resemble two half moons. Because these deities were revered for protection and well-being, their symbol, the crescent, later found replicated in the shape of the horseshoe, developed into amulets worn against evil influences.

Contributing to the mystery surrounding the horseshoe was undoubtedly the once inexplicable fact that this piece of metal could be nailed to a horse's hoof without causing any visible signs of pain. Hence, to the medieval person's mind, the horseshoe became an object of powerful influence and superstitious awe, not something to simply be discarded after it had become worn and served its purpose. In countries as far apart as Turkey, Italy, Spain, Greece, Egypt, Morocco, and Tunisia, amongst Christians and Muslims alike, a common custom still found in rural areas is that of fixing old horseshoes and cow horns on doors, doorways, and above barn doors. The horseshoe is not only believed to bring good luck, but also to avert the evil eye and to protect against spells, witches, and the devil. In England it was firmly believed in the past that the devil, thought to always travel in circles, was interrupted when he arrived at one of the two points or heels of the horseshoe, and was consequently forced to take a retrograde course. Witches were also believed unable to cross any threshold with a horseshoe nailed above the door.

Opinions are divided over which way around the horseshoe should be fixed. Most people hold that the points should face upward for the luck to 'hold out' or to 'catch the good luck'. Luck was seen to disappear into the ground, literally 'dripping out', if the shoe was hung with the ends facing downwards. Yet horseshoes have been known to be pointed downwards, as the good luck might then be directed towards anyone walking beneath it. Among good wishes common during the seventeenth century in England, it was customary to say: 'May the horseshoe never be pulled from your threshold'.

Doubly strong was the luck of finding a horseshoe on the road or by the wayside, instead of using a horseshoe removed from a horse's hoof. To keep a sailing vessel safe at sea and to protect against storms and misfortune, horseshoes were in the past nailed to the main mast by many naval commanders. If popular legend is believed, Horatio Nelson's ship Victory is but one example.[12]

The Providential Shoe

Amongst the many items purportedly bringing good luck and most frequently found on charm bracelets, in cars, and games, is the humble shoe. The shoe, especially the left shoe, particularly if it is old, has been considered a luck-bringer since way back in time and is most significant in terms of the wealth of curious beliefs surrounding it.

In the past the majority of people possessed only one pair of shoes, which was worn over a period of many years and only re-soled when necessary. Consequently shoes were perceived as becoming 'charged' with the soul essence of their owners and seen as imbued with propitiatory or protective qualities – hence 'bringing luck'. Tennyson expresses this in his 'Lyrical Monologue':

> For this thou shalt from all things seek
> Marrow of mirth and laughter;
> And whereso-er thou move, good luck
> Shall throw her old shoe after.

In modern society, throwing an old shoe after someone might be considered a dangerous act, but in the past, this action was invariably seen as providentially serendipitous. Hence, the ancient Romans used to throw their sandals after wedding processions for good fortune. In England, raining down shoes on newlyweds on their wedding day was regarded as fortuitous, as the following rhyme indicates: 'There is nothing like well-worn leather to propitiate fate'. In Yorkshire, a custom called 'thrashing' was prevalent until only a few decades ago. It signified pelting newlyweds with shoes on their return from church after the wedding ceremony. Similarly, a tradition in Turkey encouraged all guests to touch the bridegroom with their sandals after the ceremony.

Formerly, it was also customary in many European countries for brides to throw their right shoe, instead of a bouquet, a tradition that must have been painful for some guests! Whoever managed to catch the thrown shoe was assured to be happily married soon. Another wedding custom was to tie old shoes and boots to the newlyweds' departing carriage or car to ensure a lucky future for them. This tradition is still found in certain parts of Europe and the U.S. but is generally dying out.

Although the shoe is perceived as a symbol of luck at weddings, its original connection to matrimony had no link to good fortune. Throughout the ages, the shoe symbolised domestic authority and ownership. Therefore, Anglo-Saxon marriage custom required the bride's father to present one of his daughter's shoes ceremoniously to the groom. This action symbolically transferred the authority he once held over her, giving the groom full command over his new wife. As a token of submission to her husband, the bride was required to receive a tap on the head with her husband's shoe after the marriage ceremony. The shoe therefore also embodied a transfer of ownership of the bride from her father to her husband. In Ireland, an ancient ceremony formerly performed whenever someone was elected to office, was to throw an old shoe over the person's head to signify authority.

Similar customs can be found in the Middle East, where shoes or sandals were once given or exchanged as confirmation of a sale and regarded as a symbol of authority. Amongst Jews, the exchange or delivery of a shoe was the token of confirmation of an agreement or contract: 'Now this was the manner in former times in Israel [...] for to confirm all things, a man plucked off his shoe and gave it to his neighbour: and this was a testimony in Israel'.[13]

In Western society, the chief act of investiture is linked with the head – the 'crowning' of a monarch, 'saluting' with respect, or the 'capping' ceremony connected with graduation. Amongst Moslems, Hindus and Buddhists in the East, however, uncovering the head is replaced by uncovering the feet in mosques and temples and, on solemn occasions, to denote respect. The shoe in these cultures is regarded as a symbol of dignity and authority, hence to uncover the feet signifies humility and servitude. In ancient Egypt, the bride and groom customarily wore only one sandal, each on the opposite foot, during the betrothal ceremony. However, at the wedding ceremony, neither of the newlyweds wore sandals. This is depicted on Tutankhamen's golden throne chair, discovered in his tomb in the Valley of Kings and displayed at the Egyptian Museum in Cairo.

The Old Testament refers to 'loosing the shoe' as a mark of respect: 'And the captain of the Lord's host said unto Joshua: Loose thy shoe from off thy foot; for the place whereon thou standest is holy'.[14] Another example of 'loosing the shoe' in biblical times was connected to widowhood. A widow customarily married her dead husband's brother. If, however, contrary to convention, a widow was refused in marriage by her husband's surviving brother, she asserted her anger and independence by 'loosing his shoe from off his foot and spitting in his face'.[15] Called the Halisa Ceremony this procedure had to be enacted in front of the rabbi, who then gave her permission to marry again, this time, a man of her choosing. By formally unstrapping her husband's brother's shoe, the widow renounced a union with him.

In Europe, shoes were once popularly used in divination to see one's future husband by throwing them over one's shoulder on New Year's Eve. Alternatively, they could be placed in the form of a 'T' at right angles to one another before going to bed to enjoy glorious dreams of one's future spouse. A bridegroom had to pay particular attention to his shoes during the wedding ceremony, taking care to leave the buckle of his left shoe undone or the laces untied, to prevent the secret influence of witches on his nuptial night. To prevent nightmares, shoes were placed one 'going in', one 'going out', at the door, or they could be placed in the form of a cross at the side of the bed. Great care, of course, was taken, when putting shoes on, not to start with the left foot. To put shoes on a table was always considered taboo – today for hygiene – as this symbolised a hanging. Therefore, shoes on the table were linked with bringing bad luck, and the saying 'to die in one's shoes' refers to someone dying on the scaffold.

As good luck charms, old shoes when burned, were believed to drive all contagion from a house and to prevent infections from diseases and fevers. In seventeenth-century England, a sure cure for tonsillitis and haemorrhoids was to burn a well-worn old shoe to white ashes. These were then mixed with lard and rubbed on the afflicted part for several days. Burning old shoes was also thought to protect women and their newborn babies, when they were at their most vulnerable, from being abducted by fairies. An interesting parallel is found in rural Rajasthan in India, where women possessed of spirits are still made to drink out of old shoes in order to be 'cured' and accepted back into society.

Is it not amazing to note how an unassuming, common object such as a scuffed, scruffy, old shoe comes suffused with such a wealth of symbolic meaning, tradition, and custom?

The Protective Tattoo

Tattoos are markings made on the skin with indelible pigments rubbed into small punctures. In fact, the word tattoo means 'to puncture'. Tattooing is an ancient and widely distributed custom used at some time or another by nearly all cultures. Tattoos were once universally used as charms to protect the wearer from maleficent forces responsible for illness and misfortune. This belief is endorsed by Hindu myths that recount Lord Vishnu imprinting specific designs on his wife Lakshmi's hands to protect her from evil entities.

Tattoos, applied as protection and to ensure acceptance into the afterlife, were found on Egyptian mummies thousands of years old. Similarly, in China, mummies dating to 1500 BCE, found in 1989 in a remote corner of the Taklamakan desert in Xinjiang, China's westernmost province, were elaborately tattooed. Ancient mummies discovered in Peru and other parts of South America dating to 4000 BCE, the oldest ever found, bear elaborately tattooed designs on the shrivelled skin of their faces and limbs. The interesting fact about these tattoos is that they seem to have been applied as charms to relieve various aches and pains, worn as a medical remedy and placed on specific body areas.[16] The 5300-year-old Neolithic iceman Otzi, discovered in 1991 by a German couple in the Italian Alps, was found to have elaborate tattoo markings on his ankles, above the kidneys, and on the left knee. To keep away the evil forces causing pain to these body parts?

The Arabs tattooed their fingers at the joints as protection against sprains. As many cultures shared the tradition that snakes had protective influences, tattoos often took the form of intricately designed snakes. In Burma, tattoos also functioned as love charms, and many Burmese women wear a special design depicting a triangular love charm tattooed on their lips or tongue or between their eyes. In India, tattoos were widely used as caste marks and for protection. Hinduism is a source of countless tattoo designs, such as the popular gods Siva, Ganesha, and Kali, as well as sacred symbols, such as 'om', adorning the skin of devout followers.

Although tattooing had a predominantly protective function, many cultures also considered it essential for the soul's passage into the afterlife. The Maoris believed elaborate facial tattooing gave acceptance and vision in the hereafter to find one's way. The Dayak tribes of Borneo thought hand tattoos illuminated the darkness of the hereafter, whereas the Inuits of Alaska used such markings to prepare for death rituals.

Tahitians claim that the gods were the first to use tattoos and that the tradition therefore dates to the times when the gods lived on Earth. Amongst those tribes, where most, if not all, people were illiterate and wore minimal clothing, tattooing provided much useful information about rank, age, and tribal connection. These markings also identified a person as a member of a specific social group. In some cultures, tattoo markings began as celebrations of maturation from boy to warrior and hunter. After every successful headhunting expedition, the young man added a tattoo mark to his chest, thereby affirming his status as a warrior within the tribe.

Solomon Islanders punctured their tattoos with the sharp claws of fruit bats or flying foxes; Florida Islanders used the fine bones from bats' wings, whereas Maoris made use of sharks' teeth. Other cultures used thorns, cactus spikes, and various fish bones. Primitive tattooing was an excruciating process, and hours or even days of intense agony were spent by tribal members covering themselves from head to toe in tattooed designs. Tattooing gave the appearance of being covered without the physical encumbrance of clothing.

Often there was no choice in the matter, as many cultures imposed punishment on those who neglected wearing tattoos. Polynesian men considered not being tattooed as unmanly. Thus, despite the painful ordeal, tattooing was common. Because it involved blood shedding, it was not only seen as a mark of courage, but also as a sacrificial gesture. Each tribe practising the art of tattooing developed its own distinctive technique and style. Some tattoo designs were truly artworks, and amongst many peoples of the Pacific Islands and the Maoris of New Zealand, tattooing reached an exceptionally high standard.

The Christian Church banned tattooing under Pope Adrian I at the Ecumenical Council held in Nicaea in 787 CE, labelling it as a 'savage and barbaric practice'. From then on, tattoos were seen as an action of protest, opposing religious or social dictates. For sailors, however, adorning the body with many tattoos remained one of the many precautions taken to guard against misfortune. Most seafaring superstitions reflected a need for protection from the most feared mishaps while at sea, specifically being shipwrecked or drowning. In the days when floggings on board ship were still common, sailors often had tattoos depicting the Crucifixion on their backs in the belief that whoever carried out the punishment would not only be impressed by their piety, but also flinch at striking the image of Christ!

In modern times, tattoos have increasingly become a fashion statement in some Western countries, worn by men and women around their ankles, on their chests, or on one arm and shoulder, as a decorative feature. Clan or tribal tattoo marks and tattoos still worn as protective charms are still found amongst peoples of the Middle East, the nomads of Asia, the North American Indians and the native peoples of Africa.

Sacred Salt Spilled

Throughout history, salt has universally been regarded as a protective agent or charm, thought to possess magical powers and drive away all malevolent forces. As a preserving and curative agent, salt has been essential to humankind since prehistoric times. While salt is cheap and ubiquitous in modern times, its significance and value in the past was enormously important. The many English phrases referring to salt indicate the longstanding importance given to this mineral. We take something with a 'pinch of salt', call someone a 'pillar of salt', speak of 'salting' a mine, and discuss the most 'salient' points of an argument. In the New Testament Book of Matthew, Jesus tells his disciples that they are 'the salt of the earth'.[17]

In the past, salt was an important medium of exchange in commercial ventures across the Mediterranean, Aegean, and Adriatic Seas. Salacia, originally paired with the Roman sea-god Neptune, was the goddess of salt water. Salt was already mined in the Alps when Rome was founded,[18] and the so-called salt routes were specifically established for trade in this commodity. The ancient Phoenicians built saltpans on the Mediterranean island of Ibiza as far back as 600 BCE. To them, salt was known as 'white gold'. Germanic tribes living around the North Sea area traded amber, a much desired fashion accessory by Roman ladies, for salt from the Mediterranean Sea.

Salt was subject to taxation by many governments around the world, from the ancient Chinese and Romans to late medieval Burgundy, where salt was taxed at more than 100 percent when it came from the salt-works. This tax was so lucrative for various governments that the income from a saltpan in southern Spain is said to have largely financed Columbus' voyages.

Food can effectively be stored by drying in arid climates. However, in any normal humidity, fungus and bacteria will rapidly destroy stored food. Even when kept in ice during winter, it quickly rots as it thaws during spring. Therefore, in societies lacking refrigeration, freeze-drying, and canning, salt was used to preserve food – an absence of salt could mean the difference between life and death.

Because salt was such a precious commodity, many peoples customarily paid for contracted work in measured amounts of salt. Salt in the form of small cakes served as monetary exchange in ancient Tibet and Ethiopia. Roman soldiers and workers were paid a salarium in the form of salt or given an allowance with which to buy it, hence, the term 'salary', meaning 'of salt'. Therefore, we still say someone is 'not worth his salt', meaning not worth the expense of the food he eats, or 'he won't earn salt for his porridge', indicating he will never earn a penny.

Salt has traditionally been used in religious ritual amongst various nations and was commonly used in altar offerings and sacrifices. The ancient Greeks, Romans, and Hebrews regarded salt as sacred and a repository of life. They mixed it in their sacrificial cakes and used it in their lustrations. Salt has always been an emblem of purity and sanctity. Holy water consists of a mixture of water and salt, both solemnly exorcised for the banishment of devils and blessed for the infusion of divine grace. The primary use of holy water is for the rite of the Asperges, the sprinkling of the congregation immediately before High Mass each Sunday. The Catholic Church uses holy water on most occasions. For example, when objects are blessed for holy use, in stoups or small basins at the entrance of churches, and by the faithful in their homes.

Salt also features in various mythologies. The Finns have a myth of Ukko, their sky-god, who flung a spark of heavenly fire into the ocean, thereby turning it into salt water, essential to life. Similarly, the ancient Aztecs worshipped Huixtocihuatl, their salt goddess. In some parts of the world, salt mining was regarded with great reverence. Laotian salt miners were obliged to observe sexual abstinence during their term of work, because of the sacred reputation of the substance they were handling. Salt was used to solemnify social transactions and to ratify important agreements; as a symbol of incorruptibility, salt stood for perpetuity. The Old Testament mentions 'a covenant of salt',[19] indicating a covenant that could not be broken. Similarly, Germanic and Celtic tribes used salt for binding oaths by dipping a finger in salt before swearing an oath, and in the English North Midlands, it was customary in the past to use salt as a substitute for the Bible when oaths were pronounced.

To appreciate the many superstitious beliefs connected with salt, it must again be pointed out how precious and rare a commodity this was to many people in the past. Anyone who has eaten totally unsalted food, especially meat, can understand how valuable salt must have been to those lacking access to it. As salt was so vital to the maintenance of life, it was inevitably attributed with magical powers due to its preservation properties. Therefore, salt signified incorruptibility and immortality, and because it was not only essential but also difficult to obtain, it was believed that even spilling a small amount accosted bad fortune.

Spilling salt was considered an unlucky omen by the Romans, and this superstition has descended over the millennia to modern times. Spilling salt was believed to rouse evil spirits and bring bad luck. Many believed that every grain spilt represented a tear to be shed. In Leonardo da Vinci's famous painting of The Lord's Supper, Judas Iscariot can be identified by the saltcellar accidentally knocked over by his arm.

The superstition that the bad luck caused by spilling salt can only be averted by throwing some salt over the left shoulder with the right hand is widely known. This was an add-on to the existing superstitions about salt and developed with the spread of Christianity in Europe and the resulting belief in the devil. Why the left shoulder? This is where the devil and evil spirits were said to lurk. As most people are right-handed, the left side was regarded as the weak side, and using the left hand was seen as inviting misfortune and ill luck.

As the symbol of incorruptibility and immortality because of its magical preservation properties, salt was regarded as harmful and hostile to evil forces, fostering the notion that salt could drive them away. It was therefore used in various stages of human existence, from infancy to death. Newborn children were often 'salted', meaning that immediately after birth, they were bathed in saltwater to ward off the threat of witchcraft, as it was generally believed that unbaptised children were readily seized by fairies. Alternately, a pinch of salt in a newborn baby's mouth or in the cradle protected it from harm and maleficent forces. Another preventive was to sew a little salt into the child's dress.[20]

In many European countries, the belief persisted that a saucer of salt placed on a corpse before burial kept the devil at bay. The devil was thought to abhor this symbol of eternity and immortality. Salt, an emblem of the immortal spirit, together with some earth, was placed on a small plate on a corpse's torso. Besides keeping the devil away, it was thought to keep the deceased's ghost from walking about. 'There is no weight so heavy as salt gets, when it is on the dead' is a popular saying in the British Isles. This custom was widespread in Europe and still practised as late as the 1950s.[21]

The protective qualities attributed to salt are reflected in many curious beliefs of the past. A pinch of salt in daily wash water guarded against evil spirits, and salt carried on one's person at night, protected against the wicked intentions of ghosts. Salting a house served the same purpose of protection and was traditionally observed worldwide. To throw salt after a gypsy was believed to nullify any evil curse the nomad might have pronounced. To keep unwelcome visitors from calling again, salt was spilled on the doorstep or thrown after them as they departed!

Salt was also used as powerful protection against witches and witchcraft. To throw a handful of salt into the fire was believed to neutralise the evil influence of witchcraft. Witches were thought to hate salt, and during the witch trials in Europe, anyone complaining that food was too salty was immediately suspected. Formerly, dairymaids sprinkled salt on their milk pails and butter churns to prevent any interference from witches, and cows were rubbed down with salt after calving to prevent milk fever. In his Teutonic Mythology, Jacob Grimm writes: 'When a witch walks into your house, give her a piece of bread with three grains of salt sprinkled on it, and she can't hurt anything'.[22]

As salt was thought to keep evil at bay, it was known as a luck-bringer, and in Europe, it is still customary in rural areas to give a gift of salt to newlyweds for good luck, hoping they will want for nothing in their future life together. Salt was traditionally carried over the threshold on New Year's Day to ensure good fortune throughout the year. In the past, when moving into a new house, a box of coals and a plate of salt were the first things taken inside to ensure warmth and good fortune;

when moving house, salt was thrown into the fireplace of the old home to leave all sorrow behind, and only fresh salt was brought to a new home to ensure luck, following the saying: 'Travel salt, travel sorrow'.

Borrowing and lending salt has always been considered most unlucky. However, if it was essential, then the salt should be promptly paid for. Similarly, passing salt at the table was considered unlucky, hence the saying: 'Help me to salt, help me to sorrow', or 'pass the salt, pass the sorrow'.

Being a natural preservative, salt symbolises friendship in many countries. To eat a man's salt means to partake of his hospitality. No one who has eaten of another man's salt should speak ill of him or do him a bad turn. This was taken especially seriously in the East. Amongst the Arab people, to share salt created a sacred bond between host and guest, hence the Arabic expression: 'There is salt between us'. The Greeks said: 'Trespass not against salt and board', and Iranians described disloyalty as being 'untrue to salt'.

Interestingly, in European countries during the Middle Ages, salt formed a line of social demarcation at the table, separating family and retainers. Hence, the expression 'to sit below the salt' described the position of servants and staff when taking meals. The family saltcellar of those fortunate enough to afford servants was of massive silver and was usually placed in the middle of the high table. All persons of distinction sat 'above the salt', in other words, at the high table, and had access to the salt, whereas all the servants sat at lower trestle tables, therefore 'below the salt'.

It should be noted that the term 'salt' was, and still is, used for the salt container as well as the condiment, and when entertaining, the salt should always be placed next to the guest of honour, thereby distinguishing the guest from the host.

'Saved by the Bell' or Curfew

Today, many of the original functions behind the use of bells have been forgotten and lost in obscurity. In the past, bells were not only sounded as a part of religious ritual before and after a church service, but also to announce good news; to celebrate occasions such as weddings, christenings, or funerals; to signal ships arriving in port; to spread an alarm about fires or wars; and to frighten away the ever-present evil spirits.

In modern times, it is difficult for us to appreciate the psychological significance of pealing bells throughout the Middle Ages. These were times when ignorance and superstition were widespread, when settlements and villages were often isolated and remote, and werewolves, wild animals, harmful spirits, demons, and many other imagined or real threats were believed to inhabit the countryside. The reassuring sound of powerfully resonating church bells, therefore, constituted a protective magic circle. Within this perimeter, a divinely ordained order prevailed, dispelling the forces of darkness and evil in the minds of the people. The bell's sound, a constant comforting presence, divided every day into hours, regulating the order of the days, summoning the pious to prayer, and terrifying demons and unclean, maleficent entities.

Bells were even fabled to disperse plagues and storms.[23] Therefore, when the Black Death arrived in England, Edward III ordered London to be '…cleaned of all bad smells, so that no more people will die from such smells'.[24] Cannons were fired to clear the air, and bells were rung to dissipate the 'corrupt airs', which physicians of the time believed responsible for the cause and spread of pestilence.

Church bells were also thought highly effective in chasing away witches and sorcerers populating the night skies. In many European countries, therefore, bells were used to protect the harvest from witchcraft. Bells were also considered effective against the powers of the evil eye, which is why they were, and still are, attached to domestic animals, camels, goats, and horses in some countries. In this context, we only have to think of the splendour of horse shows and parades worldwide – the horses decked out with charms, talismans, and numerous little bells attached to their harnesses.

Bells still feature prominently in maritime jargon. In the past, bells regulated life on board ship, rung after each half-hour and hour until 'eight bells' marked the end of a four-hour watch. In poor visibility and fog, the ship's bell was used as a warning signal to any vessel in close proximity. Interestingly, even on modern nuclear and missile-oriented naval vessels, the ringing of the bell at specific intervals has its time-honoured place.

Throughout the ages, bells have been used for ritual, magical, and social purposes, and many superstitions surround bells and bell ropes. The Chinese once rang bells to summon rain, and they still hang protective or 'safe' bells in the entrances of their houses and in cars to ward off ill luck.

It is difficult to ascertain when bells were first used. They played a significant role in the religions of the Assyrians, Babylonians, and Egyptians, whereas the Romans seem to have been summoned by tintinnabula bells to their hot baths and, on certain occasions, to public places. China and India were long famous for using bells, whereas the ancient Hebrews used trumpets instead of bells. The Greek Orthodox Church followed the ancient custom of using wooden boards or iron plates pierced with many holes. These were knocked with a hammer or mallet to call the faithful to church. The first bells used in Christian religious ritual were small hand bells rung as a call to prayer, mentioned by Gregory of Tours (538–594 CE). From the eighth century onwards, church towers were built expressly to house bells, which implies that bells must have increased in size, whereas the very large bells used in churches and cathedrals today became integral to Christian observance from the tenth century onwards. Bells are still used in various Christian, Buddhist, and Hindu rites.

The casting and consecration of church bells were once accompanied by elaborate ceremonies. Legend has it that during the Middle Ages, human sacrificial victims were at times dropped in the cauldron filled with the seething metals destined to become a church bell to give the bell a 'voice' to cry to heaven![61] When casting was completed, bells were officially and ritually blessed, sprinkled with holy water and salt and anointed with oil, to make all devils flee at their sound. The ceremonial baptism of a bell, usually dedicated to a saint in Catholic Europe, required a bishop or his deputy to officiate. The first such baptism of a bell took place in 968 CE when Pope John XIII had a very large newly cast bell consecrated and gave it the name John. Vestiges of this custom are still found in the names various bells are called, such as Great Tom at Christ Church in Oxford and Big Ben housed within the clock tower of the Palace of Westminster in London.

From about 800 CE, it was customary in Europe to sound a single, ominous, woeful bell, the 'passing' or 'soul bell', when someone died. The ringing of this bell was to ensure the prayers of the whole community for the soul of the departed and to keep away evil spirits imagined as waiting to molest and terrify the soul in its passage to the netherworld. Consequently, the soul could get a good head start – like a hunted rabbit – in making it to the hereafter.

The following curious story, from the Dictionary of Superstition by Iona Opie, illustrates the function of bells in dispersing evil entities. In 1911, the vicar of Upton Grey in Hampshire in the United Kingdom noted that when the time came for tolling the passing or soul bell, his sexton tolled all the bells instead. When he enquired as to the reason for this, the vicar received the following delightful reply: 'You know, Sir, devils can't abide o' bells. And there's some devils as are feared of some bells, and there's other devils as are feared of other bells, and so we tolls them all to fear them all'.[26]

Until a few decades ago, it was still customary in many parts of Europe to make numeral distinctions when ringing the soul bell: nine knells were meant for a man, six for a woman, and three for a child. Shakespeare refers to the soul bell in Henry IV: 'And his tongue sounds ever after as a sullen bell, remember'd knolling a departing friend'.[27] This bell is still sounded in rural areas of various European countries as a sign of mourning, giving new meaning to the phrase 'for whom the bell tolls'.

Another interesting bell is the so-called 'cover fire' bell, commonly believed to be of Norman origin. A law was made under William the Conqueror in the eleventh century that with the ringing of the couvre-feu bell every evening, all people had to put out their hearth fires, lights, and candles. The couvre-feu bell or, in translation, 'cover fire' bell, was a common and approved regulation at the time. This bell was used in most northern European monasteries and towns, mainly to prevent accidents from fires, which had unintentionally been left to burn. As all common houses consisted of timber, and dwellings were built very close to each other, house fires were frequent and usually fatal, spreading rapidly from house to house. Although ascribed by some to William the Conqueror and imposed on the English by the Normans as a token of servitude, the same custom seems to have also prevailed in France, Spain, Italy, and probably all other European countries at the same time. Our modern word 'curfew', meaning 'the restriction of movement of people after a certain time deadline', is a corruption of the French couvre-feu, the bell signifying when all people were once expected to douse their fires and turn in for the night.

Equally fascinating is the origin of the expression 'saved by the bell', meaning 'to be rescued by last-minute intervention'. Most sources attribute the origin to popular boxing slang, which came into being some time in the mid-1850s. A boxer is 'saved by the bell' marking the end of each round. Especially if he is in the process of losing a bout, the sound of this bell must be most welcoming!

However, there is an alternative explanation regarding this phrase, involving a curious invention thought to have originated at the end of the eighteenth century. Although there is no evidence of the phrase ever being used in this connection, it may however describe people saved from being buried alive by using a coffin with a bell attached. Several such devices, called safety coffins, were in fact patented in England, on the Continent, and in America, though it is unknown whether such coffins were ever used.

The fear of being buried alive is an ancient one but drew public attention especially during the cholera epidemic of the eighteenth century when bodies were more hastily buried than usual. In the past, medical diagnoses were rudimentary and conditions rendering the body motionless, cold, and unresponsive were not competently and adequately recognised. Basically, it was impossible to establish with certainty that a person was dead until putrefaction had set in. Therefore, doctors devised several tests: Salt and pepper were blown up the nose to see if a corpse would sneeze, or pieces of horseradish, onions and garlic shoved up the nostrils to revive the person; trumpets blown very close to the ears; vinegar, salt and warm urine poured down the throat; stinging nettles applied to the body; scalding hot wax dripped on the scalp and most extreme of all a red hot poker applied to the rear end of the corpse in an attempt to make it flinch.

However, in spite of such extreme measures, the undisputed fact reported throughout history, of coffins found with scratch marks on the inside attests to people actually having been buried alive. Hence, there was considerable public anxiety about this topic voiced by various prominent figures, especially during the Victorian Age. The macabre writings of Edgar Allan Poe tapped into and fuelled public fear, with short stories such as The Premature Burial, released in 1844. Such fears and anxieties therefore resulted in the timely, reassuring invention of various curious devices that could be incorporated into coffins, yet had a means of communication to the outside, such as a cord with a bell attached. The presumed dead unfortunate, enclosed six feet under, could then indeed be saved by the bell!

III

WITCHCRAFT AND THE DEVIL

Ancient Practices of Witchcraft

A belief in magic practices through the agency of spirits and demons is universal, found in all cultures, and together with references to witchcraft, was practised by men and women going back to the beginnings of history. Egyptian records tell of soothsayers deriving their powers from devils. The Old Testament speaks of a male sorcerer in the Pharaoh's court,[1] in the court of the king of Babylon[2], and amongst the Jewish people.[3] Although the code of the Babylonian king, Hammurabi, prohibited witchcraft, the practice continued to flourish amongst Babylonians, Chaldeans, and Egyptians millennia before our current era. The scriptures acknowledge the existence and power of witches. This is confirmed in Deuteronomy, where it is written: 'There shall not be found among you any one that uses divination, or an observer of times, or an enchanter, or a witch, or a charmer, or a consulter with familiar spirits, or a wizard, or a necromancer, for all that do these things are an abomination unto the Lord'.[4] The biblical command: 'Thou shalt not suffer a witch to live',[5] was a main justification for the terrible witch persecutions of later times.

Contrary to popular opinion, ancient witchcraft consisted primarily of medium-like skills in evoking spirits such as the Old Testament witch of Endor whom Saul consulted in defiance of his own edict: 'Then said Saul unto his servants: Seek me a woman that has a familiar spirit, that I may go to her and enquire of her. And his servants said unto him: Behold, there is a woman that hath a familiar spirit at En-dor'.[6] The witch of Endor subsequently calls up Samuel's spirit at Saul's request: 'Then said the woman: Whom shall I bring up unto thee? And he said: Bring me up Samuel'.[7]

Besides attributing mediumistic skills to witches, the Old Testament sometimes links sexual immorality to witchcraft. With reference to Jezebel, the king of Sidon's daughter, we are told: '...the whoredoms of your mother Jezebel and her witchcraft are so many'.[8] A similar connection, one persisting in Europe during the Middle Ages when women accused of witchcraft were thought to have caused miscarriages and immoral behaviour, can be deduced from the prophet Nahum's words when he compares Nineveh to 'the well-favoured harlot, the mistress of witchcrafts....'.[9]

In the New Testament, the term 'witchcraft' is commonly equated with the divination practices of the Romans: 'O foolish Galatians, who hath bewitched you, that ye not obey the truth, [...]'.[10] Similar references are also found in the Acts of the Apostles and Galatians.[11]

Witches, magicians, soothsayers, and necromancers also figured prominently in the cultures of ancient Greece and Rome. However, it is important to note that in all the ancient cultures, witchcraft referred mainly to divination and magic, and there is no mention of any woman killed for the crime of witchcraft. It was not until the Middle Ages,[12] through the powerful influence of Christianity, that the concept arose of witches receiving their powers from Satan. Medieval witchcraft thus became defined as using supernatural powers derived from dealing with the devil and evil spirits. The witch was considered able to perform her antisocial magic acts only through the co-operation of these dark forces.

Witchcraft during the Middle Ages

In early Christian times, the Church's attitude towards witchcraft was one of leniency because the Church was still struggling to consolidate its power throughout the Roman Empire. Witches and sorcerers were believed to cast spells, mix potions, call up rain or fair weather, and perform many acts typically executed by witchdoctors and tribal shamans since the dawn of time. Although the Church frowned on such people, they were not considered a threat to society. Likewise, the Church did not yet seek to challenge the many devotees of the old religions and tolerated the ancient rites of worship. Most scholars agree that surviving remnants of the old pagan religious rites, which prevailed in Europe before Christianity, later became labelled as 'witchcraft'. These witches served the old gods and practised their rituals with no evil intent, combining remnants of pagan rites, folk medicine, and a curiosity for the unexplained. The old religions probably existed side by side with Christianity for several centuries, slowly losing adherents and significance. But, as Christianity gained in ascendancy, the Church increasingly demonised the old religions, persuading people that the pagan gods were devils and that those who continued practising the ancient ways were surely witches.

The fact that adherents to the old religion did not accept and follow the established order and were unwilling to submit to the Church's ruling authority condemned them outright from the growing population of converts. Consequently, these diehards began to practise the old ways in secret, making their actions all the more mysterious and clouded in superstition. At that stage, the Church required only penance to atone for performing the so-called black art of witchcraft.

The Church's attitude became austere towards witchcraft under two main influences: First, the Church had become so powerful that it could afford to annihilate openly any remnants of the old faith. Second, the increasing social unrest during the Middle Ages found expression in various forms of secularism. As these tendencies threatened to undermine the Church's ecclesiastical authority, it set about eradicating them by treating secularism as heresy and identifying heresy with witchcraft. Interestingly, the word 'heresy' is defined as a belief or practice contrary to orthodox doctrine. It derives from the Greek term hairesis, meaning 'choice'. Therefore, a charge of heresy was a denial of the right of choice.

Ordinary people had always been fascinated by astrology, horoscopes and various methods of divination. They bought love potions, amulets, charms, talismans, magic rings, and magic mirrors and feared comets and signs in the night sky. Superstition was ever lurking in people's minds. During the Middle Ages, the term 'witchcraft' was extended to include all the black arts so popular amongst the general populace and openly practised at fairs and festivals. The Church condemned all these concepts and instilled the fear of everlasting hellfire and damnation in those resorting to divination or magic.

Unleashing the Witch Terror

Social disorganisation, hysteria and inter-denominational tensions in the Christian world were only a part of the collective issues that laid the foundations of the witch terror during the Middle Ages. The outbreak of the devastating plague known as the Black Death, which killed about a third of Europe's population during the fourteenth century, also had an unimaginable impact. Spreading along the trade routes from China, the plague reached Egypt by 1348 and from there, quickly spread to Europe where it lasted for four years. An estimated 25 million people died on the European continent alone, and the population of England was reduced by almost half. The resulting terror caused uncontrolled mass hysteria on an unprecedented scale. Scapegoats for this catastrophe had to be found and minority groups, such as gypsies, various unorthodox religious groups, Jewish groups and so-called witches were held to blame for the epidemic.

A close parallel to the resulting persecutions during the witch craze in Europe can also be found in the Eket district of Calabar in Nigeria. Between 1918 and 1919, an influenza outbreak decimated a large section of the population in Eket through the death of many hundreds of people. A spate of witchcraft accusations immediately followed this epidemic, with eighteen persons being hanged for witchcraft in one small village alone. Analogous circumstances occurred in Alaska in 1957, when civil authorities were hard put to prevent an Eskimo community from killing the 'witches' held responsible for the outbreak of a viral epidemic. Many decades later, in 2014, the widespread ebola outbreak in West African countries was blamed on witchcraft and sorcery by a large number of the population. On 2 August 2014, BBC news reported that some people in West Africa were not seeking medical treatment because they blamed sorcerers for the recent deaths due to ebola, and not the disease itself. Similarly, several news reports still attest to accusations of witchcraft in modern day Pakistan and India, as well as the burning of alleged witches in Papua New Guinea in 2009. With such superstitions still extant in modern times, it is no wonder that witchcraft was blamed for the unprecedented loss of life many centuries earlier during the Black Death outbreak of the fourteenth century.

Social and economic change was already well underway when the great plague reached epidemic proportions in Europe during the fourteenth century. Aside from the Black Death that was prevalent throughout Europe, and in addition to inter-denominational tensions, deep anxieties amongst the faithful strengthened the conviction that Satan's powers were ascending. The church father, Thomas of Aquinas (1225–1274), had already concluded in his writings two hundred years earlier that witches could cause epidemics, storms, and other abnormal weather conditions and that they could fly through the air, carried by Satan on broomsticks, and transform themselves into animals. Once this belief became generally accepted amongst the people, the inevitable conclusion was for an institution such as the infamous Inquisition to be called to seek out those dabbling in witchcraft as servants of Satan.

Pope Gregory IX formally created the Holy Office of Inquisition in 1231 to expurgate heresy. Two years later, Gregory transferred the control of proceedings against heretics from the bishops' courts to special commissioners chosen from Franciscan and Dominican friars. Pope Innocent IV (1243–54) added torture to be administered by the secular authority. When torture to elicit confessions proved problematic to some, inquisitors and their assistants were given permission to absolve one another for such acts, to 'promote the work of faith more truly'.[13]

Even religious groups such as the Albigenses, Waldenses, Templars, and several minor orders were considered heretics during the thirteenth century. For two hundred years, the Inquisition concentrated its efforts towards their elimination. Confiscating properties of those accused of heresy and witchcraft was a profitable business for the Church, and often, accusers might have been motivated solely by the acquisition of wealth. Therefore, the very rich, especially those with powerful political enemies, feared the inquisitors even more than the poor did. Inquisitors were given added incentive to tackle their duties with zeal by receiving part of the proceeds of confiscated property. There were various methods of dividing the spoils of the condemned, and once the scribe and executioner had been paid, the remainder went into the Pope's treasury.

In 1484, Pope Innocent VIII issued a bull defining witchcraft in all its aspects as heresy. The witch-hunt mania then took hold irrevocably and obsessed Europe with unquenchable fury from the fifteenth century to the end of the seventeenth century. Charges viewed as heretical by the Church included sorcery, sacrilege, blasphemy, sodomy, and non-payment of taxes to the Pope and the clergy. Spurred on by the bull issued by Pope Innocent VIII, the first important and most damning book on the subject of witchcraft, the Malleus Maleficarum, a handbook of European witch-finders, appeared in Germany in 1486. This book's wide circulation was made possible by the printing press, which Johannes Gutenberg had invented in 1440. Many hundreds of the faithful who could read were now given formal authority to all the fables and phenomenal assertions allegedly collected about witches and their craft – all contained in the Malleus Maleficarum.

Although there had always been the occasional 'witch' in a village or hamlet, the pontiff began receiving many reports that witches had begun multiplying alarmingly. Christendom was suddenly thought to be threatened by the infestation of thousands of malevolent witches, present in almost every town, village, and hamlet. Even though hundreds, and eventually thousands, were tortured and burned, their numbers were believed to be ever increasing, resulting in a frenzy never before witnessed on the European continent.

However, it would be wrong to construe the witch-hunts solely as a means by which the Church sought to control society. Even though the execution of witches was officially sanctioned and brought about by the manoeuvrings of the Inquisition, it was often instigated and carried out at a local level and frequently depended on the settling of personal grudges and superstitious fears.

Witch-Finders

The general procedure for finding witches during the Inquisition varied only slightly among different European countries. First came the accusation of witchcraft by someone allowed to remain anonymous and only made known to the accused by permission of the accuser. Witnesses were well paid for their testimonies, resulting in the rise of gangs of so-called witch-finders who, for handsome payment, then handed hapless victims over to the Inquisitors.

Witch-finders tended to single out especially older women, who, living alone, were tolerated in former times for their strange yet harmless ways or spells and respected for their herbal remedies. Now, the village healer and wise woman, skilled in using herbs as medicine, the aged eccentric spinster, the haggard old crone known for her love potions, or those generally mistrusted by the community as being odd, were erroneously called witches. Often, they were accused of the black arts because of jealousy, hatred, spite, or suspicion. Many accused old women were physically weak and haggard looking, with hairy growths on their faces or missing teeth. Sometimes these old hags kept pets for companionship – a psychological need we well understand today, especially for the lonely – which caused the traditional image of the witch-figure accompanied by her cat, typically found in today's fairy tales, with the pointed hat, tripod, and broomstick added later. Witch-finders targeted these unfortunate old women and then proceeded to search their homes for potions, herbal mixtures, or poppets, which were small effigies of human figures used for evil intent.

Those accused had no advocates. Children were encouraged to bear attestation against their parents, whereas spouses, relatives, and neighbours informed the Church authorities of their suspicions of one another, especially in times of conflict. Not only were old people targeted, but thousands of young women, men, and children – some as young as eight – were accused of making a pact with the devil.

After having their homes searched, the accused were also tested for evidence of complicity with the devil. All witches were believed to have a mark somewhere on their bodies made by the devil as proof of belonging to him. Any physical abnormalities, such as an unusual skin blemish, a hairy growth, a mole, a wart, a birthmark, a spot insensitive to pain, or one that did not readily bleed, were suspect – all regarded with great suspicion and proof of alliance with the Evil One.

Today it is general knowledge that skin covering old scars becomes thicker and does not bleed easily and that old people often have moles and marks on their bodies, insensitive to pain – a fact not considered during these terrible persecutions. Any raised protuberances on the body of the accused were believed to be nipples through which familiars suckled the witch's blood. Witch-finders employed pins, knives, and sharp probes to prod and poke their victims, thus determining any areas on the body insensitive to pain. Sometimes, knives with retractable blades and hollow handles were used on suspects – a most fiendish, devilish ploy, as it convinced the poor victim and all witnesses that she must be guilty as charged because she did not feel the probe!

The accused, head shaved, totally naked, and subjected to scrutiny, was often examined in public before a gathering of leering men, women, and children. The shame, embarrassment, and psychological stress for the victim must have been dreadful. Not only spots on the victim's skin became proof of witchcraft, but also the inability to weep, an aversion to salt, or failure in the water test.

It was firmly held that witches were unable to weep or to shed more than three tears and anyone complaining that the food was too salty was immediately suspected. The water test was carried out by throwing the unfortunate, who had been 'cross bound' – that is, the right thumb tied to the left big toe and left thumb to right big toe – into a body of water to test her innocence. The theory was that a witch would float, as the water would reject a servant of the devil, who inevitably renounced baptismal water. Whether the victim stayed afloat or sank, death was a certainty. If the accused sank and somehow managed to survive, the test was simply not considered adequate proof that the victim was innocent, but proof rather of Satan's great powers to protect his own kind.

In many instances, old women accused of witchcraft were demented and confessed freely to enjoying aerial rides with Satan, prowling the countryside as cats, or giving birth to terrifying monsters after coupling with the devil.

The Alleged Powers of Witches

Many supposed influences and capabilities of witches were imaginary and depended largely on the powers of superstitious suggestion. The mere notion that a witch had cast a spell on someone or was sticking pins in a waxen image of that person possibly resulted in illness and even death. Witches were charged with causing injury to others, ranging from minor afflictions to poisoning and murder. A murder charge was made for the witch's practice of sticking pins in waxen images of victims and slowly melting these over a candle flame.

The concept of witches' sabbaths, their pact with the devil, their bestial rites, anointing themselves with oils from murdered infants' bodies, and nefarious ideas propagated about witches and witchcraft all evolved as accusing allegations instituted by the Inquisition and documented in the Malleus Maleficarum. Inquisitors and bounty witch-hunters were convinced that blasphemous horrors formed the basis of all witchcraft, and none of them ever imagined they could be wrong in their assumptions. All information about witches' powers and their activities came from the infamous witch trials. Such information, extracted under the most unimaginable tortures, simply reflected what people believed to be true about witchcraft.

Every witch was assumed to be a servant of the devil. In this respect, the practitioners of witchcraft differed from warlocks, sorcerers, and other black magic conjurers thought to be traditionally educated and presumed to have learned to master the devil. Witchcraft therefore presupposed the reality of the devil and all subordinates in the form of demons, imps, incubi, and succubi, and the possibility of a physical relationship with these powerful forces. The belief in the devil's power to assume human or animal form, so pronounced during the days of witchcraft prosecutions, was responsible for the widespread acceptance of accounts of intercourse occurring between the devil and humans. At various witchcraft trials, such powers of metamorphosis were affirmed, admitted, and accepted by judges, prosecutors, and defendants alike.

In return for serving the Evil One, it was believed that witches received certain powers such as the ability to cure or inflict illness, to transfer illness from one person to another, to cause impotence and sterility in humans and barrenness in livestock, to sour milk, to raise storms, cause drought, cause crop failure, and to cause many other disasters. Any uncommon sickness of man, beast, and crops was attributed to their demoniacal practices.

It was generally believed that a witch could see spirits, and by her supernatural gaze, could enchant and bewitch people through a single glance. A witch could arouse love with love potions or destroy it with spells and charms. It was also believed that she could revive the dead, animate inanimate objects, conjure up spirits, transform herself into certain animals, make herself invisible with certain ointments, and fly through the air.

Flying has always been attributed to supernatural beings – both good and evil – and the belief in a witch's power to travel through the air was widespread and persistent. In seventeenth-century records of witchcraft trials, the words 'not guilty, no flying' appeared several times. So-called flying ointments, allegedly used by the accused by rubbing them on the skin, were referred to in witch trials. Such ointments usually consisted of a mixture of toxic plants such as belladonna, hemlock, and wolf's bane,[14] now known to cause symptoms of dizziness and even delirium accompanied by a feeling of falling through the air. Rubbing such a potent potion into the skin was just as effective as swallowing it. Many of those convicted of being witches actually believed that they could fly through the air. The blood of bats was believed to be a main ingredient in the purported flying ointments – the association obvious in that the blood of a flying night creature undoubtedly let a witch acquire the same abilities.

During the Middle Ages, witches were thought to travel through the air on various flying objects, including animals, shovels, eggshells, forked sticks, or broomsticks, without any visible support. The whole question of witches flying was thrashed out in an English court of law towards the end of the eighteenth century. Lord Mansfield, the judge, delivered the judgment that he knew of no English law prohibiting flying and, for him, anyone so inclined was free to do so. Interestingly enough, all reports of English witches flying stopped immediately from the moment British law sanctioned it.

A Scientific Explanation?

In modern times, there is perhaps a valid scientific explanation for some symptoms experienced by those accused of witchcraft during the witch-mania in Europe. In 1976, Linda Caporael, a behavioural scientist, offered the first evidence that the Salem witch trials in colonial Massachusetts in 1692 followed an outbreak of rye ergot.[15]

Ergot is a parasitic fungus found on cereal grasses, especially rye. This fungus thrives in a cold winter followed by a wet spring. Ergot naturally produces a wide range of chemical compounds, all of which generate psycho-activity to some degree. Ergot also narrows and constricts the blood vessels, which if severe can lead to gangrene of the extremities. Ergot alkaloids include lysergic acid, from which LSD is made. Toxicologists now know that symptoms of ergot-poisoning include hallucinations, severe mental disturbances, delusions, convulsions, vertigo, vomiting, crawling sensations on the skin, and tingling and painful burning sensations in the extremities – all these symptoms were reported during the European and Salem witch trials. In severe cases of ergot-poisoning, peripheral vaso-constriction leads to gangrene and death. Interestingly, livestock fed with infected grain often become sterile, reminding us that causing barrenness in livestock was one of the many charges so often levelled at the accused.

In her book, Poisons of the Past: Moulds, Epidemics and History,[16] Mary Matossian, tells a story about rye ergot reaching far beyond Salem, encompassing seven centuries of demographics and weather and crop records from Europe and America. Her research determined that during the Middle Ages, ergot was a widespread parasite of cereal grains in Europe, growing especially well during excessively damp springs and summers. As heat does not break down the psychoactive compounds in ergot, they would have been present in bread baked from ergotised grains. Besides the symptoms of 'bewitchment', ergot seriously weakens the immune system, leading Mary Matossian to argue that drops in population because of epidemics such as the Black Death followed diets heavy in rye bread with climate ideal for ergot to flourish. Witch-hunts hardly occurred in those European areas where rye was not grown as a staple food and climate was not conducive to ergot.

In 1951, the publicity surrounding an outbreak of ergot poisoning in Pont St. Esprit, a small town in France, gave insight into what might have been experienced over centuries in medieval times when grains made up the people's staple diet. The local bakery in Pont St. Esprit inadvertently sold bread contaminated with ergot. Consequently, four people died, and countless others suffered hallucinations, vomiting, crawling sensations under the skin, violent convulsions, and other typical symptoms of ergot poisoning. Although inevitable speculation by the superstitious arose about possession, bewitchment, and a belief that the devil occupied the bakery, ergot was unquestionably found to be the culprit through laboratory testing.

The Weaker Sex

On May 4, 2009 the Daily Mail Newspaper in the United Kingdom carried the following article: 'The remains of a 14th century teenager, believed to have been beheaded on charges of witchcraft and buried in unconsecrated ground, has been laid to rest in a proper funeral…700 years after her death. The girl, named Holly by archaeologists because her remains were found beneath a holly bush, had had her head laid at her side, a sign that she might have been suspected of witchcraft. […] the decapitation – which it was believed would deny eternal life – meant Holly was shamed'. About 80 percent of those once accused as witches were women. Women, unlike men, were believed to possess supernatural powers and, hence, were suspected of witchcraft more often than men were. Theology of the time assumed women were much weaker than men and therefore more likely to succumb to the devil. On sorcery, King James I of England wrote in his Daemonologie in 1597: 'There are twentie women given to that craft, where there is one man'.[17]

Traditionally through the ages, a magic aura was believed to surround women. Much of this can be attributed to the ignorance that has always surrounded female physiology – a physiology only now understood and accepted by most civilised societies. Horror, awe, and the stigma of uncleanness were characteristic reactions to menstrual flow, pregnancy, and childbirth. The Christian Church further strengthened this attitude.

Archbishop Theodore's seventh-century Penitential forbade women to enter a church or receive communion during their monthly periods, as well as pregnant women until forty days after childbirth.[18]

Underlying the prevailing attitude towards women at the time was the position taken by the Church and by men in general. The fall of humankind in the Garden of Eden attributable to Eve permeated Western culture – Eve had become the focus of sin in the world. Being the daughters of Eve, women were therefore perceived as seducing even without trying. As women are receptive during sexual intercourse and can receive indefinitely, whether willingly or not, this generated the idea that women were insatiable and prone to leading men astray. St. Jerome (circa 340–420 CE) summed up the existing mindset: '... women's love in general is accused of ever being insatiable; put it out and it bursts into flame; give it plenty, it is again in need; it enervates a man's mind and engrosses all thought except for the passion which it feeds'.[19] St. Paul's ascetic views further strengthened the elements of misogyny. The church father, Tertullian (circa 160–235), himself married, also condemned sexuality as illicit and referred to women as 'gateways to the Devil'.[20] Other church fathers followed suit. Whereas St. Jerome was not even sure women were human, St. Augustine (354–386 CE) declared women were morally and mentally inferior to men and Thomas Aquinas (1225-1274) regarded women as a temptation to evil.[21] The key archetypes of womankind at the time were the virtuous, immaculate Virgin, the pox-ridden prostitute and the witch.

Furthermore, it was propagated that women were to be feared as child bearers. Because they were traditionally viewed as deceptive, no man could be sure that the children he was raising were his own. It was thought that chaos would ensue if women were to have the fear of childbirth removed from them. Therefore, women had to regard sex with the utmost apprehension; it was joyless, nothing but a marital duty, and invariably led to suffering and even death in childbirth. In the sixteenth century Martin Luther bluntly expressed the views still popularly held at the time: 'If women die in childbirth that does no harm. It is what they were made for'.[22] The very fact that midwives knew how to alleviate the pain of birthing was considered a threat, coupled, with the fact that they kept their potions a secret, automatically surrounding them with a mysterious aura. Hence, the Malleus Maleficarum singled out especially midwives as deserving the worst possible treatment.

Such unanimous misogynist declarations by the leading church fathers of the time spurned a scornful attitude towards women, evident in the sexual charges levelled against so-called witches. They were accused of wild orgies in which they were believed to copulate with their master, the devil, and with subordinate demons. They were also deemed solely responsible for causing impotence in men and sterility in women.

Witches' Servants

Beliefs surrounding witchcraft were concerned mainly with the need to obtain protection from activities involving the black arts. In popular imagination, the typical witch was an old hag deriving pleasure from inflicting harm and misfortune on others. Witches were traditionally depicted in black garb, accompanied by their most trusted familiars – a black cat, bat, or raven – pointed black hat, cauldron, and book of spells. Witches' creature familiars, derived from the Latin term famulus, meaning 'servant', were believed to be demons in human or animal form feeding on the witches' blood and doing everything by their mistresses' bidding. It was generally accepted that the witch could take on the shape of these familiars. Usually familiars appeared in the form of small domestic animals, although they could also appear as monsters, toads, or flies. Demonic flies were specifically a feature of northern European sorcery. These tiny and very mobile creatures naturally had access to anyone suspected of witchcraft.

The cat's role as a witch's familiar was tragic indeed. In the ancient world, this animal was invested with an aura of holiness, but in Christian Europe, the cat was decidedly not destined to be venerated. With its violent repudiation of paganism, the Christian Church succeeded in reducing the status of this once sacred animal to that of a devil. In most European countries, the black cat was considered the embodiment of Satan. In Britain, the white cat assumed this role, whereas the brindled cat was notorious as a witch's familiar. This reminds us of the ominous witch's cry in Shakespeare's Macbeth: 'Thrice the brindled cat hath mew'd'.[23]

During the witch-mania in Europe, anyone could indiscriminately be accused by hostile neighbours or acquaintances to have assumed the shape of a cat. In Scotland, in 1607 a woman named Isobel Grierson was hanged on the evidence that she entered the house of Adam Clark at Prestonpans in the likeness of a cat.[24] One of the last people to be tried for witchcraft in England was Jane Wenham, accused of assuming a cat's form to terrify her victims. Towards the end of the witchcraft mania in Britain in 1718, William Montgomery of Caithness claimed he was driven berserk by a crowd of cats gossiping in human language outside his home. He attacked the animals with a hatchet, killing two and wounding others. The next day, two old women were found dead in bed, whereas another had an unexplained gash on her leg.[25] This was considered indubitably positive proof of shape changing during the night. Witch-hunters were inclined to have very vivid imaginations and saw exactly what they wished to see.

Not only the cat, but also the hare or rabbit were thought of as witches' familiars. It was firmly believed that witches themselves appeared in hare or rabbit form. This is why various parts of the animals' bodies feature in mischief-making spells and potions. The belief that it was unlucky to meet a hare originated in medieval times, as any hare was thought to be a witch in disguise. According to popular opinion, this transformation was achieved by rubbing the skin with fat from a hare. Usually, a hare concealed in the form of a witch could talk to and play tricks on hunters in the forest, leading them astray. This theme is central to many fairy tales and folk tales. If a hare was killed or wounded, it was firmly believed that a witch would be found the next day, either dead or with a wound corresponding exactly to the one inflicted on the hare. Countless old women were either hanged or burned because of such sketchy evidence. The almost-human plaintive cry and the upright sitting position of the hare might have contributed to such beliefs.

Confession and Condemnation

The Church considered it unjust to condemn someone for witchcraft without a confession. But, to extract a confession, the most fiendish, and terrible tortures were sanctioned and applied in the name of God. Limbs were wrenched from their sockets, and then tightly bound in contorted positions; fingers, arms, and legs were crushed slowly or smashed to pulp; tongues were wrenched out and red-hot iron poured into the mouth; or hair set on fire. Often, these were only considered the preliminaries before the real torture started. Unspeakable atrocities were carried out on mostly innocent victims, until finally, they admitted any accusation levelled at them to end their ordeal. The victim was then told to name accomplices, or the torture would continue. This resulted in more innocents being arrested and, hence, the consequent notion amongst those in authority and the public, of an apparent growth in the numbers of witches! Witch-hunters never seemed to grasp that they were creating witches, as their victims said whatever was expected of them to make the pain stop.

The avowed purpose of the Inquisition was not only to condemn the guilty, but also to save the poor creature's soul. Those confessing under torture were allowed to be given the sacraments and then often allowed an 'easy' death by hanging or beheading before being burned. Although most victims fervently recanted their confessions on the way to their executions, this was considered invalid.

The number of victims condemned under these circumstances must have been enormous, although exact figures are unknown. However, estimates given by modern scholars run into tens of thousands. Most of Europe was engulfed in the terrors of witch trials. In the German states, the situation became acute during the Reformation, when both Catholics and Protestants zealously pursued witchcraft with a pious severity only partially dampened by the terrible ravages of the Thirty Years War (1618–1648). In England, Inquisitional courts were never established, as the English judiciary strongly disapproved of torture, thus hanging witches instead of burning them.

In 1631, the Netherlands was one of the first countries to end the persecutions. It was eventually recognised that too many convictions had targeted the innocent out of malice and envy and that magistrates' leading questions tended to govern the content of so-called confessions, not to mention the guaranteed methods of extracting confessions under fiendish tortures. During the second half of the seventeenth century, the Inquisitio Sancta Romana in Italy urged judges to apply torture only under suspicions of genuine guilt and to cease prosecuting those suspected of attending witches' sabbaths.

Finally, witch trials started declining in most parts of Europe after 1680. Slowly, prosecutions diminished, and in England, the death penalty for witchcraft was abolished in 1736. The last legal execution of a witch occurred in Switzerland in 1782. Eastern Europe largely escaped the terrors of witch-hunts, simply because the Orthodox Church did not expound on the theory of diabolism with as much fervour as its Western counterpart.

As witchcraft was universally believed responsible for all kinds of misfortunes and natural disasters, countless charms and amulets were devised to protect humans, livestock, and homes against its evil workings. Central to European witchcraft was the worship of the devil or Evil One.

The Horny Devil

Medieval society regarded the devil as a constant threat waiting to exploit the smallest of human weaknesses, offering temptations of wealth, power, and sexual gratification to those who lacking them, further urging every imaginable type of crime to be committed. The devil was believed an immediate presence, apt to appear instantly whenever his name was mentioned. Feared by everyone, people were reluctant to mention the devil's name, referring to him instead as Old Nick, not to provoke dark and evil forces. The adjective 'old' stemmed from a time when referring to someone as old denoted great respect for their maturity. Thus, by speaking of Old Nick, or the closely related term, Old Harry, it was sincerely hoped that the devil was favourably humoured.

In the expression, 'there'll be the dickens to pay', the devil is cleverly referred to with a euphemism by only using his initial. Shakespeare alluded to the devil in this way in his Merry Wives of Windsor when Mrs. Page says: 'I cannot tell, what the dickens his name is'.[26] The saying that someone will have 'the devil to pay' derives from a time when it was believed that to gain wealth or enjoy earthly pleasures meant that a bargain first had to be made with the devil.

In folk tales and fairy tales, the devil is often depicted as rather stupid and easily outwitted by clever tricks. In medieval art, literature, and philosophy, the devil was a familiar figure, depicted as ugly, evil-smelling, and often with goatish attributes such as horns, tail, and cloven hooves. Although it was thought he could partly transform himself into various shapes, he could not change his cloven hooves, which always identified him and singled him out at every appearance. These characteristics were derived from the first theological definition of the devil, composed in graphic detail by the early church fathers. It dates to the Council of Toledo in 447 CE. Here, the devil was described as a black, monstrous apparition with horns on his head, cloven hooves, an immense phallus, and an unpleasant sulphurous smell surrounding him.

The typical features of the devil, with cloven hooves, tail, and horns, come from the most ancient descriptions of a demon. An ancient Syrian mythological text, stemming from Ugarit, tells how the god El was once terrified by the appearance of a demon with 'two horns and a tail'. In Hindu, Buddhist, and Persian mythology, evil powers are also frequently represented as horned.

Another explanation for the representation of the devil with cloven hooves might have originated from rabbinical writings in which the devil was called seirizzim, meaning 'goat'. The Jewish scapegoat ritual also tended to connect the goat with evil. This association is strengthened in the Matthew Gospel,[27] which relates Jesus likening the righteous to sheep and the wicked to goats that will be condemned to 'everlasting fire, prepared for the devil and his angels'.

The descriptive definition of the devil by Christian church fathers at the Council of Toledo was probably influenced, not only by the scriptures, but also by the various pagan cults prevalent in the Roman Empire at the time. Greek and Roman horned gods might have become prototypes for the later conception of the Christian devil, surviving through the principle of henotheism in which the old gods became demonised in the new religion.

Judging from the confessions of those accused of witchcraft and subsequent pictures drawn by artists, the devil often looked remarkably like the half-man, half-goat, Greek god, Pan, depicted with cloven hooves, goat's horns, and a beard. Christianity represented the devil as a creature as lascivious as the goat. In ancient Greece, Pan was worshipped with great reverence as the god of flocks, herds, and pastures, in charge of reproduction. The horned Pan was an amorous god linked with fruitfulness, as his chief function was to make flocks fertile, a function of great importance when livestock formed the basis of subsistence. The goat's love of copulation explains why sexually aroused people are often referred to as being horny. Interestingly, the association of horns with fertility accounts for the metaphoric use of 'horn' for phallus found in the Old Testament,[28] as well as the worldwide consumption of powdered horn as an aphrodisiac. Therefore, the half-man, half-goat devil of European folklore is often still referred to as 'Old Horny'.

IV

DIVINATION, OMENS
AND PORTENTS

Divining the Future

The art of divination might be defined as a specific method used to gain insight into the unknown and to discover events in the past, present, and future by supernatural means. From the earliest times, humankind has tried to enquire and penetrate into the future through practices believed to access predictive knowledge. Among ancient civilisations, divination was always closely allied with religion. As the word indicates, divination is derived from the Latin term divinare, meaning 'to divine', which implies a superior knowledge obtained from the supernatural by specific communication with divinities. In Latin, the art of interpreting signs was simply called divine activity or divinatio and in Greek, the word for God, theos, is closely linked to the work of seers. Today, divination has lost its connection to religion but persists in the category of superstition. Fortune telling in modern society refers mainly to predictions pertaining to an individual's own future and does not refer, as was customary in the past, to society as a whole

Divination has ancient origins and was practised by the Babylonians as far back as 2000 BCE. Proof of how important the art of divination was to the ancient societies of Assyria and Babylon was found in the unearthing of thousands of clay tablets on which diviners had catalogued and collected individual omens. Similarly, in China thousands of bones bearing inscriptions, belonging to the Shang Dynasty (ca 1300 BCE) have been unearthed. Such divination bones, consulted on a daily basis, would be heated over a fire and the cracks and crackles 'interpreted'. All the bones bear the inscriptions of questions asked of higher powers, as well as the prognostications and actual outcomes for future reference.

Universally, in ancient times, any public or private activity first required a good omen before being carried out. The Babylonians had a great interest in omens, and seers used various methods of divination to determine the outcome of almost every important activity. Demons were greatly feared for the suffering and misfortune they could cause, prompting priests to use various magic rituals to drive them away. In ancient Mesopotamia, all divine signs were observed and reported to the king. Divination also proliferated among the ancient Greeks and Romans, where oracles were of supreme importance.

Essentially, there are two types of divination: a mediumistic method and an interpretive method. The mediumistic method, which included the oracle, was in ancient times often frenzied and obscure. It can still be observed amongst some modern fortune-tellers experiencing or feigning a trance or amongst medicine men in traditional societies. In this type of divination, the diviner might enter into a trance or a state of possession and offer advice through an attained mediumship.

Conversely, under the interpretive method, omens are construed and deciphered according to certain established principles from long-term observations of the relationships of certain events and objects. In this context, Herodotus tells us: 'The Egyptians [...] keep written records of the observed results of any unusual phenomenon, so that they come to expect a similar consequence to follow a similar occurrence in the future'.[1] The diviner might use intuitive insight brought on and aided by certain materials such as bones, sand, shells, cards, dregs in a cup, or any object considered suited to interpretation. In ancient times, the behaviour of birds, sacred fish, or tame serpents was regarded and interpreted as a sign that could be applied to human behaviour. Sluggish movements of these creatures would be interpreted as an indication of a slow growth of crops and hence a lean harvest. Alternately, if their movements were frenzied, a fast-growing crop and a plentiful harvest could be expected. Especially birds of prey, called oionoi in Greek, were thought to give important signs. Legend tells us twelve eagles appeared when Rome was to be founded, which was the greatest augury for Romulus. In Homer's Iliad, Kalchas 'the best of birdwatchers' leads the Greek army to Troy through divination. Even during Christian times, it remained difficult for emperors to ban the bird-watching ceremonies by which the Roman army had been guided for so many centuries.[2]

Many Celtic and Germanic tribes used cauldrons, thought endowed with sacred magical properties, for divination. Strabo (circa 64 BCE–19 CE), Greek historian and geographer, gives a detailed description of the ritual killing of prisoners by the Cimbri, a Germanic tribe: 'Among the women who accompanied their war-like expeditions were priestesses who possessed the gift of prophecy. [...] Sword in hand they walked through the camp towards the prisoners, decorated them with garlands, and then led them to a huge bronze cauldron. Mounting a step they bent over the cauldron and cut each prisoner's throat as he was lifted up to them'.[3] The priestess then interpreted the patterns formed by the blood dripping into the cauldron to predict victory or defeat for impending battles.[4] Similarly, vessels filled with water or for that matter any liquid were used by the ancients for divination.

In the history of Christianity, traditional divination has always been in implicit conflict with the Church. The exception, however is prophecy, as it is found in the Old Testament. Prophecy is regarded as the ability to foretell future events through divine inspiration.

Various forms of divination include extispicy, hepatoscopy, the oracle, astrology, palmistry, numerology, the Tarot, bibliomancy, the reading of tealeaves, the dowsing rod, dice, and various forms of scrying. Most of these forms of divination are still popularly used, and are abundantly on offer in psychic expos, newspapers, and on the Internet.

Lily-Livered Coward

Extispicy and hepatoscopy were two important forms of divination, enabling the diviner to make predictions concerning future events. Both forms of divination, originated from the ancient Babylonians, and were practiced by the ancient Greeks and Romans, in Celtic and Germanic societies, in Asia, Africa, and by cultures indigenous to Central and South America.

Extispicy refers to the scrupulous examination of the entrails of sacrificed animals or prisoners. Signs seen as predicting instant disaster included excessive 'bloodiness', malformations, or discolouration. The Greek historian and geographer, Strabo, reports: 'They [...] cut open the prisoners' bellies and read the omens from their entrails, proclaiming victory in the battle to come'.[5]

Divination by means of hepatoscopy was very popular in the ancient world. Babylonian clay models of sheep's livers used for omen divination date from circa 2050 BCE. Similarly, the Etruscans fashioned models of the liver out of clay, as well as bronze, hundreds of which have been unearthed by archaeologists. The liver was seen as a reflection of the macrocosm, the 'mirror of heaven' as it were, reflecting the will of the gods in the same way the zodiac was perceived as doing. The liver was also seen as the source of blood in the body, hence, the life force. This gave the organ special occult significance. All those wanting a prediction had to bring a sheep to the temple for sacrifice. The question the person wished answered, was written on clay and laid at the feet of the god's statue. The priest's assistant would then kill the animal, deftly remove the liver, lay it out before him and inspect it carefully. For the purpose of divination it was considered important that the liver be freshly plucked from the sacrificed animal or victim. Any discoloration, malformation, deficiency, or depression, especially on the left side of the liver, was seen as an ominous sign, linked with bad tidings. When royal diviners were at work, armies consisting of thousands of battle-ready men literally stood for days until diviners could report favourable omens. This is vividly described by a student of Socrates (469–399 BCE) named Xenaphon, historian, essayist and soldier, who functioned as a mercenary in the Greek army for a time.

From the custom of hepatoscopy derives the notion that the liver of a coward was as light as a lily, hence we still use the term lily-livered to describe cowardice.

The Ancient Oracle

Oracles typified the mediumistic method of divination through a medium or diviner and figured prominently in the beliefs of all ancient peoples, often forming an integral part of religious rites. The meaning of the term oracle, derived from the Latin term orare, to 'speak' or to 'pray', is varied. Not only might an oracle be defined as the answer of a god or an inspired priest to an inquiry concerning the future, the term might also allude to the deity or personage giving the response. Alternatively, the word can refer to the place where the deity is consulted. In his work De Superstitio, the Greek philosopher Plutarch, explains that seeking out the oracle is an act of religion while the interpretation of omens is an act of superstition.[6] Oracles not only delivered cryptic verbal messages in a trance, but also practised oneiromancy, divination by means of dreams, and necromancy, the art of securing revelations from the spirits of the dead.

Oracular divination had its origin thousands of years ago. In the world of antiquity, no important decisions were ever made by emperors or kings without first seeking the advice of an oracle.[7] Oracles were usually feminine, and in Greece this type of divination was represented by a priestess called a Pythia who uttered cryptic and often epigrammatic revelations under the influence of certain drugs or vapours. The sanctuary dedicated to the power of oracular divination was given the name 'oracle', meaning 'place of invocation' or 'place of the sacred word'. Such a place was the ancient town of Delphi, situated high in the mountains, dominated by the Temple of Apollo, surrounded by a vast enclosure, housing great treasures. Near the temple was the entrance to the crypt in which the god pronounced his oracles through the famous Pythia.

The Greek historian Diodorus (circa 90–21 BCE) recounts the legend concerning the origin of the Oracle of Delphi: A goat herder named Coretas was grazing his herd, when some goats grazing among the rocks approached a cavity from which rose intoxicating vapours. Inhaling these vapours, the goats were inexplicably struck down by convulsive seizures. When Coretas went to investigate, he discovered a cleft in the ground, and bending over it, also breathed in the fumes emanating from the cavity. Suddenly, he began to speak in a peculiar way. As other herders approached and listened to him, they realised in utter astonishment that Coretas was prophesying their future. The priests, hastily consulted on this mysterious phenomenon, decided these signs indicated the presence of a god desiring to communicate his wisdom through the medium of human speech from the location of the cavity in the rocks. The sanctuary of Delphi, comprising dozens of buildings including the Temple of Apollo, which is comparable to the Parthenon in size, was consequently built around this legendary spot. So, once a month, a virgin bearing the sacred name of Pythia – a name commemorating Apollo's victory over the serpent Python – sitting on a tripod, gave voice to prophetic hallucinations produced by heady vapours and stupefying fumes, which emanated from burning laurel, pinewood, henbane, laudanum, and other intoxicating materials.

On the seventh day of every month, the town of Delphi was overrun by milling crowds coming to consult the famous oracle, bringing lavish votive offerings, most of which they had purchased in the local stalls and shops. In this way, the town profited and prospered economically. It was thus in the interest of the priests of all oracle sites throughout the ancient world to maintain popular interest in their specific locations. This was achieved when an oracle site attracted renowned persons who received advice and prophesies that were allegedly fulfilled. Such news would spread the fame of the oracle like wildfire. Clearly, the priests always cleverly exploited the situation. In his book, The Mystery of the Oracles, Phillip Vandenberg describes ancient Delphi at the time of oracular divination: 'What took place here on the seventh day of every month was a perfectly rehearsed mechanism, compounded of para-psychological, power-political, and material interests. In this prophetic machinery the Pythia was nothing but a supine tool; but she knew this and it filled her with pride to be the medium through which the god spoke'.[8]

Procedures at the oracular sites varied greatly. The Roman historian, Tacitus (circa 56–117 CE), in his Annals,[9] describes everyday events at the Oracle of Claros in modern-day Turkey, which in antiquity was ranked in importance alongside the Oracle of Delphi. According to Tacitus, a male priest presided at the Oracle of Claros, and when asked specific questions, he would descend into a cave at the sacred site, drink water from a sacred spring, and though generally illiterate and ignorant of meter, he spontaneously produced a set of verses on whatever subject the visitor questioned him. Unfortunately, the wonder of this art disappeared two thousand years ago.

With regard to the Pythia, or pythoness, it is interesting to note that the modern female African diviner is also known as 'pythoness'. In her book, Africa through the Mists of Time, Brenda Sullivan writes: 'As far as I have been able to learn, African diviners today use techniques which may have been ancient when the Greek pythonesses plied the same trade at the shrine of the Delphic Oracle'.[10]

Typically, responses made by the oracles were so ambiguous and obscure, as to be utterly misleading and misunderstood. For example, when the Lydian King Croesus consulted the Oracle of Delphi about a planned invasion, he received the answer 'When Croesus crosses over the river Halys, he will overthrow the strength of an empire'. King Croesus naturally assumed the message alluded to his armies overthrowing the enemy's empire, only to learn too late that it was in fact his own empire destroyed when the Persian King Cyrus defeated him.

It's All in the Cards

One of the most popular methods of divination is with ordinary playing cards or by the larger and more elaborate pack known as the Tarot. This type of divination is thought to involve intuitive stimulation believed to provide answers lying dormant in the subconscious of the diviner.

The origins of our modern card packs are still disputed, and the number of theories propounded is about as numerous, as the variations of card games. Over the course of time, cards have been made from bark, skin, ivory, bamboo, or pasteboard, and in modern times, plastic, while designs have been painted by hand, printed with blocks, or lithographed. According to some sources, cards were known in China as early as 969 CE, although Hindu legends claim they were originally invented in India by a maharajah's wife to keep her husband, suffering from a nervous disorder, occupied. Wherever the origin, all playing cards eventually found their way to Europe around the thirteenth century.

One of the earliest known examples of playing cards can be seen in the Bibliotheque Nationale of Paris. They are said to have been prepared to amuse Charles VI of France (1368–1422) when he was suffering from a bout of melancholy. The four suits in playing cards represent the four classes of society at that time: spades – the military (like the points of spears), hearts – the clergy, diamonds – the merchants, and clubs – farmers and peasants.

During the Middle Ages, religious authorities were set against the practice of playing cards, and in later times, Puritans regarded it as sinful to even own a pack of cards. In modern times, playing cards are sometimes referred to as the 'devil's picture books'. A maze of superstitions still surrounds any card gambling game, and the summoning of lady luck is ever dependent on varying auspicious factors. Hence, superstitious gamblers are known to cross their legs for good cards, snap their fingers to drive away negative forces, or blow on the down turned cards before picking them up. All these actions are considered to bring luck to the gambler.

Any deck of cards designed for divination or meditation is now loosely called a Tarot deck. Many people have become fascinated with New Age practices, and consequently, hundreds of different packs or decks, all emblematic of the 'encoded mysteries of the universe', depicting the symbolism of various ancient civilisations, myths, and legends, have appeared. Celtic, Gothic, Anglo-Saxon, Egyptian, and many other Tarot decks are available; all based on mythical cycles, specific psychological theories, or channelled information. However, most Tarot cards on the market in modern times were created in the last couple of decades.

The true origins of the Tarot are unknown, although a great many theories link this divination to different cultures and beliefs. One theory concerning the origin of Tarot cards is that the Knights Templar recorded their beliefs in the twenty-two cards of the Major Arcana, and that this was done before their dissolution in 1314. Although there are some Christian elements contained within Tarot cards, the connection with the Knights Templar seems unlikely. Another common myth is that the Tarot was brought to Europe from Asia by gypsies. A further suggestion holds that the Tarot is of Arabian origin and was introduced to Europe by the Crusaders, as the Tarot is most closely related to the Mamluk card deck of the Islamic world. A further suggestion is that the Tarot is a very early form of chess originating in India or that a form of Tarot goes back to ancient China. Another theory holds that while the alphabet of Thoth is the indirect origin of modern Tarot cards, the Tarot is in fact of Jewish origin. The most commonly believed, though unlikely, assumption is that the Tarot is derived from Egyptian hieroglyphics, a theory explored and elaborated on extensively by the Parisian Protestant pastor, Antoine Court de Gebelin (1728–1784).

Whatever the true origin, the Tarot, as we know it in modern times, has its roots in the Renaissance Period, when all playing cards found their way to Europe. The earliest records of the existence of the Tarot indicate that it was first known as a card game with the title Les Tarots in France and as Tarocchi in Italy. This game is a distant cousin to the game of bridge and bears no resemblance to the current use of Tarot cards for divination. In medieval Italy, Tarocchi, using the Tarot deck was very popular, especially amongst royalty. Artists were commissioned by the aristocracy to create beautiful decks of Tarocchi cards, and some of the surviving Tarot decks come from this source. The cards depict mythological symbols and figures, archetypical images conveying mystique and universal spirituality. The earliest surviving Tarot cards were made in 1450 and belonged to the Visconti family in Milan. Many packs regarded as historically genuine are, however, not Italian, but French. Plain decks were also in use, but have not survived the centuries.

From the card game called Tarocchi, the Tarot slowly evolved to being used for divination. The entire esoteric tradition of the Tarot stems from the work of the relatively obscure Parisian Protestant pastor, Antoine Court de Gebelin, a Freemason and savant, who wrote about the Tarot in 1781. De Gebelin 'invented' most of the standard myths linked with the Tarot, that is, that the Tarot originated in Egypt, that it is related to Cabbalism, and many more. According to de Gebelin, whose view was accepted when little was known of Egyptian inscriptions, the most ancient form of fortune telling by cards was the Egyptian Tarot. De Gebelin proclaimed that Thoth, the Egyptian god of writing, knowledge, and magic, invented the Tarot. While studying the occult, de Gebelin developed the theory that a connection existed between the Tarot and the Book of Thoth. This postulation took hold when there was an enormous interest in all things Egyptian. In the mid-nineteenth century, another Frenchman with an intense interest in the occult, Alphonse Louis Constant, popularised the Tarot deck by revising and 'adjusting' it for divination. Through the system he had developed, he inspired the printing of several Tarot decks. Later, the English mystic Aleister Crowly, his interest piqued, created lengthy literature on using the Tarot.

Most Tarot decks contain 78 cards: four suits consisting of numeral cards, four suits of court cards, and a series of non-suited emblematic cards. Over the years, the trumps, triumphs, or trionfi eventually became numbered, with one card, the Fool, remaining without a number or sometimes designated a zero.

In modern times, Tarot cards are still immensely popular, with dozens of available versions offered at New Age shops, on the Internet, as well as at Psychic Expos.

Seven Years of Bad Luck

The art of divining certain information from mirrors is called catoptromancy or scrying. Not only did mirrors throughout the ages fulfil the same practical role they do now, but they also played a key role in divination and religion.

In western China, mirrors made of highly polished metal were found in ancient graves dating from about 1500 BCE. The Aztecs used mirrors made of highly polished obsidian, whereas the ancient Greeks and Romans used burnished bronze and silver discs. The method of making mirrors was known in the Middle Ages, but these were rudimentary and nothing like the mirrors we have in modern times. However, glass mirrors also seem to have been used by some ancient cultures, as the Roman historian, Pliny, specifically mentions glass mirrors produced in Sidon, Syria, centuries before his time.[11]

Mirrors have always been held to expose and scare off demons and evil spirits. Like pools of water and lakes, mirrors have been perceived among varied cultures as entry points into another world or dimension. According to myth, the ancient Aztec god, Tezcatlipoca, whose name is interpreted as 'smoking mirror', had a magic looking glass in which he saw everything happening in the world. Similarly, in ancient Egypt, Hathor, the goddess of love, music, and dancing, was entrusted, not only with Ra's sacred eye, through which she could see all things, but also a shield that reflected all creatures in their true light. This became the first magic mirror with the power to observe everything, no matter how far or how distant in the future. This theme, of course, is found in many fairy tales. We only have to think of Snow White's evil stepmother requesting: 'Mirror, mirror on the wall, who is the fairest of them all?'.

Universally, mirrors were believed to deflect the evil eye's malignant rays. Therefore, during the Middle Ages, those fearful of being bewitched resorted to purchasing witch-balls, probably a corruption of 'watch-balls'. These were small reflective glass balls, reputed to ward off evil influences by reflecting everything in miniature and keeping watch so that no witch approached. In the seventeenth century, it was customary in many European countries for men and women to wear small mirrors in their hats or clothing to avert the evil eye's influence. In modern society, it is still common practice, especially in countries such as China, Indonesia, India, and the Middle East to use small mirrors hung in doors, windows, and cars, sewn on clothing, or carried on one's person to deflect evil.

From earliest times, mirrors have been linked with divination and the occult. It was believed that by dipping a mirror into water and then reading a sick person's reflection, the severity of the malady afflicting that person could be diagnosed. Formerly, when someone was seriously ill, all mirrors in the house were covered. This was done because it was feared that the soul, thought to be temporarily separated from the body during illness, might not find its way back and, hence, become eternally trapped in the mirrored world. Another widely believed superstition intimated that any person who saw his image reflected in a mirror hanging in the same room in which a corpse lay would shortly die. This superstition's origin is based on the belief that one's soul is contained in one's reflection – hence, the ghost of the deceased would be able to carry off the person's reflection caught in the mirror, unless the mirror was covered. As the invisible world was believed to closely overlap the visible one, superstitious dread also existed at possibly seeing the spirit of the deceased in a mirror.

The superstition that breaking a mirror portends death as well as seven years of bad luck was once widely believed. The belief's origin stems from the idea that a person's reflection seen in the glass partly contained the soul. Breaking the mirror shattered this reflection, hence the soul would come to harm and ill luck, or the person's early death would follow. Vampire legend substantiates this notion, as it was held that a vampire had no soul and, therefore, no reflection. Similarly, the idea of the soul contained in the reflection explains why, in ancient times it was regarded as dangerous to see one's likeness in water – in case the denizens of the deep, the water spirits, and sprites, pulled the reflection and, hence, the soul into the unknown depths or into rapidly flowing waters.

A more practical explanation for the various beliefs concerning the breakage of mirrors is the simple fact that in the past they were very expensive and, therefore, irreplaceable. Although crude looking glasses were available during the Middle Ages, mirrors, as we now know them, have only been manufactured since the mid-1800s. Once the making of sheet glass had been mastered during the sixteenth and seventeenth centuries, but at prohibitively exorbitant costs, mirrors became a symbol of wealth only afforded by royalty. Hence, every major European palace boasted a room or hall of mirrors, its size indicating the degree of prosperity and status its owners held. It was thus naturally seen as ominous to break something as valuable as a mirror. The seven years of bad luck associated with the breakage comes from the belief that the body changes its physiological make-up every seven years – a number sacred to all nations of antiquity. Thus, it was thought that only when the body had renewed itself after seven years would the ill luck incurred after breaking a mirror eventually dissipate.

Breaking a mirror was seen to portend the loss of a family member or dear friend, and superstition contended that preserving the broken pieces would only add to the ill luck. Several antidotes, however, were proffered to solve this dilemma. One method of averting misfortune was to collect all the pieces of the broken mirror carefully and to throw them into a fast flowing stream where the water literally 'washed away' the ill luck. Alternatively, the broken pieces were promptly buried, thereby neutralising any evil influence, the effectiveness of which was subject to the place of burial – the more sinister the place, the more effective this neutralising effect!

Too numerous to mention are the past curious notions centred on mirrors. Probably in acknowledgement to the sin of vanity, the superstition arose that to look at oneself too long in a mirror conjured up the devil or other 'things you did not want to see'. It was also considered unlucky to see one's image in a mirror by candlelight, and superstition dictated that two people looking in a mirror at the same time risked a quarrel.

To Walk under a Ladder

The fear of walking under a ladder is one of the most widely known superstitions still observed in Christian and non-Christian countries. The many beliefs of various cultures, linked with the ladder, indicate how far back symbolic and religious ideas underlying these superstitions go.

Already, the ancient Sumerians (circa 3000 BCE) viewed the ladder with fearful reverence and saw it as a symbol of the way to the gods, depicting an 'ascent to goodness'. To the ancient Egyptians, the ladder represented a means by which the dead could gain access to the netherworld. The Egyptian god, Osiris, used a ladder that his father, Ra, created to ascend into heaven, the ladder representing a transition from the material world to a higher consciousness. The Greek philosopher, Plotinus, preached about the 'Ladder of Virtues', the progress towards perfection taken step by step or rung on rung. The same ideas are expressed in Dante's Paradiso.[12] During the Middle Ages, religious symbolism was especially plentiful in representations of ladders surmounted by a great variety of sacred symbols, such as the Cross, the Trinity, the Star of Bethlehem, and angels.

Inevitably, all ancient symbolism and reverent apprehension surrounding ladders must have led to the belief that walking under a ladder propped up against a wall is unlucky. The original ancient reasons, however, have been lost and substituted by many ones dating to a much later time.

Although the fearful belief of walking under a ladder is very ancient, it has been linked to the devil since the spread of Christianity. A ladder leaning against a wall was perceived to form a natural triangle with the wall and the ground. To walk through such a triangle not only showed great disrespect for God, but also, above all, indicated an alliance with the devil, as the triangle was seen to symbolise the Holy Trinity. All God-fearing persons considered themselves barred from passing through this sacred arch.

Another explanation often given for the ill-luck related to walking under ladders is that in the old type of gallows, a ladder was propped up against the supporting beam. Someone about to be hanged was forced to climb the fateful rungs to reach the noose, hence the ladder's association with bad luck. Alternatively, those about to be executed were walked under the ladder to reach the rungs; hence walking under a ladder was linked with death.

A further explanation holds that the belief comes from a wide-ranging taboo that applies to walking under many objects. The fear of walking under ladders might be the survivor of the so-called head taboo, known and practised by the ancient Persians and still practised by many native races. The underlying reason for this curious belief is connected with the notion that the head is the seat of the spirit, and nothing should ever overshadow it or be placed over it. A taboo amongst Aboriginal societies in Australia, the Solomon Islands, Burma, and most South Pacific countries was for males never to walk under sharply leaning trees or any other objects. The Cambodian natives, for example, will never let anything be suspended over their heads and will desperately avoid places where this could naturally occur.

Superstitious notions concerning the ladder extend further than merely walking under it. Some believe that even reaching through or handing anything over the rungs is ill-fated. However, if a ladder has an odd number of rungs, it can bring the climber good luck, as odd numbers are linked with good fortune. To slip on a rung, however, means a financial setback. To step between the rungs of a ladder lying on the ground is still considered unlucky. To avert the ill luck attracted by walking under a ladder, fingers should immediately be crossed or the sign of the cross made.

The superstition about walking under ladders is still prevalent in modern times, and it is interesting to observe how city people would rather step out onto a busy street to walk around a ladder placed across the sidewalk than walk under it.

To Be Moonstruck

Although astronauts have once and for all cleared up the myth that the moon is made of green cheese, earthlings might never be quite willing to surrender the many notions and beliefs about this heavenly light. Since time immemorial, humankind has held the moon in awe and surrounded it with myth and fearful superstition.

To our ancestors, the moon revealed not only that death is indissolubly linked to life, but also that death is not final, because it is always followed by a birth. As the sun-god ruled the day, so the moon-goddess ruled the night. Both deities were worshipped and revered as sources of the life force and often linked in mythologies. Therefore, the Egyptian goddess, Isis, was both goddess of the moon and the sun. Similarly, Caotlicus, the Aztec moon-goddess, was the sun-god's wife. In time, as our ancestors' hunter-gatherer way of life gave way to agriculture, the fruitfulness of the earth and all her inhabitants became synonymous with the moon-goddess' fertility.

As the moon waxed and waned, this heavenly body was seen to swell like a pregnant female, thereby associating it in all mythologies with growth and fertility, birth and regeneration. As a fertility symbol, the moon plays a part in the ancient folklore of people worldwide. This contention is underlined by an old European folk belief that suggests that if a woman drinks at night from a pond holding the moon's reflection, she will become fertile. In Greenland, young girls dared not stare at the moon lest they become pregnant. Fascinatingly, the exact same belief exists on the other side of the world. According to Australian Aboriginal myth, the moon brought the gift of fertility and was perceived as a fertilising male who conferred the power to reproduce on women, as well as on plants, and animals.

The universal belief that the moon is linked to women's physiology has prevailed throughout the ages. The Greeks, Indians, Romans, Germanic people, Celts, Egyptians, Arabs, Chinese, and Aboriginal Australians all had creation myths recognising the mysterious and sacred nature of the moon's cycle in relation to human menstrual blood flow. As the moon was seen to influence the Earth's waters, so it was thought to affect the liquid in human bodies and the bodies of all living things. From ancient times, people recognised the connection of the moon's cyclical nature with women's menstrual cycles – Mensa was the Roman goddess of measurement, numbers, calendars, and record keeping.

The cycle of human ovulation is said to approximate the lunar month, a fact that is preserved in the term menstruation, signifying 'monthly'. Many cultures throughout time have referred to a woman's menses as her 'moon time'. The Maori of New Zealand call menstruation mata marama, meaning 'moon sickness'. Because of its connection with female rhythms, life cycles, and the mysteries of nature, the moon was seen as feminine in most mythologies. The moon-goddess soon came to represent all females –the young maiden, the woman, the old crone, and the wise woman.

Traditionally, the moon is also linked with witchcraft, magic, and sorcery; hence in Christian times, all pagan goddesses closely related to the moon became the queens of witches. Witches were thought to perform their magic spells and meet according to the lunar phases. The ancient witches of Thessaly were believed to have the power of drawing the moon down from the sky at their command. It was believed that the Thessalonian witches wished to bring the moon down to Earth to concentrate its beneficial influence on the various plants they used for spells and potions. The symbolic ritual of 'drawing down the moon', also called 'drawing down the goddess', is still performed in modern times amongst Wiccans, adherents of the modern, peaceful, pagan Wicca movement.

As an amulet, the crescent or horned moon, symbol of the moon-goddess, was believed to protect powerfully against all malevolent influences, especially the evil eye. Charms, such as the moon-ornaments mentioned in the Old Testament,[13] were used to adorn humans and animals. A relic of this tradition is still preserved in the brass accessories, many in the shape of the crescent, adorning horse harnesses.

Because the 'ruler of tides' symbolises dark, mysterious, and often negative forces, it has been believed throughout the ages that those gazing too long at the full moon risk lunacy. It was firmly believed that the moon could turn people mad; in fact the moon was believed to cast a spell. The word lunatic is derived from the Latin term luna. Lunacy means 'possessed by the spirit of luna'. An English saying reiterates this belief: 'When the moon's in the full, then's wit in the wane.' The moon's control over all body fluids, including those in the brain, was believed to cause moon-madness. People of unstable character were said to be 'ruled by the moon'. Shakespeare refers to the moon's power to drive men out of their minds in Othello: 'It is the very error of the moon; she comes more nearer earth than she was wont, and makes men mad'.[14]

Sleeping in the moonlight was regarded as dangerous, and young girls were especially advised never to let the moonlight stream in their window at night, lest they beget monsters if exposed for lengthy periods to moonlight. The moon's rays were thought to be harmful and cause moon-blindness. The sleeper could also be moonstruck, perceived as harmless idiocy and generally alluded to as being loony.

Resulting from the conviction that the moon could harm and injure, respectfully greeting this heavenly body at every opportunity was once traditional. In many parts of England, in the early 1990s, children first glimpsing the new moon still customarily invoked the following: 'I see the moon and the moon sees me. God bless the moon and God bless me'. This couplet was recited aloud to escape bad luck or some dire calamity that the moon could otherwise cause.

Pointing at the moon was considered unlucky, as it offended the 'man in the moon'. Pointing at any object or person meant concentrating bad luck in that direction by drawing evil spirits' attention. It was believed that the man in the moon, sent there because he had gathered sticks, that is, firewood, on a Sunday, would not stand for being pointed at and would cause ill luck for the person pointing. Superstitious awe about pointing at the moon can be found throughout Europe, although the reasons for not doing so vary. A German tradition, for example, holds that to point at the moon or the stars in the sky hurt the angels' eyes.

The three main phases of the moon – the full moon, its waxing, and its waning – were seen to emulate all of life on our planet, that is, birth, maturity, and death in nature – animals and humans. The moon's waxing and waning was thought to affect not only birth and death, but also all enterprises to a large degree. The moon in its increase, full growth, and wane was regarded as an emblem of rising, flourishing, and declining fortunes, whereas the times between the various phases were considered most ominous. For example, no new venture should be started when there was no moon, and children born during this time were thought to have no chance of success in life. Therefore, to our forefathers, the felling of wood, the thatching of houses, the cutting of turf, and all other activities depended fully on the phases of the moon. The growth of crops, hair, nails, and even corns was attributed directly to the phases of the moon.

Generally, the new moon was considered a lucky period. In England and Germany, turning over a silver coin in the pocket while bowing to the new moon was customary and believed to ensure good fortune and prosperity throughout this heavenly body's next cycle. The new moon was considered especially lucky for lovers, and in the past, marriages were ideally arranged on the new moon. The mating urges of large animals seemed to be heightened during the moon's waxing, and a lunar periodicity was observed in the movement of certain ocean fish. In all ancient communities, peasants sowed 'by the moon'. Many rustic gardeners today only plant seeds when the moon is growing and increasing in light, and many farmers use only this time to cure their bacon and sow their corn. Some hairdressers still believe hair growth is linked to cutting the hair during the moon's waxing. Killing livestock, especially pigs, was better done when the moon was on the increase, as the meat was believed to swell, rather than shrink, during cooking. Bacon was thought to be richer and fatter if slaughtering took place during the waxing moon. If sheep were shorn during this time, their wool was believed to grow thicker and longer.

The waning moon was believed to have an unlucky influence, especially on births and weddings. To cut hair and fingernails during this period was inadvisable, as it was believed that they would not grow again. It was, however, a good time to cut down trees and let blood. The best time for picking herbs and flowers was considered to be when the moon was on the decline.

The moon was also traditionally observed by country folk to predict the weather. For example, if the horns of the new moon pointed upwards, forthcoming weather would be fine; if, however, a haze covered the moon, then rain was imminent.

When considering this beautiful, heavenly body on a starlit, tranquil night, is it not amazing to consider how much this enigmatical light has influenced life here on Earth – our myths, beliefs and traditions?

Auspicious or Sinister Heavenly Signs

Since the earliest times, people have believed that great phenomena in the skies foretold of massive changes here on Earth. The general idea circulating among the ancients was that the birth of a person destined for greatness was announced through celestial signs.

The appearance of bright stars was generally thought to presage happy events, especially the birth of gods, emperors, kings, and heroes. Signs in the heavens heralded the births of the founders of all major religions. The Star of Bethlehem announced the birth of Christ. The legends of Jewish patriarchs and prophets relate that a brilliant star shone in the heavens when Abraham and Moses were born. The sacred books of Buddhism state that the rising of a group of stars on the horizon accompanied Buddha's birth. When Krishna was born, his stars were seen in the heavens. Celestial signs foreshadow the birth of all Indian avatars. According to Muslim tradition, celestial signs foretold the birth of Ali, Mohammed's great disciple. The same tradition is found in China at the birth of Yu, the first dynasty's founder, and Lao-Tzu, the Chinese sage. This myth also extended to the New World, as we find that the symbol of the god, Quetzalcoatl, was the Morning Star. Similarly, the ancient Greeks and Romans considered that the appearance and disappearance of heavenly bodies symbolised the births and deaths of great men. At the birth of the various Caesars, brilliant signs in the heavens were purportedly seen each time.

Superstitious beliefs concerning the heavens originated from humankind's idea that the gods lived there. In ancient times, meteorites were seen as messages from the gods and interpreted as omens of impending death, war, and catastrophe. Shakespeare alludes to this notion in Richard II: '... meteors fright the fixed stars of heaven, the pale-faced moon looks bloody on the earth and lean-look'd prophets whisper fearful change ... these signs fore-run the death of Kings'.[15]

Meteorites, or rocks falling from space, often appear as shooting stars in the night sky. During the Middle Ages, the belief was widespread in Europe that shooting stars were the souls of children falling to Earth to animate newborn babies. Another common belief was that when a death occurred here on Earth, the flame of life lit up a new star.

Although most meteorites burn up on entering the Earth's atmosphere, some do reach the ground, and many beliefs are centred on such fragments, inspiring awe and reverence throughout the ages. A sacred ruby sent down from heaven is said to be contained in the northeast corner of the Holy Kaaba in Mecca.[16] According to Arab tradition, the sacred stone contained in the Kaaba is the guardian angel of Paradise turned into stone. It was believed to be as clear as crystal when Abraham first built it into the shrine's wall but through the ages, it has become black from being kissed by sinful humans. In a similar vein, Malaysian kings used to worship a block of iron fallen from the sky, and the Bedouins of Sinai believed that any sword fashioned from a meteorite made the carrier invincible. Medieval literature abounds with references to such magic stones, fallen from heaven. Although the Grail (Latin gradalis, meaning 'wide hollowed out vessel') in various epics is usually described as a 'vessel of gold' or a cup, the medieval German poet Wolfram von Eschenbach, in his epic poem 'Parzival' (written between 1195 and 1210), depicts the Grail as a stone 'which fell from heaven'.[17]

In modern times, shooting stars have lost their ominous meaning and are seen as bringers of good luck, hence the well-known song: 'Catch a falling star, and put it in your pocket, save it for a rainy day....'. Superstitious belief dictates that a wish should always be made on seeing a meteorite, and bad luck is sure to follow at the omission of such a wish.

Although meteorites or 'falling stars' were often viewed with mixed emotions, the sight of a comet has always inspired the deepest foreboding amongst humans. This heavenly body is universally recognised as a portent of disaster, having been linked over the centuries with war, famine, drought, plagues, and the death of monarchs. The comet's association with disaster is probably because of its swift and unexpected passage through the sky, seen as disrupting the orderly regularity of the heavens. During many centuries, the beliefs surrounding the appearance of comets caused the direst notions, coupled with fanaticism – a dangerous combination indeed.

Among the ancients, the Chaldeans alone regarded comets without fear, while amongst philosophers, the Pythagoreans – followers of the metaphysical teachings of Pythagoras founded in the fifth century BCE – seem to have had a vague idea of comets as bodies returning at fixed periods. The appearance of Halley's comet in 43 BCE was seen as an ominous sign regarding the Roman ruler of the period, Julius Caesar, who was murdered on March 15 the following year. Similarly, a comet's appearance is said to have foretold the Roman Emperor Nero's downfall. In this context, the Roman historian, Tacitus, tells us that a comet was seen in the sky, when in the minds of the public, Nero's reign had long ended, and it was time for a new ruler. During that period, there was much speculation about who his successor would be. A comet is also said to have foretold the Norman Invasion of England in 1066, which is why the Bayeux Tapestry, illustrating the Battle of Hastings, depicts a large comet in the background of the famous battle scene. In 1665 the appearance of Halley's Comet again excited a spate of catastrophic prognostications and indeed, the Great Fire of London followed soon after.

The belief that every comet is a ball of fire flung angrily from the right hand of God to warn humankind of its sins and consequent retribution was propagated by the early Church – transmitted through the Middle Ages, the Reformation Period, and beyond. This belief aroused fanaticism and strengthened ecclesiastical tyranny. The portentous character of comets was a great source of terror to humanity and was used by church authorities as an incentive for all believers to repent.

In the third century, Origen, perhaps the most influential of the early church fathers, insisted that comets indicated catastrophes and the downfall of empires and worlds. In his writing, De Natura Rerum XXIV, Anglo-Saxon scholar and historian, the Venerable Bede,[18] described comets as 'long-haired stars' with flames appearing suddenly and presaging either a change in sovereignty, war, plague, or floods. St. Thomas Aquinas accepted and handed down the same opinion. In one of his Advent sermons, Martin Luther (1483–1546) declared: 'The heathen write that the comet may arise from natural causes, but God creates not one that does not foretoken a sure calamity', and 'Whatever moves in the heavens in an unusual way is certainly a sign of God's wrath'.[19] Without a doubt, such pronouncements led to the superstition that no one should embark on a new project after seeing a comet.

Another sinister, ominous heavenly sign was the eclipse. Eclipses of the sun and moon, throughout history, have been attributed to the workings of evil spirits bent on robbing the Earth of light. Understandably, in ancient times, people feared eclipses, as the sun and the moon were recognised in their cosmo-conception as mighty gods and goddesses who demanded appeasement. All celestial phenomena, therefore, were surrounded by ominous forebodings and interpreted as signs of the gods.

In the past, performing sacred rituals during eclipses was customary worldwide. Through chanting, dancing, and sacrifice, the solar or lunar deity concerned was entreated to re-appear again. In many cultures, a hungry demon was thought to have swallowed the sun or moon, and rituals performed were aimed at persuading the demon to vomit forth the bright morsel. Ancient astrologers had little doubt that the relationship between the heavens and Earth were causal, producing outbreaks of the plague and various catastrophes and cataclysmic events.

Eclipses were traditionally interpreted as death-omens of gods and monarchs. The Greeks believed that darkness overshadowed the Earth at the deaths of Prometheus, Hercules, Aesculapius, and Alexander the Great. Roman legends contended that, at Romulus' death, there was darkness for six hours. Similarly, the earth was shrouded in darkness at Julius Caesar's death. In Christian tradition, at the crucifixion of Jesus Christ, darkness overspread the Earth from the sixth to the ninth hour.

Both lunar and solar eclipses often sent Greek and Roman armies into great panic, especially when those eclipses occurred before or during a battle. One of the most famous of the ancient eclipses, its date accurately predicted by the philosopher, Thales (640–546 BCE), was the solar eclipse of May 28, 585 BCE. This eclipse ended a five-year war between the ancient Lydians – an ancient people from the region of western Asia Minor – and the Medes – an ancient Persian people. Both armies, utterly terrified, stopped fighting at once, when 'day turned into night'. The Greek historian, Herodotus, in his Histories mentions several eclipses as having influenced battles. One such example is the eclipse of February 17, 478 BCE, which the Persian King Xerxes witnessed shortly before his armies were led into battle against the Greeks. Soothsayers interpreted the meaning of the portent to the anxious king, explaining that a darkening of the moon by the sun's shadow meant the destruction of Greek cities, as the sun was the symbol of the Persians, whereas the moon was the symbol of the Greeks. However, the soothsayers' predictions of a favourable outcome for the Persians in the naval battle of Salamis proved to be inaccurate.[20] Similarly, an eclipse of the moon on the night of August 27, 413 BCE, so terrified the Athenians, prepared and ready to sail into battle against the Syracusans, that they retreated – a decision that cost them thousands of lives.[21]

On his fourth voyage to the Americas, Christopher Columbus is said to have saved himself and his companions because of his knowledge of an impending eclipse, indicated on one of the many calendars he carried with him. The Calendarium, issued in Venice in 1485 by the astrologer Regiomontanus, indicated an eclipse of the moon for February 29, 1504, expected to last for one hour and forty-six minutes. Nearly two years after sailing from Spain, Columbus and his disgruntled, restless crew were stranded on the north coast of Jamaica, their ships worm-eaten and leaking. After several incidents of plundering by the crew and various disagreements with the islanders, the locals were no longer prepared to supply food to the stranded sailors. The situation was becoming untenable, and Columbus, tired and weary, was forced to find a solution. When going through the Calendarium, he noted the predicted eclipse, its exact time, and duration. He then proceeded to arrange a meeting with the hostile natives and then warned that the moon would disappear from the heavens if they did not cooperate. When the eclipse happened soon afterwards, the natives were greatly terrified, begging and entreating Columbus to restore the heavenly body to the sky. Needless to say, Columbus and his men received all the food they needed and were rescued not long after by a Spanish vessel.

At one time, eclipses were widely believed to be responsible for all the ills of humankind. Shakespeare refers to this belief in Othello: 'O, insupportable! O heavy hour! Methinks it should be now a huge eclipse of sun and moon, and that the affrighted globe should yawn at alteration'.[22] So ingrained was the notion that all eclipses foretold disease and misfortune that European astrologers traced the Great Plague, also called the Black Death, beginning in 1348 CE, to a lunar eclipse that occurred in that same year. The plague spread along the trade routes from China to Europe, where it lasted for four years and killed about 25 million people. Not only plagues, but also natural disasters and wars, such as the outbreak of the First World War in 1914, were thought by the superstitious to be foreshadowed by an eclipse.

Messengers of the Gods and Other Omens

An omen or portent can be an occurrence or object presaging good or evil. An omen is a prophetic sign or augury, which when interpreted, is a message about future events. Since ancient times, certain phenomena and unusual events were taken as a prediction of good or evil, from the belief that coming events cast their timely shadows before them. Omens and portents, throughout history, have been regarded as warnings of dangers to be avoided and opportunities to be seized.

Based on long-term observations, of the relationships of certain events and objects, omens were of great importance to the affairs of ancient rulers and every public or private activity first required a good omen, before being carried out. In the daily lives of the Greeks and the Romans, no public action or decision was ever taken without specifically requesting signs from the relevant divinities. The ancients were firmly convinced that the gods communicated with them by inscribing such signs or messages of things to come into the natural surroundings. The information given by the gods was thus abundantly available. However, the challenge for ancient diviners was to first recognise and define these signs, and then to correctly interpret them.

Omens could be read from signs in the heavens, such as celestial phenomena. Because the sky was seen as the orderly and regular procession of stars, any disruption such as an eclipse, a meteor, or a comet, was regarded as an omen. In King John, Shakespeare alludes to this belief: 'But they will pluck away his natural cause, and call them meteors, prodigies and signs, abortives, presages and tongues of heaven'.[23] Similarly, thunder and lightning were often viewed as expressing the anger of the gods. The ancient Greeks considered lightning a good omen when it was seen on their right side, and a bad omen when on the left. Those killed by lightning were thought of as obnoxious to the gods and either buried apart not to contaminate others or simply left to decay in the place where lightning had killed them. All omens coming from an easterly direction were regarded as positive in ancient Greece, as the life-giving force of the sun emanates from that direction.

Omens were also obtained from the blood, liver, or entrails of sacrificial animals or prisoners and from the behaviour of animals and insects. In ancient times, the behaviour of sacred fish or tame serpents was interpreted as a sign that could be applied to human actions. For instance, sluggish movements of these creatures were interpreted as indicating slow crop growth and, hence, a lean harvest. Alternately, if their movements were frenzied, a fast-growing crop and a plentiful harvest could be expected. If ants were seen fighting, the omen warned of an enemy approaching. But, to see a swarm of bees land in one's garden was regarded as an omen of impending prosperity.

From the earliest times, birds have been regarded as the harbingers of good and evil, their behaviour carefully observed and auguries drawn from their flight and actions. Because birds have always been seen as having a close relationship with the various sky gods dwelling in the heavens, the belief arose that birds were the messengers of higher powers, and hence, the possessors of secret knowledge. The ancient Greek and Roman augurs were adept at interpreting the flight of birds, a practice called ornithomancy. Especially birds of prey, called oionoi in Greek, were thought to give important signs. Hence, legend tells us that twelve eagles appeared when Rome was to be founded and Homer's Iliad, states that the Greek army was led to Troy through divination alone. Differing cultures worldwide followed the practice of bird watching for divination. For example, amongst African tribes from the south to the north of the continent, the flight or chirping of birds to the right or left of a specific point was seen as a specific omen in the same way as it was in ancient Greece and Rome.

Throughout history, special meaning was given to the sighting of specific birds. The owl, abhorred by the Romans, has always been a particularly unlucky bird to see. Equally, the peacock was regarded in European countries as an ill-omened bird, and to bring a peacock feather into one's house boded disaster and illness. In the South Pacific countries, hearing the scream of a night bird or a screeching crow flying overhead, was seen as an omen of misfortune requiring immediate appeasement of the appropriate deities. In Abyssinia, the colour of birds, if white or black, should they fly away or approach a traveller, indicated mishap or good fortune.

In northern Europe, various beliefs about the cuckoo's call were widespread and gave rise to numerous omens. To hear the cuckoo for the first time, and not have any money in one's pocket, boded ill for one's finances in the year ahead. Whatever a person was doing when first hearing the cuckoo was thought to later be the action most frequently performed throughout that year.

Traditionally, country people foretold the weather and the seasons by the behaviour of birds. For seagulls to fly low over the shore foretold foul weather, and a peacock's harsh clamour or shrill call was seen as a sign of coming rain. Although the Christian Church tried to stamp out such superstitions, they persisted and exist even today in some rural areas.

Certain birds were seen as omens of death, the strongest warnings coming from ravens, crows, and owls. Amongst Australian Aborigines, the crow was regarded as a 'death bird', especially when seen persistently hovering around a homestead, and night owls were linked with bad fortune. Similarly, in Europe, ravens croaking over a house boded evil, and a white pigeon settling on a house was viewed with great misgivings, as it was a certain omen of death. Similarly, cocks crowing at night or birds flying against windows were all considered ominous warnings that someone was about to die.

Besides all natural phenomena, the study of entrails, and the behaviour of animals, insects, and specific birds, there were various other omens to be carefully heeded. The mystery surrounding death has always instilled a sense of dread and fear amongst humans. An involuntary cold shudder, for example, is seen to be associated with someone walking over one's future grave. Every culture has differing omens warning of imminent death. Not long ago, very little was known about the causes of various illnesses, with the result that people facing any serious malady became racked with fear and anxiety, thus becoming oversensitive to surrounding sights and sounds. Some animals were credited with the gift to see death coming, particularly dogs whose repeated howling was seen as an omen that someone in the house was about to die. The howling was interpreted as the dog being conscious of spirits hovering around the house, preparing to bear away the soul of the departed. Similarly, a dog behaving strangely and uncharacteristically while someone lay ill, or the persistent neighing of a horse at night, were seen as sure omens of death.

Any change in a clock's rhythm was viewed with foreboding, symbolising a corresponding disturbance in the human life cycle. Mirrors, framed photographs, or portraits falling from their hangings and breaking for no apparent reason or old trees falling over, all indicated an imminent death in the family. Persistent knocking heard at night in a house where someone lay ill meant that the Spirit of Death was on his way to claim the soul. The creaking and cracking of beams and furniture in houses was also generally regarded as a foreboding omen. When considering that most houses were formerly constructed of wood, and families tended to occupy the same house for generations, one can imagine the sense of foreboding felt at each creaking sound and all that went 'bump' in the middle of night.

Unlucky Friday the 13th

Some days are seen as ominous, others as auspicious. This belief is very ancient and continues into modern times. On the sacred calendar of the early Mesopotamian city-states, dating from circa 3000 BCE, every month was made up of certain lucky and unlucky days. Similarly, the ancient Egyptians believed that certain days were connected with good fortune and others not. This is illustrated by a nineteenth-dynasty papyrus preserved in the British Museum,[24] which contains a calendar of lucky and unlucky days, detailed according to the utterances of ancient seers. These series of calendrical lists were believed to have originated from Assyrian sources, though more probably from Egyptian astrological practices, and were called Lucky and Unlucky Days. Good luck was always believed to come from beneficent deities, and bad luck was caused by evil entities.

Most of us have, at some time, entertained the notion that certain days, months, or seasons are unfavourable. Specific days seem not to bring any luck, while other days do; which is why we often tend to put off functions or decisions to those days that we consider favourable. Although there is almost certainly no truth in the luck or 'un-luck' of a day, month, or season, the superstition persists and is still adhered to by a surprising number of perfectly rational people. The belief is also held that some days are bad for everybody, while other days are bad for some and good for others. Generally, in Western societies, Sundays are considered lucky and Fridays unlucky, but Friday the 13th is viewed as the most ominous day of all.

Friday is an ill-fated day in superstition, the reasons varying for its unhappy reputation. The day changed from a lucky to an unlucky day because of Christian belief, and the sombre symbolism of Good Friday soon transferred to every Friday of the year. This, however, was only observed from Christian times onwards, as Friday was considered a most lucky day amongst the Roman and Germanic peoples.

The Romans dedicated Friday to Venus, naming it dies veneris or 'day of Venus', still reflected in vendredi, the French term for Friday. Thus, dedicated to the love goddess, it was regarded as a happy day on which weddings were often held. Similarly, Germanic people devoted this day to Freyja, their goddess of love and marriage, thereby giving the day a cheerful connotation – from Freyja, the German word Freitag for Friday is derived.

However, according to Christian belief, Christ was crucified on a Friday, the disciple Judas hanged himself on a Friday, and early Christians commonly believed that Adam and Eve were expelled from the Garden of Eden on this day. The Catholic Church transferred the tradition of fasting on Good Friday to every Friday, and any year beginning on this day was thought to be ill-fated.

In England and America, criminals were customarily hanged on a Friday, earning it the reputation of Hangman's Day. Accidents were believed to be more frequent on Fridays, because of the fact that evil influences were at work on this day. It was also considered a day on which to avoid seeking medical treatment, and after a long illness, it was advisable not to get up on a Friday for the first time. Children born on a Friday were believed to be unlucky and doomed to misfortune, unless it happened to be a Good Friday when the sanctity of the day counterbalanced all other misfortune related to it. Clothes sewn on a Friday would not fit, and anyone who laughed on this day was sure to cry on the Sunday. It was equally unlucky to court or marry on a Friday, to move house, or start a new job or any new venture, journey, or sea voyage. Even to cut one's hair or nails on a Friday was once considered risking misfortune. According to popular legend, the bad luck linked with Fridays was carefully heeded by great men such as Napoleon and the German statesman, Bismarck, who never began any important venture on this day.[25]

However, when the thirteenth day of the month fell on a Friday, the negative omens linked with both the day and the number became compounded; hence, the day was then considered especially unlucky. Christian authorities trace such ill omen back to the Last Supper which was attended by thirteen, but the prejudice against this number is of far older origin and is known to have existed in pre-Christian times.

The number thirteen's ill-omened associations in superstition are universal, and the number has been regarded as burdened with misfortune and ill luck since antiquity. (See Chapter IX Unlucky Thirteen)

V

SPECIFIC DAYS AND FESTIVITIES

Pervadingly Pagan

S pecial days for religious or secular observances have been set aside in the calendars of all cultures throughout the ages. In modern times, such days are marked, not only by customary celebrations, but also by the cessation of employed work on specific holidays. However, many holidays have lost their traditional or religious significance. Certain days, such as Valentine's Day or April Fools' Day, are still noted by their occurrence, but are not disruptive to employment.

The term pagan originated from the Latin term paganus, meaning 'country-dweller', as opposed to urbus (from which derives the English urban), referring to those living in the larger cities. The pagani or country-dwellers were seen as closely connected to the local ways of their village or hamlet, removed from the fast pace, new ideas, and views that had taken hold in Rome and other large centres. As the new Christian religion gained popularity in the cities, the pagani became known as those still devoted to the old ways and the old gods; in other words, they were seen as 'behind the times'. By the third century, however, the term had come to mean all non-Christians and eventually took on a distinctly negative connotation, even implying Satan-worship.

Humankind, since antiquity, has observed occasions of religious significance with fertility rites, harvest festivals, and sun festivals. A scrutiny of all significant Christian festivals reveals that many pagan rites were simply perpetuated and combined in traditional celebrations on Christian holy days such as Easter, All Hallows Eve, and Christmas. Pagan cults presented a problem to the early church fathers, who soon realised that suppressing a popular custom seldom succeeded, and thus, the Church's policy became one of assimilation rather than confrontation. Hence, equinox celebrations glorifying the rebirth of nature, the fertility of the land, and the onset of spring in the Northern Hemisphere were supplanted by the Christian Easter celebrations, traditional midsummer festivals were transformed into a feast honouring John the Baptist, Christmas replaced the winter solstice festivities, and most other pagan festivities, rites, and ceremonies underwent a similar process.

Magic trees became 'gospel oaks', and ancient magic springs and wells became holy places linked to the names of particular Christian saints. Pagan temples and buildings were consecrated as churches or inscribed with declarations that these dwellings of demons had become Houses of God. For example, Notre Dame in Paris was built on the foundations of a temple of Diana, and St. Sulpice in Paris rose on the ruins of a temple of Isis. The pagan spirits of woods and streams became monsters, appearing in traditional tales as seductive fays and nymphs leading men astray, while fauns and satyrs became linked with the horned, hoofed creatures of medieval demonology.

In many of our annual special days and holidays, superstition has played an important part. Activities performed on these specific days have lost their original meaning, and we are often unaware of the significance and reasons underlying the festivities, particularly why certain actions are performed and certain customs are adhered to. In the following chapter, the origin and historic significance of various select traditions still observed are considered in calendared order.

New Year on March 25?

Although many believe that the New Year universally begins on the first day of January, it begins on different dates for different societies and cultures.[1] In the past, for some native tribes the arrival of certain animals for the hunt or specific shoals of fish marked the beginning of the year. In some parts of the ancient Near East, the New Year was celebrated in autumn, when rains ended the long drought of summer. The ancient Egyptians, on the other hand, watched for the rising of the Dog Star, Sirius, which foretold the flooding of the Nile, bringing new life to land and people and heralding the New Year. Usually, however, the New Year officially began in spring at the beginning of the growing season, marked by the vernal or spring equinox in the Northern Hemisphere.

The beginning of spring, a season of rebirth and of planting new crops, was a logical time to start the New Year. Around 2000 BCE, the Babylonian New Year began on March 25, which many cultures in ancient times regarded as the traditional fixed date for the vernal or spring equinox. In ancient Persia, present-day Iran, the New Year, called Nowruz meaning 'New Day', began on March 21. This New Year's date is still celebrated in Iran.

The Romans similarly started their New Year on March 25. Originally, the ancient Roman calendar had only ten months, still reflected in the names of some months derived from Roman numerals. Therefore, if starting the year in March, September is the seventh month; October, the eighth; November, the ninth; and December, the tenth month. In about 715 BCE, the months of January and February were added to the Roman calendar. Over time, through continued tampering by various emperors, the calendar became out of synchronisation with the sun. Therefore, in 46 BCE, as part of a calendar reform, Julius Caesar decreed the New Year should start at the beginning of January and January 1 became a time of great festivities for the Roman people. However, with the spread of Christianity, the Church outlawed this customary celebration, banning all Christians from observing any festivities on this day by threat of excommunication, as the celebrations represented paganism and idolatry derived from the feast of the heathen two-faced god Janus, after whom January is named.

Things changed again in 567 CE at the Council of Tours! The Christian Church, now all-powerful, moved the New Year's date from January 1 back to March 25 as it had been in ancient times all along. Thus, for centuries, all European countries celebrated the New Year on March 25, a fact not generally known today.

However, it was not to remain this way. When Pope Gregory XIII in-troduced the Gregorian calendar in 1582, the New Year's date was again moved – back to January 1. However, different countries throughout Europe adopted this date for the New Year at different times: Catholic countries all adopted it soon thereafter, but Protestant countries took some time to follow suit – Germany changing over in 1700, England in 1752, and Sweden in 1753. Hence, just a few centuries ago, these northern European countries still wished one another a happy new year on March 25.

Essentially, these changes to the New Year's date were to have a lasting impact on traditions we still observe, namely April Fools' Day and the famous Easter Bunny and Easter eggs (see below).

'Be My Valentine'

For young lovers, the most popular day on the calendar is, without a doubt, St. Valentine's Day on February 14. Although at least three different Saint Valentines are mentioned in the early martyrologies under the date of February 14, it is generally accepted that the day is named after a Christian priest who defied an edict by the Roman Emperor Claudius. The imperial edict specified that soldiers should not be allowed to marry, as it negatively influenced their fighting skills. By conducting the nuptials for many young soldiers, the priest was sentenced to be executed on February 14, in the year 269 CE and has since become the patron saint of lovers.

However, it seems that the middle of February was associated with love long before this date, in ancient times, as the early Greeks and Romans observed this time to honour their respective goddesses, Hera and Juno, both related to marriage. The Greek goddess, Hera, was chiefly known as the jealous and often vindictive wife of the philandering Zeus. Although she presided over all phases of feminine existence, she was primarily regarded as the goddess of marriage and maternity. Juno, the Roman equivalent of Hera, was similarly seen in a maternal role. Roman boys and girls randomly drew names and selected their partners at this time in honour of the love goddess. As with all other heathen superstitions and lewd customs, the Church replaced pagan divinities with ecclesiastical saints, and hence allotted the festival of Juno to St.

Valentine. Slowly, the tradition of observing Valentine's Day spread to various European countries. However, the ancient custom of choosing a partner or 'valentine' on this day remained.

A contributing factor to the amorous customs linked with this day might be the common belief in England and France during the Middle Ages that all birds chose their mates halfway through the second month of the year. This would account for the many superstitions connecting Valentine's Day with our feathered flocks. The first kind of bird seen by a young girl on Valentine's Day was said to be a sign of her future husband; for example, a blackbird indicated a clergyman; a robin, a sailor; a sparrow, a farmer; and a goldfinch, a wealthy man. Another widespread belief related to Valentine's Day contends that the first person one sees on this day will importantly influence one's future destiny. Alternately, the first person seen on Valentine's Day will become one's husband or wife if one is unmarried.

Ladies Privilege Day

Leap Year is celebrated every 4 years on February 29. This extra day was added to the calendar in 46 BCE when Julius Caesar's astrologers measured the solar year at 365 days and 6 hours. To eliminate the odd 6 hours each year, the Julian calendar added an extra day to February every 4 years.

The term Leap Year originated because English courts did not legally recognise February 29 and, as in the game of leapfrog, the day was simply 'leapt' over. Hence, whatever occurred on this extra day every four years was dated February 28.

Because Leap Year has always been seen as an unusual occurrence, disturbing the orderly progression of the year, various beliefs and superstitions have been attached to this out-of-the-ordinary event. Often termed as 'Ladies Privilege Day', February 29 is the day when a young woman may propose to her reluctant young lover who has not yet popped the question. The most likely explanation for this custom's beginning has to do with the fact that February 29 was perceived as a day that did not properly belong in the calendar. Therefore, this was a day when the ordinary rules of conduct did not apply. However, according to popular belief in the British Isles, this tradition was started in fifth-century Ireland when St. Bridget complained to St. Patrick about women having to wait so long for a man to propose. So, the kindly saint granted that yearning females could propose on this one day in February during a Leap Year.

Formerly, when courtship rules were much stricter than in today's permissive society, and men customarily did the asking and women the accepting or declining, this was the only day of the year when women were allowed to pop the question. However, there is general disagreement about The Ladies Privilege – some see it appropriate only to the extra day; others consider it applicable throughout that Leap year.

To succeed in her proposal, it was apparently customary for the lady in question to wear a scarlet petticoat, clearly visible to all from under her dress, hence leaving no doubt about her intentions. Several sources claim this is the origin of the expression 'scarlet woman' to describe someone brazen or forward.

In America, Sadie Hawkins Day, which is not a set holiday, but celebrated by some on the Saturday closest to November 9, is the equivalent of 'woman-can-pursue-man day'. Named after the man-chasing female character in the cartoon strip Li'l Abner, Sadie Hawkins Day officially gives women permission either to propose or to ask their beau out on a date.

April Fool!

All of us have at some time or another played what we perceived as a successful prank on an unsuspecting friend or family member on April Fools' Day without perhaps quite knowing the exact origin of the custom.

As previously mentioned in this chapter, the New Year's date was officially moved from March 25 to January 1 in 1582, according to the changes instituted by Pope Gregory XIII, who introduced the Gregorian calendar. Different European countries followed suit at different times, some as late as 1753.

Playing tricks on people on the first day in April originated in France during the sixteenth century. In ancient times, great festivals were usually celebrated in an octave, that is, they would continue for eight days, of which the first and the last day were the principle days of celebration. Hence, according to the old calendar, March 25 signified the first day of the octave celebrations of the New Year and April 1, the last, signalling the close of the New Year's feasting. Both days were, therefore, days of extraordinary merrymaking. Then, in 1582, Catholic France adopted the new calendar – the first day in January was suddenly decreed the beginning of the year, and all celebrations on April 1 were abolished.

In the days when news travelled mainly by foot, communications were not instant as they are in modern times. Many people did not receive the news of the changed New Year's Day for a long time. Others strongly objected at having the New Year shifted to the first day of January, which was after all, a freezing time for most of Europe. Thus, the public's annoyance resulted in the taunting and tricking of friends, family, and public officials by sending them on fool's errands and playing pranks on them, hoping to indicate to everyone that April 1 was still the closing day of the New Year celebrations that had been traditionally accompanied with much hilarity.

This tradition spread to England and Scotland in the eighteenth century and was later introduced to the American colonies. In modern times, the custom of taunting and tricking is still recognised worldwide on April 1.

The Feast of Eggs

The Christian festival of Easter is marked by many rituals and customs combining various pagan and Christian elements. Easter eggs, the Easter Bunny, and hot cross buns are all of pagan origin.

Easter is celebrated as the principal festival of the Christian Church, commemorating the resurrection of Jesus Christ. In the Western Christian Churches and the Eastern Orthodox Church, the formula for determining the Easter date is identical. Easter is celebrated on the first Sunday after the first full moon on or after the spring equinox. However, the two main branches of the Christian Church base their Easter date on different calendars – the Western churches using the Gregorian calendar, which is standard for much of the world, whereas the Orthodox churches retain the older Julian calendar. This means that Easter, the celebration of a fundamental aspect of the Christian faith, is observed on different dates by these two church bodies, a theological inconsistency that remains a thorny problem for the Christian Church.

Throughout recorded Western history, ancient Mediterranean cultures have celebrated some kind of festival at or around the time of the spring equinox on March 25 – in most instances, these were New Year's celebrations. In the northern hemisphere these New Year celebrations were a way of rejoicing in the rebirth of nature, with the onset of spring. The seasonal changes were acted out ritually, from the symbolic death of the earth in winter to its resurrection through the budding and blooming that came with spring. Most of these cultures had myths of god-men born miraculously, killed, and reborn at this time each year. As far back as four thousand years ago, the ancient Egyptians annually celebrated the resurrection of their god, Osiris, while the ancient Syrians had similar festivities centred around their god, Adonis, during the same period in early spring. Similarly, the death and rebirth of the god, Attis, son of the great goddess, Cybele, was celebrated each year in ancient Rome, the festivities in his honour ending on March 25.

Marking the rebirth of the sun and of nature, each culture also honoured its respective fertility goddess. To the Germanic tribes, she was known as Ostara, which gave rise to the German term Ostern (the German word for Easter); to the Anglo-Saxons, she was Eostre, from which the term 'Easter' is thought to be derived. Similarly, from the same word originate 'estrogen', the scientific name for the hormone governing breeding, and the female reproduction cycle 'estrus'.

The custom of eating and giving eggs at this time of the year originates with the 'feast of eggs', which was part of the pre-Christian spring festivities – the egg traditionally symbolising the rebirth of nature. The feast of eggs also marked the time – long before intensive farming methods played havoc with the natural cycles of hens – when hens began laying again after the long winter.

Most nations of antiquity – the Egyptians, Persians, Chinese, Romans, Greeks, Celts, and Teutons – gave one another presents of eggs during the solar New Year celebrations. In Egypt, Persia, Greece, and Rome, eggs were dyed red to represent the womb and given at spring festivals. Eggs dyed blood red were traditionally rolled along the ground in fields to ensure the fertility of the newly sown seeds. After the spread of Christianity, the feast of eggs became attached to the Christian Easter celebrations. The colouring and ornamentation of Easter eggs continued, red on the painted eggs now symbolising the blood of Christ.

Whereas sugar Easter eggs became popular in Europe during the sixteenth century, the delectable chocolate Easter eggs we so enjoy at this time of the year are of recent origin. So-called 'eating' chocolate was first introduced to the European public in the late seventeenth century.

Today the Easter egg survives mainly as a much-commercialised economic commodity, the symbolism and ancient origins largely forgotten.

Sweet Easter Bunnies

The first edible Easter Bunnies were made from sugar during the sixteenth century in Germany. Now, these Easter treats are manufactured in all sizes and are usually made of chocolate.

Our famous Easter Bunny, which yearly brings chocolate eggs to millions of children worldwide, is derived from the sacred hare of the Anglo-Saxon fertility goddess Eostre, also known as Ostara. Often, she was depicted as hare-headed. Like all lunar deities, she represented the rebirth of nature and fertility, celebrated during the spring equinox. From her name is derived the term Easter, her hare incorrectly called the Easter Bunny.

Most ancient deities had specific patron animals. As the owl was sacred to Athena, so the hare, because of its renowned fertility, was an attribute and companion to the most prominent pagan goddesses: Venus, Aphrodite, Diana, and Ostara. This association probably contributed to the hare's sinister reputation in later times, linking it to stories of witchcraft, as pagan gods and goddesses and their patron animals were vilified by the Church after the spread of Christianity.

Fertility deities symbolising the rebirth cycle of nature were not only traditionally associated with the hare, but also the moon, as this heavenly body was linked with the concept of rebirth, disappearing from the sky for three days after each lunar cycle, and then seemingly reborn again as a crescent. Hence, there is a chain of associations – fertility gods, the hare, and the moon. The hare, a prolific breeder, is found in mythologies worldwide and goes back to ancient times. It is depicted on Assyrian reliefs and ancient Egyptian wall paintings. In mythology, the hare is invariably an attribute to lunar deities and, hence, a symbol of fertility. In ancient Sanskrit literature, the hare is the symbol of the moon-god Chandra, usually depicted carrying a hare. Similarly, the Scandinavian goddess, Freyja, had attendant hares and Celtic moon-deities were often depicted holding a hare. The hare is also the symbol of the moon in Burmese mythology, and during the Chinese moon festival, figures of hares, which represent the yin lunar power, are celebrated.

Therefore, the truth about our famous Easter Bunny is that it is simply a relic of ancient universal associations: the spring equinox and the approximate time of our Easter – to rebirth and fertility and both linked with moon-deities, who were always linked to the hare, hence, the Easter Bunny!

Hot Cross Buns

In modern times, what was once simply known as the cross bun has been reduced to a highly commercialised commodity, usually on sale in supermarkets long before Easter, and on many occasions, still on bakery shelves long after the religious festival has passed. The 'hot' was added to make the attraction more mouth-watering.

Cross buns, as a symbol of the Crucifixion, were traditionally only eaten on Good Friday or the Day of the Cross. However, current cross buns go back a long way and are related to the archaic sacred cakes and consecrated breads offered to deities at religious festivals in different cultures. Breads and small cakes have always been important in early forms of worship. In the rites of Isis, in ancient Egypt, sacrificial cakes made from the purest and most delectable ingredients were on sale outside the temples. The Old Testament prophet, Jeremiah, notes the sacrificial offering of breads: 'And when we burned incense to the Queen of Heaven, [...], did we make her cakes to worship her, [...]'.[2]

Cross buns originally took the form of wheat cakes baked with fine flour and honey for eating during pagan spring festivals in the Northern Hemisphere. The ancient Greeks stamped each piece of bread with a horned symbol, representing the new moon, as an offering to the moon-goddess. The horned symbol might have given rise to the English word bun from the term boun, Greek for ox. Eventually, this symbol evolved into a cross, representing the Crucifixion and commemorating the unleavened bread that Christ shared with his disciples at the Last Supper.

An alternative explanation given for the cross on the cross bun is that it was a pre-Christian symbol signifying the quarters of the moon in honour of the moon-deity invariably representing fertility.

Many superstitions have been linked to the cross bun, and it has long symbolised good fortune. A popular custom was to keep one or two cross buns after Good Friday and hang them in the home. This bun was believed to have magical powers and to act as a charm against evil influences throughout the year. Being as hard as a rock after some weeks, it probably made a handy missile as well!

Trick or Treat

Hallow Even, Hallowe'en, or Hallow's Eve, which eventually became known as Halloween, is on the Eve of All Saints' Day, when Catholics commemorate the saints and martyrs. Hallow is an Old English word for 'saint'. Protestants, however, commemorate Reformation Day on October 31 because, on this day in 1517, Martin Luther affixed his epoch-making ninety-five theses on the castle church doors in Wittenberg in Germany.

The modern celebration of Halloween is a descendant of the ancient pagan Celtic fire festival Samhain. All attempts to Christianise this festival by making it Hallow Even on October 31, All Saints' Day on

November 1, and All Souls' Day on November 2 failed to obliterate the festival's pagan character. Halloween is still typified by the ubiquitous imagery of grotesque masks, hollowed-out pumpkins, and broomstick-riding witches to frighten away evil spirits and demons. Even the phrase 'trick or treat' harks back to the giving of food as compensation for frightening or tricking away evil spirits.

Before Christianity, the Celts in Europe celebrated two great fire festivals each year: Beltane on the eve of May 1 and Samhain on October 31. Despite these dates, lacking a connection with the equinoxes or the solstices or with sowing and reaping, the festivals of Beltane and Samhain marked the beginning of summer and winter, respectively, because the Celts were primarily a pastoral people, as opposed to an agricultural people. In high latitudes, the solar year was often divided into two instead of four seasons. Exactly when Germanic and Celtic people discovered the solstices remains unknown, although it is believed that this knowledge came from the ancient Egyptians during their trade in tin and salt with the ancient European peoples.

The festival of Samhain was held from sunset on October 31 to sunset on November 2. In northern Europe, it signalled the beginning of the long winter season, which lasted until May and marked the end of harvest time. The ancient festival of Samhain recognised the dead and the powers of darkness. Therefore, sacred bonfires were traditionally lit during Samhain on the tops of hills.

Universally, the sun was seen as the source of all life and nourishment. The presence of the sun was, however, not constant, as it died every evening to be reborn the next morning. Especially in northern European countries, the daily duration of the sun's presence varies greatly throughout the year; in midwinter, it seems as though the sun vanishes altogether. This must have been a frightening concept to the ancients who, through rituals involving fire, which was considered a representation of the sun, aimed to ensure the lengthening of the days. With fire, the sun was also symbolised by wheels or discs, which were found in tombs and burial mounds throughout central and Western Europe and in Eastern and Asian countries, probably to light the way in the land of the dead.

Samhain, meaning 'summer's end', marked not only the onset of the long northern winter, but also the beginning of the Celtic year. Similar to a child being born from the darkness of the womb, it was thought that nature sprouted forth from the blackness of the ground, and thus according to Celtic belief, the New Year was born from the dark gloom of winter. This was the time when cattle were brought indoors from the surrounding pastures, and domestic animals and humans then spent the long winters indoors under cover together.

All turning points in the cycle of life were viewed by the Celts as magical times, especially the transition from the old to the New Year. Mythology and folk traditions in Ireland, Wales, and northwest England associate this time with visitations from ghosts, goblins, and fairies. This was perceived as a brief period when the screen separating our real world from the supernatural was thin, when spirits suddenly became visible to humans, and supernatural forces returned to the physical plane and influenced people.

The Celts believed that with the onset of winter and the disappearance of the sun, the poor shivering souls of the dead were stalking the countryside and, therefore visited the living on this night, seeking shelter. Their ghosts were likely to come indoors seeking cover and protection, which is why food was fearfully left for them in the parlours of houses and fires kept continuously burning in hearths. Most of all, it became imperative to frighten these forces away and to guard against them by any means available. Masks were worn in order not to be recognised by evil entities and fairies, which might otherwise spirit a person away. Disguises to fool or trick evil spirits ranged from soot-blackened faces to clothes worn inside out or back to front. Hollowed-out turnip heads inserted with lighted candles and placed on windowsills were also believed to frighten these forces away. Because this night belonged to neither the one world nor the other, it was also a night for horseplay and practical jokes before the gloom of the long winter set in.

Bonfires on hills were a conspicuous feature of the old Halloween rites in northern European countries. In England, these bonfires were transferred to November 5 to mark the arrest of Guy Fawkes. Some of the traditions of the ancient festival of Samhain can still be perceived on

Guy Fawkes Night by the knowledgeable observer. In northern Europe, the belief is still common that if one hears footsteps approaching from behind on this night, one should not look back, as it might be the dead, and one might soon join them!

During the 1800s, many Europeans immigrated to America, with the result that holidays and traditions from different cultures merged. Halloween was now also called Devil's Night or Hell Night and to many, became 'mischief night', a time to play tricks on others. In America, the hollowed-out pumpkin has taken over the role of the turnip used in Europe. Most beliefs once surrounding this day have been forgotten, and the festival of Halloween has become disguised in commercialism. Halloween has become a family event in the U.S., and the masks and disguises have remained. In addition, funny plastic hats are sported, adults go to masked balls or fancy-dress parties, families enjoy favourite recipes and get-togethers, and children go trick-or-treating. Going from door to door, trick-or-treaters collect sweets, biscuits, apples, and other goodies. If no treat or present is forthcoming, a trick or practical joke might be played on the householder.

In Catholic South and Central America, the festival of the dead is called El Dia de los Muertos or, alternatively, Los Dias de los Muertos,[3] as the celebrations last for three days. No other nation has embraced this 'Festival of the Dead' to the extent that the Mexicans have. Beginning on October 31 and lasting until November 2, it is one of the most important holidays of the year for them. Candles are lit in the memory of ancestors; altars in homes are decorated with fruit, bread, sweets, and flowers; and people dress in costumes and fancy dress, marching in parades and processions through the streets.

Why Is Christmas Celebrated on December 25?

The Christian Bible is silent about any religious or secular celebration of Christ's birth, called Christmas. History confirms that in the first century after Christ's birth, such a celebration was unknown. During the first three centuries of the Christian era, there was considerable opposition within the Church to the pagan custom of celebrating birthdays, as it was considered that only pagans celebrated the birthdays of their gods, emperors, and kings. The Greek church father, Origen, voiced his opposition in 245 CE to any efforts of establishing a birthday for Christ as though the Lord was some earthly pharaoh. In modern times, historians have determined that Jesus' birth occurred between 8 BCE and 4 BCE (not in CE 1 as most people presume). But the celebration's specific date is traditional and believed to have been influenced by various pagan festivals.

The celebration of Christmas was an invention of religious men, removed by many centuries from Jesus' birth. Thus, the exact date of Jesus' birth was unknown to these people and could not be determined with any accuracy from the scriptures. The Gospel of Luke suggests that it might have been some time in May as '…the shepherds were tending their flocks by night'.[4] Shepherds tend their flocks at lambing time, which must have been in the spring, and not in the dead of winter when sheep are kept in pens and not tended by shepherds.

There is evidence to suggest that Christ's birth was observed on various dates. At the beginning of the fourth century, there was no consensus about when this date should come on the calendar, or even if it should be there. As it was impossible to determine the exact date of Christ's birth, or any other tradition, from the Gospels, the early church fathers appointed January 6 for the celebration of Christ's birth, even though the Church celebrated Epiphany on that day. Although this had nothing to do with Christ's birth, the Church turned January 6 into Jesus' birthday during the early fourth century.

Choosing January 6 as the date for such an important feast seems to have its antecedent in Alexandria in Egypt, where, during Roman times, there was a large temple called the Koreion. In Alexandria, possibly the most civilised city in the world in Jesus' time, the birth of the god Aeon was celebrated yearly on January 6. The pagan feast of Aeon is recorded in the Christian writings of St. Epiphanius (circa 315–402 CE) and seems to have been still strictly observed in his day. He writes: 'At Alexandria, in the Koreion, as it is called – an immense temple – after they have kept all-night vigil with songs and music, chanting to their idol, they descend with lights into an underground crypt and carry up a wooden image lying naked on a litter [...]. And they carry round the image, circumambulating seven times the innermost temple, to the accompaniment of pipes, tambors and hymns [...]. If they are asked the meaning of this mystery, they answer: "Today at this hour the Maiden Kore, that is the virgin, gave birth to the Aeon...".'.[5] This implies a startling connection between a virgin birth and the setting of the date for the festival of Christ's birth. The Church's decree to commemorate Christ's birth on January 6 helped many pagan Alexandrians convert to Christianity, as they were accustomed to celebrating this day. They could accept Jesus as Aeon and Kore as the virgin, without having to change the date of their principal feast.

'It is well known that in the transition from pageantry to Christianity, the Christian clergy, finding it impossible to wean the people from old customs or to eradicate primitive beliefs, discreetly met the situation by diverting pagan festivals to the honour of Christ'.[6] It became general practice by the Church to adopt and superimpose the introduction of Christian festivals onto existing periods of pagan festivities. Thus, by adopting the feasts of the Greeks and Romans and adapting them to the most striking events in the life of Christ and his disciples, the pagan worshippers' prejudices were shaken and new converts easily obtained. In this way, the Christian Church, always anxious to meet the heathens halfway by allowing them to retain the feasts they were used to, grasped the opportunity to turn the people away from pagan observances held in Rome and throughout Europe at this time.

After Constantine's triumph,[7] Christianity became a state religion throughout the Roman world in 324 CE. However, strongly linked to the Christianisation of Rome was the 'Romanisation' of Christianity. Whereas the Eastern Orthodox Churches have kept January 6 as the date for their Christmas celebration, the Church in Rome under Pope Julius I changed the celebration for Christ's birth from January 6 to December 25 in 353 CE.

The early Church in Rome was forced to legitimise December 25 because of a competing religion that had long captured the hearts and minds of Romans. It must be remembered, that the majority of Romans were still pagans by 300 CE, and during this period, countless religious cults still flourished side by side in the Roman Empire. One of these was the cult of Deus Sol Invictus, 'God the Unconquerable Sun'. This cult reached extraordinary heights during the reign of Constantine the Great (306–337 CE), its followers commemorating Dies Natali Invicti, 'the birth of the unconquered god' festival on December 25.

Another cult, very popular in the Roman Empire during the second and third century CE, was Mithraism. Not only was Mithra, the central figure of the Persian mystery cult, born on December 25, but he offered salvation to his adherents by being an intermediary between humans and the good god of light.[8]

Around this time, Romans also celebrated the winter solstice festival and the festival of Saturnalia from December 17–23, in honour of Saturn. During the festival of Saturnalia, the reversal in nature marked by the solstice was celebrated with wild revelry, rejoicing, and festivities, when the usual restraints on law and morality were unfettered. Class distinctions were temporarily and playfully abolished, masters even accepting taunts from their slaves, which, under ordinary circumstances, would have been punished. The community selected a mock King of Saturnalia, who directed his subjects to drink, dance, and carouse. After the festival, the mock king pretended to expire on Saturn's altar, and order was restored. During Saturnalia, it was customary among the Romans to suspend all public business and give presents to friends and loved ones.

At this time, on December 25, the ancient Germanic races in northern Europe also celebrated a great festival – the festival of the winter solstice, known by the Druids as Yuletide and by the Scandinavians as Mother-Night. Yule comes into modern English from Anglo-Saxon geol, the feast of the midwinter solstice, one of the most important festivals on their calendar, when the gods were consulted about the future, agreements were renewed, and time was spent in jovial merrymaking. Many features of this festival, such as the burning of the Yule log and decorations of mistletoe and evergreens, survive.

By fixing the celebration of Christ's birth on December 25, which was already a longstanding date of many diverse festivities, the Christian Church gave meaning to existing pagan observances – not by eradicating them, but by simply adopting them.

Many people believe that to put an 'X' in Xmas is disrespectful and an attempt to cross the Christ out of Christmas. In reality, however, the 'X' in Xmas is of Greek origin. 'X' is the first letter of the Greek word for Christ. This term was popular in Europe by the sixteenth century and is still customarily used, although its origin has been lost in obscurity.

Christmas Celebrations Banned?

Imagine not being allowed to celebrate Christmas! This was however the case for a brief time in seventeenth-century England under Puritan rule.

Puritans, an extreme group of Protestants within the Church of England, thought the English Reformation had not gone far enough in amending the doctrine and structure of the Church. Their aim was to purify their national church by eliminating every shred of Catholic influence. The Church of England was also to be cleansed of all liturgies, ceremony, or practices not found in Scripture. To Puritans, the Bible was the sole authority, and they believed it applied to every aspect of life.

Puritans disapproved of Christmas, Easter, and other festival and saint days on the grounds that these holidays were invented by humankind and not prescribed by the Bible and, as such, could not be considered holy. Christmas was especially labelled as pagan and an unwelcome survival of Roman Catholic faith. Nowhere in the Bible was there a call to celebrate Christ's birth in this manner.

In the early 1640s, power passed from Charles I – later executed – to a largely Puritan parliament known as the 'Long Parliament'. The Long Parliament forthwith forbade all church services and festivities relating to Christmas, condemning the celebration of Christmas altogether. Parliament sat on Christmas Day, and it was business as usual for everyone. All shops and markets had to stay open on December 25. Soldiers even went into private homes, looking for anyone celebrating on this day, and took away any festive food. Although there was rioting in the streets, Christmas remained suppressed. Instead, Puritans demanded stricter observance of Sunday, the Lord's Day, and legislated thus. It was not until the Restoration under Charles II in 1660, when the bleak Puritan Age ended, that Christmas festivities were restored with renewed exuberance and public vigour.

Meanwhile, Puritan settlers carried over their zealous piousness to America. Hence, Christmas celebrations were not permitted in Massachusetts between 1659 and 1856. In Boston, public schools held classes on Christmas Day until 1870, with all pupils not attending school on that day subject to punishment. But, with the wave of Irish and German immigrants to America in the late nineteenth century, the enthusiasm for the feast was revived and old traditions taken up again, spreading nationwide.

Santa Claus

The well-known, red-suited, roly-poly, jolly American symbol of festive cheer and commercial activity emerges from historical, mythological, and legendary figures in folklore. Historically, Santa is probably based on the kindly Christian Saint Nicholas, Bishop of Myra,[9] who lived during the fourth century CE.

St. Nicholas was well known for the many miracles attributed to him and his acts of kindness, especially towards children. He also had a reputation for gift giving. A legend about him recounts how he went to the homes of those living in abject poverty and threw several coins through the smoke holes in their roofs. On one specific occasion, the gold pieces fell into stockings left hanging to dry, instead of landing in the hearth. This is believed by many to have given rise to the traditional belief that Santa comes down the chimney on Christmas morning to fill stockings, which expectant children have left out for him. It is, however, likely that this legend evolved to distract from the deeply ingrained parallel pagan story told of the god, Odin.

Many comparisons have been drawn between Santa and the Nordic Odin, chief god in Norse mythology, before Christianisation. The Anglo-Saxons knew him as Wodan, and during the winter solstice festival known as Yule, Odin, riding his eight-legged horse Sleipnir, was thought to command a great hunting party across the heavens. This led to comparisons with Santa's procession of reindeer. A further point of comparison is that it was customary during this time of the year for children to leave their boots filled with carrots and straw near the smoke hole as fodder for Odin's horse. To show his appreciation, Odin is said to have rewarded their thoughtfulness by placing gifts inside the boots. This custom continued in northern European countries after Christianisation, became linked with St. Nicholas, and is still seen in homes when children hang their stockings by the chimney, to be filled with presents.

The legend of the kindly Saint Nicholas travelled from Myrna (modern-day Turkey) to northern European countries, and the saint eventually became a popular figure in Holland where he was known as Sinterklaas. The Dutch brought Sinterklaas to the New World, and around 1870, the Americans turned the name into Santa Claus. Sometime later, this celebrated character merged with the Elizabethan Father Christmas, a jolly old man, who the British believed provided the Christmas feast. He is still known as Father Christmas in the United Kingdom and Europe, although his depiction is identical to the American Santa. Another interesting fact is that the two characters live in different locations – Father Christmas residing in Finland, while the American Santa purportedly lives at the North Pole.

Santa's present depiction as a rotund white-bearded old man dressed in a red-and-white outfit eventually emerged in the 1920s, after portrayals by dozens of artists. This new image, however, was universalised by none other than Coca-Cola in their 1931 advertising campaign, as Santa matched Coca-Cola's red-and-white logo. Encouraging Americans that Coke was the solution to a 'thirst for all seasons' entrenched Santa as an icon of contemporary commercial culture.

The Christmas Tree

Explanations for the origins of the Christmas tree vary. In tracing the custom of decorating a tree for Christmas back to its likely origin, we find it as distinctly blended with pagan influences as many other Christmas observances. The Christmas tree epitomises many ancient ideas and is perhaps the only remnant today of humankind's history of tree-reverence. The Tree of Knowledge, the Cosmic Tree, the May Tree, the Harvest Tree, as well as the universal idea of regarding trees as embodiments of deities, have all disappeared.

The tradition of the Yule Tree or Solstice Tree during the winter solstice probably goes back to early Indo-European tribes, who decorated trees with blazing torches as part of their fire festivals to persuade the sun to shine again. Ornaments and offerings were hung on trees in sacred groves, and evergreens were brought into homes to symbolise life in the midst of wintery death.

With the spread of Christianity, a popular possibility why a decorated tree might have become associated with Christmas was linked to the legend of Adam and Eve. The early Church had consecrated the 24th day of December as a feast day to Adam and Eve, and Christian legend has it that Adam and Eve took from Paradise a cutting from the Tree of Knowledge. During the Middle Ages, Bible stories were often taught to the illiterate masses through stage plays. For the story of Adam and Eve in the Garden of Eden, the 'tree of temptation' was always depicted by using a fir tree – a logical choice during cold December in the Northern Hemisphere. This so-called Paradise Tree was decorated with apples, symbolising the forbidden fruit. Gradually, people began setting up Paradise Trees in their homes with little figurines of Adam and Eve under the tree to celebrate their feast day. Besides this decorated tree, many Germans also set up a Christmas Pyramid called a Lichtstock, an open wooden frame with shelves for nativity figures, candles, and evergreens, topped with the Star of Bethlehem. A popular contention is that the Paradise Tree and Lichtstock gradually merged to what was to become the Christmas tree.

In Germany, generally considered the land of origin of the Christmas tree, it can be traced back to the beginning of the sixteenth century in churches and guildhalls. During the seventeenth century, the tradition entered family homes. According to Lutheran theologian Johann Dannhauer, Christmas trees were then decorated with apples, paper roses, Communion wafers, sweets, gold foil, and dolls. By the nineteenth century, this German custom had become popular amongst the nobility of many European countries, spreading to royal courts as far as Russia.

Prince Albert of Saxe-Coburg-Gotha, the husband of Queen Victoria, made the Christmas tree a tradition in Britain by introducing one from his German homeland to Windsor Castle in 1841. Eager to emulate the royals, Victorian families took up the tradition, although Charles Dickens still referred to the Christmas tree as the 'new German toy' in 1850.[10] In America, the Christmas tree was probably first used in the early eighteenth century, introduced by German settlers to western Pennsylvania.

Since the nineteenth century, the diffusion of the Christmas tree throughout the world has been so rapid that there is nothing to compare with it in the entire history of popular customs. The Christmas tree is ever popular and forms an essential feature of the Christmas festival. Modern decorations consist mainly of plastic baubles, electric lights, miniature Santas, and angels. Because of commercialism, plastic and even fibre-optic trees, which can be folded up and re-used yearly, are available in stores worldwide.

To Kiss under the Mistletoe

During the winter solstice celebrations, several traditions were observed in the Northern Hemisphere. To entice the sun's return, it was customary to light ritual fires; and to persuade trees, which had lost all their foliage, to replenish their green covering, it was traditional to decorate homes with evergreen garlands. This was especially true of the northern European nations who brought solstice decorations indoors during the icy winters. Evergreen decorations were also customary amongst the Romans during the festival of Saturnalia, which was held from the 17th to 23rd December. Temples were decorated with greenery, especially holly, a symbol of health and happiness sacred to Saturn. Christians took this practice over during Christmas celebrations, and it prevails in modern times, when houses, churches, streets, and shops are decorated with holly, mistletoe, and other evergreens.

In the past, the mistletoe was considered sacred and used in religious ceremonies by the ancient Greeks and the northern nations of Europe, in particular, the Druids of Britain, France, and Ireland. Although the mistletoe, a parasitic plant, grows on various trees, the Druids held it in greatest veneration when found growing on the oak.

The mistletoe is an evergreen, its fresh green foliage growing on the bare leafless branches of trees during winter. Naturally, this was construed in ancient times as definite proof of a magic life force present in the plant. Hence, the mistletoe came to symbolise eternal life and fertility and was linked with sacred religious rites since antiquity. In all likelihood, this plant was brought into homes for protection during the winter solstice celebrations to shield occupants.

Because of the mistletoe's explicit connections with pagan practices, it was declared profane by the Christian Church and promptly prohibited from being brought into their sacred portals. However, traditional plants do not easily lose their ceremonial function, and the mistletoe is still found as a Christmas decoration in our homes during Yuletide. It is traditional in many parts of Europe to keep mistletoe and holly throughout the year from one Christmas to another, only to be renewed and replaced with fresh branches, thereby bringing good luck and ensuring protection from harm.

To associate kissing under the mistletoe with good fortune might be for several reasons. The Romans regarded the mistletoe as a symbol of peace, and when enemies met under it, it was said they discarded their weapons and declared a truce. The English custom for lovers to kiss under the mistletoe or a man having the right to kiss any lady beneath its branches dates to ancient times and was already traditional amongst the Saxons. No doubt, this is partly because of the mistletoe's strong connection with fertility and sexual potency.

However, the most likely origin of the mistletoe as a 'kissing plant' is linked to Norse mythology, relating to the god, Baldur's, death and resurrection. When Baldur was born, his mother, the Norse goddess, Frigga, made every living thing promise not to harm him. Unfortunately, she overlooked the mistletoe plant, later used by the evil god Loki to kill the vegetation god Baldur. His death brought winter into the world, and then all creation was in deep mourning. One version explaining the custom of kissing under the mistletoe is that after Baldur was restored to life, the mistletoe was declared sacred, ordered by Frigg to bring love into the world instead of death and for all standing below its branches to share a kiss. But, there is also a different tale accounting for the custom. The plant so offended the gods of Norse mythology that it was consequently cursed by them to always have to look on while pretty girls were kissed under its leaves. No wonder then, that Shakespeare refers to the plant as the 'baleful mistletoe' in Titus Andronicus, alluding to its calamitous, woeful associations in myth and legend.[11] According to superstition, any girl refusing to be kissed under the mistletoe risks dying unmarried.

VI

RITES OF PASSAGE

Rites of passage are ritual acts conducted in most societies at all major events of a person's life, particularly at the great transitional points such as birth, the onset of puberty, marriage, and death. Rites of passage, therefore, mark the entering and initiation of an individual into a new social or religious standing.

The function of such rites, which might take the form of baptism, circumcision, confirmation, bar mitzvah, school graduation ceremonies, marriage customs, retirement functions, or funerary practices, is to preserve a harmonious relationship within a particular society by adhering to its customs, rules, and social values. All societies have very specific traditions and ceremonies surrounding the three most significant events in human life, namely birth, marriage, and death, and in many cultures, there are specific rituals also attached to the transitional states between these events.

In 1909, the Belgian anthropologist, Arnold van Gennep, coined the phrase 'rites of passage' to describe these rituals. They confirm that individuals have passed from one stage to another in their relationship and acceptance within the rest of the community. In every society, the adolescent is initiated into a religion or into the secrets of certain rites of that society. In ancient Rome, a boy became a man in the ceremony of the toga praetexta. Christian societies celebrate a child's baptism, Confirmation, and First Communion to mark religious maturity, while the same occasion is celebrated when a Jewish boy becomes a bar mitzvah, or 'Son of the Commandment', at the age of thirteen.

Everywhere, the step from the irresponsibility of childhood to the world of adults is marked by ceremonies, which, depending on whether they are religious or lay, modern or ancient, highly evolved or simple, take different forms. It can be said that human existence attains completion through a series of passage rites, by successive initiations, and that the occasion is invested with a sense of importance and ceremony, not only for those undergoing such rituals, but also the entire community.

The stages critical to a person's life vary from one culture to another. In some communities, a child's first haircut might mark the end of infancy and the beginning of childhood, with the cuttings fastidiously treasured and put away as a keepsake by the mother. Similarly, the first clipping of fingernails is considered important. Among many non-Western societies, various puberty rites such as circumcision, clitoridectomy, and infibulation, often unpleasant and painful, mark the entrance of boys and girls into adulthood. In his book, The Masks of God, Joseph Campbell expounds on this point:

'Throughout the world the rituals of transformation from infancy to manhood are attended with and effected by excruciating ordeals. Scourgings, fastings, the knocking out of teeth, scarifications, finger sacrifices, removal of a testicle, cicatrization, circumcision, subincision, bitings and burnings are the general rule. […] the natural body is transformed by the ordeals into an ever-present sign of a new spiritual state. For even in the gentler and higher societies where the body is no longer naked and mutilated, new clothes and ornaments are assumed, following initiations, to symbolise and support the new spiritual state. In India the caste marks, tonsure, clothes etc. represent precisely the individual's social role. In the West we know the military uniform, clerical collar, medical goatee, and judge's wig. But where people are naked it is the body itself, which must be changed'.[1]

In order to adhere to the customs, rules, and values of various rites of passage in certain cultures, specific ritual behaviour is observed. Ritual behaviour can be viewed as a prescribed action repeated systematically from time to time, forming a common part of human life especially important within a religious context. Rituals, such as prayers, songs, processions, sacrifices, feasts, and festivals, differ among various religions and societies. However, although the rites of passage of birth, marriage, and death might differ in content, they are common and equally important to all cultures.

Born Lucky or Friday's Child

Every stage of life is accompanied by various customs and traditions that have filtered down to us from the earliest times. Many of these now appear meaningless, but originally, they were the natural outcome of perceptions and beliefs prevailing at the time of their inception.

In the past, it was thought that countless influences assailed newborns from the moment of birth. Consequently, mothers had to be constantly vigilant that correct procedures were put in place well in advance to protect their infant children. The planets' influence was believed to affect the child's future fortune and character. Between conception and the birth of a child, astrologers were called on to gauge the position of heavenly bodies and to cast a horoscope at the time of a child's birth. From the moment the baby arrived, superstitious conclusions were drawn about every apparent characteristic the infant displayed: being born with a tooth was regarded as unlucky; having fists which were clenched or open determined if the child would be generous or tight-fisted; plenty of hair on the head was thought to lead to abundance and wealth in later life; a blue vein across the forehead pointed to an ugly temper. A cradled child who did not look at its mother directly was believed to be a witch. All these observations indicated how the child would grow up and what kind of person he or she would eventually turn out to be.

Generally, it was thought that babies born on a Sunday would be blessed with luck and would never suffer drowning or hanging. Sunday's children have always held special birth rites. In Yorkshire, they were regarded safe from the evil eye. In Germany, they were seen as especially privileged. In most parts of Europe, they were considered able to see things hidden from others, such as the spirit world. In some parts, it was believed that a child born on Christmas Day would not live beyond the age of thirty-three, the age at which Christ died on the Cross. If born in a leap year, the baby or the mother was destined to die soon.

Those unfortunate to be born on a Friday were believed unlucky, a psychological impediment that they carried with them for the rest of their lives. Friday changed from being regarded as a lucky day, to one fraught with misfortune, as a result of Christian belief and the sombre symbolism of the day soon became transferred to every Friday of the year.

The hour of birth was also highly significant. A child born at chime hours, in other words, at three, six, nine, or twelve chimes, was believed to develop clairvoyance. Babies born in the dead of night were not considered as lucky in later life as those born during daylight hours.

It is easily understood how the wealth of intricate beliefs surrounding every aspect of an infant's life, from conception and birth to infancy, caused parents and relatives to follow various protective measures strictly. For instance, in many European and Middle Eastern countries, babies were greeted by spitting at them, a custom still found in some of these cultures. This was considered highly effective in keeping evil forces at bay. For the same reason, it was customary in the northern parts of England to 'sain' a baby shortly after birth.[2] This shielding procedure entailed whirling lighted candles and an open Bible three times around the bed on which mother and child were lying. It was considered important to do the whirling in a sunwise direction, that is, clockwise, to heighten effectiveness.

Another means of protection from evil forces was to wrap the infant in a garment belonging to the mother. It was commonly held that any item, which had been in close contact with the body, especially the mother, hence symbolising protecting maternal forces, was charged with significant and lasting power. It was thus believed that a baby should never be wrapped in new sheets or new clothes, where these shielding forces would be absent.

When nursing for the first time it was of utmost importance for the baby to drink from the right breast first, lest it be in danger of growing up left-handed, which was formerly regarded as very unlucky. Similarly, it was considered imperative always to lay a newborn baby on its right side first, or else the child would turn out to be 'awkward' in later life.

To compliment a mother on her beautiful baby was widely regarded as inviting harm from the evil eye. Similarly, calling the baby an angel tempted fate to take the child directly to heaven. In many European countries, it was thought that cutting the baby's hair or nails with scissors or anything made of iron within the first twelve months of life risked considerable misfortune. Often, mothers bit the infant's nails, rather than cut them, to prevent the child growing up light-fingered or dishonest. It was considered very unlucky for a baby to see its reflection in a mirror, as this was believed to kill the infant, and stepping over babies crawling on the ground or passing them through a window was believed to stunt their growth.

So numerous were the various beliefs and superstitions, which had to be adhered to and closely followed that parents and family must have been continually occupied and mindful to avert all perceived possible dangers, evils, and dire consequences for the child's later life.

The Holy Hood

A belief once prevailing universally, concerned the navel cord and the placenta. It was commonly believed that these two body parts would remain in sympathetic union with the body after physical connection had been severed. Therefore, the condition and treatment of the navel cord and placenta were thought to influence the fortunes of the child, for good or bad, throughout his life. In Africa, Melanesia, Polynesia, and on the Australian continent, it was customary amongst most indigenous people to bury the afterbirth carefully to prevent evil spirits from reaching it. The same protective care was taken with the umbilical cord. In most regions of Australia, for example, among the Aborigines, a length of umbilical cord was left attached to the baby's navel until it withered and fell off. The withered cord was then the object of a specific ceremony. It was on no account to be burned or destroyed, as harm would later befall the child. This correlates with beliefs prevailing around the world regarding the navel cord. Until the early nineteen hundreds, it was still believed in some European countries that a person's destiny was bound up with the umbilical cord and the afterbirth.

Similarly, many strange customs and superstitions were associated with the caul, a thin membrane sometimes found covering the head of a newly delivered baby. Commonly known as a 'caul' is the amniotic sac surrounding the foetus in the mother's womb. Containing the fluid surrounding the foetus, it acts as protection to the unborn child. Shortly before birth, the amniotic sac bursts and is later expelled with the afterbirth. Occasionally, however, the caul or parts of it cling to the child's head during the birth process. Known in Scotland as the hallihoo, or 'holy hood', elsewhere in the United Kingdom as the 'happy hood' and in some American States as 'the veil', the caul was regarded as presaging exceptionally good fortune for the person born with it.

The caul was treasured and highly prized by anyone able to obtain one, as it was believed that it would continue to protect in life as it had done for the foetus in the womb. Usually, it was carefully put away in safekeeping for the lucky person who had been fortunate enough to be born with it. A child born with a caul was not only believed to be assured of protection and good fortune throughout life, but also to acquire the gift of second sight. People born with cauls were said to have special psychic powers. However, the preservation of the caul was considered closely connected with the health of the person to whom it belonged. Therefore, it had to be well looked after, as damage or destruction to the caul meant illness or death to its owner. It was further believed that when the owner of a caul died, the object was to be buried with the corpse, or else the deceased was destined to walk about in spirit form in search of the missing body part.

Curiously, a caul not only ensured good luck and success to those born with it. In other words, the magic properties linked with the object were not restricted to whoever was born with it, but could in effect be transferred to others. For instance, ancient Roman midwives lacked scruples about selling a caul on the sly, without the consent or knowledge of the child's mother. Interestingly, their best market was the Roman Forum, where practitioners of the law paid high prices for a caul, as they believed that anyone wearing a dried caul on their chest would be sure to win their case. Curious indeed!

The caul was also held to be effective in preventing drowning at sea, probably because it originally had contained the amniotic fluid in which the foetus was safely surrounded – without having drowned. Therefore, the caul's power to protect against drowning made it especially prized by sailors. Its presence on board ship was believed to prevent the danger of shipwreck, and sailors were prepared to pay large sums of money to obtain this body part. Such was the intensity of superstition surrounding cauls, that they were regularly advertised in the press during the eighteenth and nineteenth centuries. In the London Times of February 20, 1813, the following typical and very popular advertisement was placed: 'A child's caul to be sold in the highest perfection. Enquire at No.2 Church Street, Minories. To prevent trouble, price 12 pounds'. During the German submarine campaign against merchant shipping in the First World War, sailors eagerly sought cauls near the London docks for prices varying between 13 and 15 pounds sterling.

Such superstitious beliefs surrounding the 'holy hood' are universal and can be found on every continent in places as far apart as Timor and Holland.

Boys in Girls' Clothes

A curious fact, not generally known, is that European and American boys were traditionally dressed in gowns and dresses until the early nineteen hundreds. At the time, dresses were generally perceived as children's wear and not specifically associated with little girls. Hence, the occasion when small boys were first dressed in breeches or trousers, known as 'breeching', was anticipated with great excitement by family and friends and celebrated as an important rite of passage.

During the seventeenth and eighteenth centuries, breeching generally corresponded with what was regarded as the age of reason, considered to be about seven. However, in the nineteenth century, the age of breeching fell closer to two or three years. But breeching was not the first important change of clothes in a young boy's life. Before they were breeched, they were 'shortcoated'. Shortcoating, however, applied not solely to boys, but to both boys and girls, signifying the time when they were taken out of the very long dresses worn by babies. Such baby garments extended well beyond the infant's feet and survive as christening gowns in modern times.

The main reason for keeping boys in dresses was probably a very practical one, namely to facilitate toilet training. Additionally, dresses could more readily accommodate spurts of future growth in children, at a time when garments were after all considerably more expensive than they are today. However, another explanation, which is of a superstitious nature, is sometimes given with regard to this custom. It concerns a fundamental attitude towards female children at the time. As children were thought to be in special need of protection from evil forces, and since girls were at one time in Europe considered far inferior to boys – as is still the case in many non-western countries – it was argued that no demon would bother to attack a girl, which is why boys dressed as girls were considered safe. The exchange of clothing between the sexes was also seen by many as an attempt to avert the evil eye. Amongst European royals, the tradition was considered protective because young heirs to the throne were thus shielded from would-be assassins who could not easily distinguish between the sexes.

Because all young children wore dresses, it was often difficult to differentiate between boys and girls by looking at their external appearance. Therefore, commissioned portraits of the wealthy sometimes included distinguishing props for boys, such as whips for toy horses, drums, and bows. In a well-known portrait depicting the children of Charles I by the Flemish painter, Anton Van Dyck, only the absence of a necklace and his dress colour set the four-year-old James I apart from his little sister Elizabeth. Some decades later, several other subtle distinguishing features evolved. For instance, girls' hair was usually parted in the middle, whereas boys displayed side paths; girls' bodices generally reflected adult styles and never had buttons down the centre of the bodice – this was reserved for the boys.

After World War I, the tradition of young boys wearing dresses finally seemed to die out.

True Blue for Boys

In the past, the wealth of intricate beliefs and notions surrounding every aspect of an infant's life, from conception and birth to early childhood, kept parents and family ever conscious of averting all possible dangers and evils.

All colours chosen for children's clothes were considered of primary importance, because of the symbolism attached to each specific colour. Children were never to wear black, which in European countries has always been linked with death and mourning, while red was the colour of blood, passion, and vitality, and also linked to witchcraft. Blue, however, was regarded as protective against all evil forces and, hence, considered especially suitable for boys.

Throughout history in all cultures worldwide, blue – the colour of the heavens – was considered divine and symbolic of purity and truth, therefore warding off all malevolent forces. In the Persian mythological epic Shahnameh, blue is the colour of kingship and sovereignty. The Mesopotamian monarchs in ancient Sumer and Akkad are reputed to have worn crowns and garments decorated with blue lapis lazuli stone, indicating kingship. The god Odin is said to have always worn a blue coat, and Druidic high priests and Jewish high priests alike are reputed to have worn blue robes, signifying holiness. To the Yezidis of northern Iraq, blue is the most sacred colour and, therefore, never worn by them. In modern times, blue is regarded as a canonical colour.

To signify their exalted and heavenly character, the gods were often painted blue in Egyptian and Indian mythological paintings. The Egyptians conceived the supreme god Kneph, the father of Ptah, as a man of blue. The Egyptian god Osiris is invoked as the 'god of Turquoise' and the 'god of Lapis Lazuli'. In India, elemental blue is still the colour of the unsullied, holy lotus and the long-eyed gods. The colour of Krishna was blue, and his name means 'blue-black'. To the South American Mayas, blue, the colour of the vault of heaven, represented holiness, chastity, and sanctity. Until the time of the Spanish conquest of Mexico, those who offered themselves as propitiatory sacrifices to their deity smeared their bodies with blue paint, signifying the exalted and heavenly character of their gods. The ancient Britons observed a similar custom. Caesar found the ancient Britons facing his troops in battle smeared with blue war paint, pointing to the probability that these men went into battle with the full intention of sacrificing themselves.

Humanity has always feared and revered the colour blue and considered it the most powerful protector against evil influences. Moslems and Christians alike use the colour to keep unwanted influences at bay, and one has only to think of the well-known Victorian rhyme regarding the bridal ensemble, 'Something old, something new, something borrowed, something blue'.

In the Middle Eastern, Eastern European, and North African countries, blue is still used in averting the evil eye. Discs consisting of blue and white concentric circles representing an evil eye are common apotropaic charms, the contention being that the staring eye bends the malicious gaze back to a potential sorcerer. The same blue symbol is also found on the prows of Mediterranean boats and common in Turkey and Morocco on houses, in cars, or worn as personal charms. The blue eye is similarly found on protective hand-shaped amulets known in the Middle East as the Hamsa Hand, or Hand of Fatima, and amongst Jews as the Hand of Miriam.

Blue is widely seen as the symbol of truth, which is why we still speak of something being 'true blue', meaning unwavering, constant, stable, or steadfast. However, the origin of this expression might be derived from a certain type of blue cloth made in Coventry, England, during the Middle Ages. The dye of this specific cloth apparently remained fast or true when it was common for colours to run and fade, contending that the literal meaning of fast-coloured was transferred to figuratively imply steadfast in character.

Similarly, there is a popular notion that the term blue-blooded, to indicate royal or aristocratic bloodlines, might have originated from a physical characteristic. The Spanish expression sangre azul meaning 'blue blood', is thought to refer to the blueness of the veins visible on the very light-skinned, fair Castilian nobles who were proud of their old heritage. They claimed never to have intermarried with the Moors, Jews, and other races populating Spain during the Middle Ages, hence the term 'blue-blooded', signifying high rank and birth. However, because of the association of the colour with the divine and sacred, since ancient times, it is most likely that the term blue-blooded is a relic of the ancient doctrine of the divinity of kingship.

The Changeling

In Christian countries, it was firmly believed in the past that those unfortunates who died unbaptised were claimed by the devil in the afterlife unless they were babies, in which case, they were fated to wait in limbo until the Last Judgment. Another tradition held that if a child died before baptism, his or her spirit was doomed to wander restlessly about in deserted, ruined places. In northern European countries, these children were thought to turn into will-o'-the-wisps, the tiny lights seen to hover over marshy, swampy countryside. Now, these small flickering lights are scientifically explained as emanating marsh gasses.

In the past, it was thought that many dangers threatened the unbaptised child and the superstitious, therefore, recommended many safeguards to mothers before the actual baptism took place. Traditionally, unbaptised babies were kept at home and given protection from all evil influences by various amulets. Often, infants were protected with a knife wrapped in its swaddling – any object made of iron, was regarded as suitable. Alternately, some salt or a communion wafer tucked into the crib offered protection. In Ireland and other parts of Europe, it was considered dangerous to pick up an unbaptised child without first making the sign of the cross over it. The earliest possible baptism of a newborn child, therefore, was considered essential, not only to save it from limbo should it die in an unholy state before baptism, but also to ensure the baby's future health and to prevent it from being carried off by fairies that would leave a so-called changeling in its place.

In Europe, belief in the changeling was firmly established in the past. Legends describe the changeling as a wizened, misshapen, hairy baby with a monstrous head, left in the cradle as a substitute for a human child, who had been snatched by fairies or underground elves. The changeling was thought to cry continuously and to eat ravenously but never grow – or if it did grow, to be horribly deformed.

At a time, when medical diagnoses could provide no answers, poor nutrition inevitably stunted the growth of impoverished children, and society was suffused with superstitions, the concept of the changeling provided a convenient explanation for backward, spastic or deformed children. When their offspring suddenly stopped growing or acted and looked strange, parents were bewildered, bereft of any explanations, save that such a misfit could not possibly be their child. It had to be a changeling! Often, such children had high-domed foreheads and were undersize, only to confirm the already held conviction that fairy children were believed to look like freaks.

For the child deemed to be a changeling, life was difficult. Numerous methods were employed for unmasking the changeling and forcing the perceived abhorrence to reveal its true age and identity. In the Scottish Highlands, a presumed changeling infant was placed as close as possible to a fire piled high with peat. If the child were truly a fairy child, it would inevitably escape up the chimney, or as the Scottish would say, 'up the lum'. The deception of raising a changeling could also be discovered by making it reveal its true age, for they were always thought to be very old. Often the whipping method was used to make the changeling known, or alternatively, the child was made to sleep outdoors. All these methods of unmasking a changeling, in modern times, would be irrevocably labelled child abuse. However, in the past, this belief was so ingrained that, as late as 1843, the West Briton newspaper reported an incident from Cornwall about a child being mistreated by his parents. The child had been severely beaten from 15 months onwards, but the case was dismissed out of court when the parents explained, in all seriousness, that this was not their own child, but a changeling.[3]

The Name-Giving Ceremony

The name-giving ceremony is generally associated with baptism in Western culture. The term baptism originates from the Greek term baptizein meaning 'to dip' or 'to bathe'. Baptism, specifically the ceremony of admitting a person to the Christian community, is a sacrament of the Christian Church and is performed by applying water in various ways for the remission of sin. This predominantly takes the form of immersion in water or the sprinkling of water over the head.

Besides being a sacrament, The Random House Dictionary of the English Language also describes baptism as '...to cleanse spiritually, initiate or dedicate by purifying'. Regarding baptism, the Wordsworth

Dictionary of Beliefs and Religions states, 'The practice of cleansing by water was known in some pre-Christian religions, where it represented transformation, promising immortality or regeneration'. Hence, spiritual purification by water was a pagan rite long before the spread of Christianity.

Water from seas, rivers, fountains, wells, rain, or dew has universally been used as a symbol of cleansing and invigorating the spirit. In this sense, baptism is a common observance found in all cultures. The purification of sin by water pertains to the religions of Asia, Africa, Europe, and America. Among all nations on earth, from the very earliest times, water has been used as a religious sacrament and has been linked with magical properties and spiritual cleansing. Every major religion in the world uses water in its rites, and all societies know of the healing properties of magic lakes, wells, and springs. The rites of cleansing with water universally represent transformation, regeneration, and immortality. Water was the element by which everything was reborn and re-created, hence the ceremony of dipping, plunging, or immersing. Ritual washing and cleansing is practised in Hinduism, Buddhism, Judaism, and the Islamic faith.

The name-giving ceremony has from ancient times been universally linked with ritual cleansing by water. In India, Mongolia, and Tibet, Buddhists celebrate the birth of a child in the presence of a priest, burning incense and candles at a domestic altar and intoning prescribed prayers, while dipping the child in water and imposing on it a name.

The ancient Persians carried their newborn infants to the temple to be blessed by a priest, purified by water, and for the father of the child to bestow a name on the infant during the ceremony. Similarly, the ancient Etruscans performed the rite of baptism or initiation, during which the child was blessed, marked with water on the forehead, and then named. Infant baptism linked with the naming of a child was also practised among the ancient inhabitants of northern Europe, namely the Danes, Swedes, Norwegians, and other Germanic tribes, long before Christianity. Water was poured on the head of a newborn child, while its father or the elder brother of its mother ceremoniously named the child.

Similarly, ceremonies that seem to correspond to Christian baptism were carried out on children in ancient Rome on the eighth or ninth day after their birth, when they were named. Besides sprinkling water on a child's head, the child was also daubed with spittle to avert evil influences. A similar custom prevailed in Scotland, where it was believed necessary that the parson use spittle to christen a child. Amongst many African tribes, the custom of spitting to ward off evil prevailed. The child to be named was spat on in the face three times to protect it in later life.

In the past it was considered unlucky to call a child by its name before baptism, even to let the name be known to anyone except the parents. It was believed that public knowledge of its name before baptism would expose the hapless infant to great risk. This superstition has its roots in the ancient past and is found universally amongst all cultures. (See Chapter I, What's in a Name?)

Children are often named after living or deceased parents and relatives, all depending on the culture to which the person belongs. In the past it was considered unlucky to name one's son or daughter after a child who had died in the same family, as the dead child was believed to return and call away the living child of the same name. Only when a father died, did the son take his name, lest it be forgotten. However, newborn children were often given the names of relatives who had passed on, not so much to honour the ancestor's memory, as we would be inclined to rationalise, but because it was believed that the child would be 'ensouled' with the spirit of the dead ancestor. The Scottish highlanders called this traditional custom 'raising the spirit'.

In Scandinavian countries, it was customary to name children after a deceased relative, as it was held that children would inherit the virtues of the ones whose names they bore. Similar to the Scottish custom of ensouling, Scandinavians named their children after deceased relatives to call up those who had died, attesting to the Old Norse belief in the transmigration of souls. Besides the custom of naming children after deceased relatives, alliteration and variation influenced name-giving in Germanic cultures. Either the same sound at the beginning of one name was repeated in another, or new names were formed to differ from those of others by changing one element in the name. For example, the Norwegian name Végeirr was varied to Vébiorn, Vésteinn, Vémundr, and Végestr.

Amongst many societies, it is customary to give succeeding generations identical names, distinguished merely by adding 'junior' or 'senior', or following the example of aristocracy by numbering the names of their progeny as Charles I or Henry VIII. However, the Puritans of the seventeenth century named their children after admired moral qualities such as Faith, Hope, Mercy, Constance, and even Praise-God.

In former times, an infant's baptism was attended by many curious beliefs, some of which are prevalent. The Christian doctrine of original sin decreed that evil spirits lie in wait for the soul of an unbaptised child, not protected by the sanctity of the Church, and that they must be driven out during the baptising ceremony. Therefore, if a child cried at the ceremony, it was considered a lucky sign, as it meant that evil spirits had been driven out. A saying from northern England tells us that 'A child's cry at baptism is the voice of the Evil One being driven out by Holy Water'. Therefore, the tears and struggles of the infant were regarded as convincing proof that the devil himself had departed. An alternative theological explanation was that the infant's howl signified the pangs of spiritual rebirth. By this token, the person holding the infant would often pinch or prick the poor child to summon up a good loud wail, audible to all pious, anxiously waiting relatives.

On no account was the font water to be wiped from the infant's face, but left to dry naturally. Another popular notion contended that to bathe the child's eyes in font water assured it of not having to see ghosts in later life. It was also a common custom that male children always be baptised before female children. Of course, the specific day on which a baptism was to be held had to be carefully considered. Sundays were held to be the most favourable, although all other days, except Fridays were also deemed suitable. Those baptised on a Friday were thought to grow up as rogues and inevitably end up under the hangman's hands. Naturally, a baptism was never to be held in the wake of a funeral, but believed to bring luck for the child, if it followed after a wedding.

'Born with a Silver Spoon'

The idea of giving children special gifts for their baptism and name-giving ceremony is said to have its origin in the offerings made to the baby Jesus by the three Oriental Kings. It is, however, highly probable that the custom of gift-giving for the auspicious occasion of naming a child was traditional amongst all nations of antiquity and did not originate with the Nativity.

Silver has always been considered a luck-bringing metal, resistant and invulnerable to all enchantment, its shielding powers unable to be deflected by magical means. It was thought to be one of the most potent precious metals with powerful protective qualities, therefore especially suitable for infants on the celebration of their baptism.

A custom going back to fifteenth-century Europe was for a child's godparents to give presents in the form of silver cups and spoons. The specific spoons given to children at the name-giving ceremony were called Apostle Spoons, as the figures of the twelve apostles were usually depicted on the tops of the handles. Some sets consist of an extra thirteenth spoon dedicated to Jesus. Shakespeare refers to these customary gifts in Henry VIII. When Cranmer professes to be unworthy of being sponsor or godparent to the young princess, King Henry replies, 'Come, come, my Lord, you'd spare your spoons....'[4] Depending on their means, godparents generally gave one or two spoons as gifts. If, however, a child was fortunate enough to have rich godparents, they would traditionally give all twelve or thirteen silver spoons, hence the saying, 'To be born with a silver spoon in the mouth', implying someone born into favourable circumstances.

Curiously, in past centuries, carved wooden spoons were frequently given as tokens of love and affection in England and other parts of northern Europe. Acceptance of such a token by a young woman generally meant confirmation of love returned. The tops of these spoon handles were intricately carved with select symbols, each having a specific meaning. For example, the heart-emblem meant 'my heart is yours', a carved chain signified 'together forever', and vines intricately entwined into the handle sent the message 'love grows'. Such 'love spoons' can still be occasionally found as valuable collectibles in select gift shops and antique shops.

Marriages of the Past

Ideas about the requirements to form a legally binding marriage underwent many changes through the ages. Ancient Romans, for example, recognised three kinds of marriages: confarreatio, which was of a religious nature and included a formal ceremony in front of witnesses; coemptio, in which the two parties, in the presence of five witnesses, solemnly bound themselves in marriage, sealing the agreement by the mutual giving of a coin; and usus, a form of marriage that constituted continuous cohabiting of a couple for one year, without the woman being absent for more than two nights during that period. If the couple were still together after this time span, they were considered legally married. In other words, only the couple's consent was necessary and no written contract or formal ceremony was required in sealing the marriage.

The Germanic form of marriage involved consummation and consent from the bride's parents, or the purchase of a bride. In northern European countries, consummation was regarded as legally sealing the marriage contract, for which, however, consent of the bride's family was of utmost importance. This point is clearly underlined by the Merovingian King Childebert II's (570–596 CE) issuing a decree in 596, stipulating the death penalty for abducting a woman by force. Even if she willingly agreed to a marriage, the couple was sentenced to exile or death unless her parents gave their explicit consent.

Amongst the ancient Danes and Normans, there was a marriage contract called hand-festing, which literally means 'hand in fist', that is, joining hands. The joining of hands to seal a betrothal was equally common in Anglo-Saxon England, as is evidenced by the term hand-fasting in Scotland and northern England to refer to a betrothal.[5] In Anglo-Saxon, the term refers to any pledge by the giving of the hand.

According to the rules of hand-fasting, it was customary at annual country fairs, the only time neighbouring rural communities got together, for persons of both sexes to choose a partner according to their liking. Done in front of witnesses, this made them officially betrothed for a year and a day, or thirteen moon cycles, following which, they could simply renew the arrangement for the same time, split up, and have the same arrangement with someone else, or renew it permanently or for 'as long as love shall last' in front of witnesses. With the introduction of Christianity, this form of marriage was considered imperfect without a priest's sanction. However, the custom of first living with a partner and then sanctioning the union through the Church still continued for hundreds of years thereafter.

Ninth-century Frankish law recognised two distinct forms of marriage: the Muntehe and the Friedelehe. Whereas the Muntehe was a formal, permanent union between partners and involved the transfer of property from one family to another, the Friedelehe was also recognised as an official marriage but was often temporary and did not include the transfer of property. Any children conceived in the Friedelehe, however, were recognised as heirs if there were no heirs from a Muntehe. Whereas King Charlemagne (742–814 CE) allowed his daughters to enter Friedelehe unions, he never permitted the more binding Muntehe, because this would have meant not only transferring property, which was part of their dowry, but also the control he wielded over his daughters to another man.

In Anglo-Saxon England, women were often purchased, although it is unclear whether payment, paid to the bride rather than her family, was for the woman or the husband's guardianship over her and her property. In Customs of Sex and Marriage, George Scott explains: 'In England under the Anglo-Saxon laws, a stipulated sum of money was paid to the father of every young woman by the man who elected to marry her'.[6] The price was fixed according to her rank and station in life.

The dowry system on the other hand was, and still is in some countries, a form of purchasing a husband. As all goods belonging to the bride originally became the property of the husband, a father's wedding gift to his daughter, was actually a gift to her husband. This custom long predates the spread of Christianity, as brides in ancient Greece already brought dowries to their husbands. Similarly, in ancient Ireland, Wales, and Scandinavian countries, wives brought dowries of household goods and land into a marriage.

Early medieval society considered concubinage, as well as marriage, socially acceptable and legally valid, but generally, a formal agreement existed for entering into such a union. Whereas marriage fulfilled the desire to maintain or improve one's social standing, concubinage provided companionship and sexual satisfaction. The Old Testament contains many references to concubines. Solomon, for instance, was said to have had three hundred, and King David, ten concubines.[7] Amongst the ancient Hebrews, living for more than three years continuously in a man's house changed the status of a concubine to that of a wife. Until the Middle Ages, the position of a concubine was one verging on respectability. However, this drastically changed with the onset of the Reformation, when she became looked upon as a woman of debased morals, not to be tolerated in respectable society.

Up to and during the Middle Ages, the only condition needed to create a marriage was for both parties and the bride's family to state their consent. The presence of the clergy was not considered necessary, nor were witnesses required. For the middle and wealthy classes, marriages could be divided into three parts: The first part consisted of the families of the bride and groom getting together and drawing up a contract. The bride was not required to be present during this part of the proceedings. The second part was the betrothal, which was legally binding, whether the marriage was consummated or not. At this ceremony, it was customary for the couple to exchange gifts (usually a ring), share food and drink, clasp hands, and exchange a kiss. The vows could simply consist of the question: 'Will you marry me?' with the expected answer given in the affirmative. The third part was the removal of the bride to the groom's home, which could take place several years after the betrothal, depending on the circumstances. The role of the clergy in this case was merely to bless the couple.

Besides rites, which were later incorporated into the wedding ceremony, certain symbolic actions seem to have been limited solely to betrothal agreements. Records from fifteenth and sixteenth century France report people drinking wine or eating a piece of fruit together in the name of marriage to seal a betrothal. Indeed, the ritual exchange of almost any object could be used to form a betrothal agreement. In England and on the Continent, it was once customary among the common people to break a piece of gold or silver as a token of a verbal contract of marriage and the promise of love. The woman kept one part of the broken piece, while the man kept the other.

Another token amongst betrothed lovers was the joint-ring. The joint-ring, made with two or more hoops, was common between lovers. The hoops turned on a hinge, and on betrothal, the groom's fingers were placed in two of the hoops while the third hoop was on the bride's finger, to indicate to everyone that the bond of union was a mutual one. On these special occasions, a 'dry bargain', where the parties did not drink a toast to one another, was not considered binding.

Weddings started to become official church policy after the Fourth Lateran Council of 1215 declared it obligatory for a marriage to be blessed and witnessed by a priest and for the banns to be published. Banns announced a couple's intention to marry in the parishes in which they resided. Despite this decree, however, the Church continued to recognise marriages entered into without a priest in attendance. Throughout the twelfth century, clergy at weddings was still uncommon but became slowly more traditional in the thirteenth and fourteenth centuries.

In 1563, during the meetings of the Roman Catholic Church at the Council of Trent, the Church's stance on marriage was reviewed. Forthwith, besides the consent of all parties concerned, a priest was required to at least say a formula such as, 'I join you in matrimony', to ratify the union.[8] However, this decree did not apply to England where the Council of Trent lacked power. Marriages in England were regulated by Common Law, and the position was that any two persons were at liberty to have their union solemnised by a priest or enter an equally binding contract without the aid of the Church. In Scotland, it was possible to marry by the exchange of consent in the presence of witnesses until 1940.[9]

Throughout Europe, the Church continued to recognise clandestine marriages, in other words, those conducted without a priest, until the late eighteenth century.[10] With decrees on marriage in place after the Council of Trent, weddings performed with a priest moved from the house of the bride to the church. But curiously, vows were exchanged in the open, in front of the church doors or in the church porch, but not in the body of the church. Chaucer (1343–1400), who lived under the reign of Edward III, alludes to this custom in his work Wife of Bath, wherein he states: 'She was a worthy woman all her live, husbands at the church door had she five'.[11]

In all probability, church-porch marriages occurred to give the nuptial ceremony the greatest possible publicity. The fact that the exact amount of the bride's dowry was customarily loudly disclosed in front of all assembled guests and onlookers greatly supports this contention, and of course, such fiscal announcements had no place inside a House of God. Once the marriage was official, the dowry became the immediate property of the husband.

Another reason given for church-porch marriages was the opinion of the priesthood that holding a marriage within a church was a sacrilegious procedure. It would have been indecent to give permission within the confines of a Christian church for a man and a woman to 'sleep' together. However, this interpretation does not merit serious consideration.

Hence, in view of the tradition of church-porch marriages, a wet day for the wedding was a very serious matter, especially because people of those days did not have our modern conveniences, such as umbrellas and awnings, to protect them from pelting rain. This is probably why rain on the wedding day was perceived as unlucky. Because raindrops were thought to symbolise tears, a wet wedding was believed to foreshadow much sorrow, as the following rhymes indicate: 'If it rains on the wedding, the bride will cry all her married life', or: 'You will shed a tear for each raindrop that falls on your wedding day', or: 'Happy the bride the sun shines on, woe to the bride the rain falls on'.

Whereas weddings in European countries were generally conducted outside the church doors, England is possibly the first country in Europe where the ceremony started to occur inside the church. An early Tudor etiquette book mentions that nobles and gentry could be married inside the church, with those of higher social station allowed closer to the altar.

Because wedding ceremonies were now performed at the church instead of at the home of the bride, this meant that the entire wedding party was obliged to travel, making the wedding procession a part of European marriage custom. Interestingly, the trend is re-emerging, especially among the more affluent, to hold the ceremony at the house of the bride, with the priest conducting the marriage ceremony away from the church.

'To Tie the Knot'

The knot, representing tightly closed links, is symbolic of a sealed bargain, the underlying implication being that anything that has the power to bind the body may similarly be used to bind the spirit. Universally, the knot has always been regarded as an emblem of love and friendship, symbolising the ties of duty and fidelity between lovers.

We speak of 'tying the marriage knot', a phrase which may have originated in the days when threads from a couple's clothes, their hands or their thumbs were actually loosely tied together. The custom of literally tying the knot is found in many countries around the world and still observed in some cultures. Traditional Hindu marriage ceremonies observe the ceremonial tying of the tali, the emblem of marriage and a thread that the groom ties around the bride's neck. In Sri Lanka, it was once customary to tie the couple's thumbs together as part of the marriage ceremony.[12] Similarly, Parsee marriage custom dictated that the groom's hands be loosely tied with a sevenfold cord, seven being a lucky number and symbolising sanctity. The Moriori natives of the South Pacific Islands traditionally tied a grass rope around the shoulders of the couple to be married, knotting the rope several times as a symbol of matrimony. In Fiji, the public tying and knotting of a short skirt, considered the symbol of womanhood, once formed part of the traditional marriage ceremony. In all the examples, publicly tying and knotting was considered legally binding as any official document.

Ancient Greek marriage custom required the bride to wear a girdle of sheep's wool fastened around the waist in a large knot, popularly known as the nodus Herculanus, which her husband was to loosen – not to tie. Roman marriage custom equally required the bridegroom to untie an intricately formed knot in the bride's girdle during the marriage ceremony. These two examples form an interesting parallel to the popular English phrase of 'loosening the virgin zone', or girdle, to indicate matrimony.

Among the northern nations of Europe, the knot pointed especially to an indissoluble tie of affection and duty. Thus, many of the ancient runic inscriptions are in the form of knots. Various Germanic peoples pledged their betrothal by joining hands or having them tied together in a symbolic gesture. The groom's right hand was joined to the bride's right hand, and the same procedure was repeated with the left hands so that if viewed from above this looked like an infinity symbol.

Another knot specifically linked with matrimony was traditional amongst the English and Scots. Known as the true-love knot, it was a popular present given mutually between lovers. The so-called bride favours, or top-knots – knots or rosettes of ribbons that were freely distributed in England at weddings of all social classes – derive from the true-love knot. In England, these knotted ribbons of various colours were worn on a gentleman's hat, and in France, they were worn on the arm. In modern times, the custom has gone out of fashion, replaced by the wearing of white carnations in buttonholes. (See Chapter II, 'All tied up in a Knot').

Bride and Bridal

The word 'bridal' literally means 'bride's ale' and originates from the Anglo-Saxon word bredale. Before the eleventh century, the word ale signified a feast or festival for the common people. So bride-ale at that time meant 'bridal feast'.

It was only much later during the fifteenth century that the word ale became synonymous with beer. The word bride-ale was then linked with the ale or beer that was especially made for the occasion and which the bride's family was permitted to sell to all guests. The bride used whatever contributions she received for the ale from friends and acquaintances gathered for the occasion to defray expenses for the wedding reception and for setting up her future household.

Sometimes, the bride-ale was also called a 'bidding', from the circumstance of the bride and groom bidding or inviting guests. Biddings were popular in Wales where guests were invited by a hired bidder or by a public notice. All strangers were welcome to attend, provided they made a contribution to the happy couple, either in the form of money or household goods. Similar to the bidding was the 'penny wedding', the only difference being that the guest list then included any ragtag stranger willing to come as long as a donation was made to the happy couple.

Right of the Lord

Under a law known as le droit du seigneur, 'the right of the lord', medieval noblemen had the right to spend the wedding night, or 'first night', with every bride in their fiefdom.

The custom of someone other than the husband being the first to engage in sexual intercourse with a bride after her wedding, hence relieving her of her virginity, goes back thousands of years. It stems from the ancient idea that God's human incarnations here on earth were the sources of all life. Initially, priests, later supplanted by divinely ordained kings, believed to have descended from heaven as the primary intermediary between humans and God, took on the role of defloration, thereby presuming to ensure a couple's fertility. The reproductive power of kings became symbolic of the overall strength and viability of their kingdoms and was seen to guarantee fertility of the land and, consequently, to ensure abundant harvests.

The first night custom is first recorded in the Babylonian Epic of Gilgamesh, considered to be the oldest story ever told, from earlier Sumerian legends of Gilgamesh (circa 2100 BCE). Gilgamesh, the arrogant and powerful ruler of Uruk, regularly exercised the privilege to be the first to sleep with a new bride. He was challenged on this account by the subhuman brute Enkidu, indicating that the custom of first night was an unpopular one even then.

The custom was similarly practised by various Roman chieftains, although by then, all pretence that it was to ensure a bountiful harvest or fertile brides had been stripped away. Roman chieftains took the custom to a new level by charging husbands for their performance of this duty, the imposed fee aimed at creating the illusion that a service was being rendered, rather than carnal desire being satisfied.

The first night custom survived in parts of Europe into the Middle Ages, solely from a position of power of noblemen over their vassals, as feudal noblemen were not of royal blood, having had their titles bestowed on them and, hence, having no claim to divinity. Of course, they also had every right to waive their performance of le droit de seigneur, especially, when on appraisal, they found the bride to be physically unattractive. However, there seems to be scant historical evidence of the actual occurrence and enforcement of le droit de seigneur in medieval Europe, indicating that it was a concept used to extort money from vassals, rather than a regular practice. In other words, the custom mostly took on the form of payments of redemption dues by vassals to avoid enforcement.

In America, during slavery, this form of rape was euphemistically known as the 'master's obligation'. Slavery was abolished in America in 1865, but until then, slaves were owned as property, and slaveholders legally could force themselves on female slaves with impunity at any time, not only on the wedding night.

Lucky June Weddings

One of the oldest beliefs concerning the date of a wedding is that all marriages in May are unlucky. Several popular sayings refer to this superstition: 'Marry in May, you'll rue the day', or: 'From the marriages in May all the bairns die and decay'.

This curious belief seems to have been passed down from the Greeks and Romans. Plutarch, the famous Greek philosopher and essayist, explains that May is linked with ill luck because it falls between two auspicious months: April, dedicated to the goddess Venus, and June, dedicated to the goddess Juno. May is also referred to by the Roman poet Ovid in his work, Fasti, where he speaks about the ill luck associated with weddings during this month. As Romans celebrated the festival of Bona Dea, the goddess of chastity, as well as the Feast of the Dead called Lemuralia during May, it is obvious why weddings were unpopular during this time.

However, there is an added reason for the month's ill-repute. May is named after Maia, an incarnation of the Earth Mother and wife of the Roman god Vulcan, a most ancient god of war, to whom human sacrifices were made. Besides being the goddess of fertility, Maia was also the patroness of the aged, hence not a suitable deity to have watching over young lovers.

A further reason May is considered the unluckiest month of the year for weddings is probably because of practicality. In olden times, the fulfilment of the promise of spring during May was welcomed with an abandonment of joy, which is perhaps difficult for us to understand in an age of comfort and excess. After the long, cold European winters, the countryside was starting to blossom in May, and there was much work to be done as this was the month best suited for sowing and planting crops. Every pair of hands was needed, and no time was set aside for frivolities, hence the saying: 'Who marries between the sickle and the scythe will never thrive'.

A fortunate month for weddings has always been June. This month was named after the Roman goddess Juno, married to the supreme god Jupiter. Juno was considered the patroness of the young and the protector of women and matrimony. It was believed that she bestowed special blessings on those who wed in her month, bringing prosperity to the man and happiness to the woman. This tradition was passed on from the Romans to other European countries, and even now, June weddings are very popular, although the original reasons behind the custom have long been lost in obscurity.

Besides May weddings being unpopular in the past, there were specific times of the year that the Church considered unacceptable for weddings. For instance, all penitential days were thought unsuitable for the joyous ceremony of marriage, hence the saying: 'Marry in Lent, you'll live to repent'. Similarly, Advent was regarded as an unlucky period in which to wed. In Scotland, December 31 was considered the most popular day for weddings. The whole world celebrates on this day, and for the rest of the couples' married life, their anniversary is celebrated by all.

Not only the month, but also the day of the week was considered of great importance for a wedding. Friday has always been regarded as unlucky in Christian countries, while Sunday was seen as a most propitious day for a wedding. The following old English rhyme advises:

> Monday for health,
> Tuesday for wealth,
> Wednesday the best day of all,
> Thursday for losses,
> Friday for crosses,
> And Saturday no luck at all.

However, despite what the rhyme intones, weddings are usually held on Saturdays in modern times, this day of the week being the most convenient and suitable for all concerned.

In the past, even the time of day for the wedding was of paramount importance. A wedding after sunset was thought to result in a joyless marriage, the loss of children, and an early grave. Postponing a wedding was also considered unlucky and seen as an almost certain sign that bride or groom would die within a short time – once the date was set, it had to be adhered to.

Another important aspect in the choice of the wedding date was for the moon to be on the increase, as falling fortunes and failure were thought to come with the waning moon. Along the coastal areas of England, the tides were also considered favorable for the marriage ceremony. From the Orkney Islands, comes the following saying: 'No couple chooses marriage except with a growing moon and a flowing tide'.

Something Old, Something New

Superstitious belief underlies many of the traditions observed with a bride's apparel. Well-known is the old English verse dealing with the bride's ensemble:

> Something old, something new,
> Something borrowed, something blue,
> And a sixpence in the shoe.

This saying dates to Victorian times, and many brides have in the past thus arranged their wedding attire. In modern times, this tradition is largely forgotten, although partially observed by some, with brides perhaps including something borrowed or a blue garter. According to superstitious belief, everything the bride wears has to be very carefully chosen to have the most beneficial possible influence on her future. To symbolise her new status in life, every item the bride wears should be new, except for something old, something borrowed, and something blue.

The 'old' represents the bride's link with the past, her family, and friends. It also refers to something previously worn or belonging to a happily married woman, thereby transferring happiness to the new bride. Formerly, the belief prevailed that any item brought into close contact with the body was charged with a significant and lasting power. Therefore, to ensure her lasting happiness, the bride held fast to something old, an item that a happy bride had already worn. It was believed that something worn during a deeply emotional, blissfully happy experience absorbed its radiation and could transmit this to the new bride. In days gone by it was customary for the handkerchief or the shoes to be old, hence the saying, 'Lucky the bride who marries in old shoes'.

The 'something new' in the rhyme represents good fortune for the new life the bride is starting – a new beginning. The 'new' refers to the wedding gown or any other apparel the bride wears on her special day. As is so often the case with superstitious beliefs, something new was also paradoxically considered a harbinger of good luck – as was something old – as humans have always believed in the potency of novelty. It was therefore considered lucky to carry a new penny, as the newness made it the source of good fortune. So the bride's new outfit, not having been seen by anyone but her attendants, is in keeping with the festive occasion, symbolic of her new status as a wife, and a powerful portent of happiness.

'Something borrowed' from someone happily married for many years, of course, will magically transfer that happiness to the wearer. Often, the veil worn by the bride's mother on her wedding day would be among the most coveted items to be borrowed. However, to borrow an object of gold guaranteed wealth and prosperity for the future. Additional good luck was believed to come to the bride wearing her mother's wedding dress. Anything borrowed was generally considered lucky, whereas to lend meant loss. An old German rhyme intones: 'He who lends money at play [card play] will lose; he that borrows for play will win'. Something borrowed was also to remind the bride that in times of hardship and strife, family and friends were there to help when needed.

The 'something blue' symbolises true love, loyalty, and faithfulness. Blue, usually the shade of sky blue, might be present in the bouquet or the garter. Throughout the ages, blue has been regarded as a symbol of truth. Through a chain of associations – God lives in heaven, heaven is in the sky, the sky is blue – blue was considered a divine colour, symbolic of purity and protective against evil forces. As is applicable on all major occasions during a lifetime, i.e. birth, christening, marriage, and death, the bride was thought to be especially exposed and, therefore, very vulnerable, to evil influences on her wedding day. Blue was hence included in her ensemble as a shield to ward off any misfortune. In the Middle East, North Africa, and certain European countries, blue is still used in averting the evil eye, this colour being considered the most powerful protector from evil.

The silver sixpence in England or the new dime in America, worn in the heel of the left shoe ensured wealth and prosperity for the couple, as these coins were considered harbingers of good fortune.

A White Wedding Dress?

White, as a symbol of purity and innocence, goes back to ancient Greece and Rome, where priestesses and vestal virgins wore this colour. However, the colour also expresses joy and happiness, which is why church vestments at Easter, celebrating the Resurrection, are white. Hence, the white wedding gown advertises the bride's happiness and joy, not necessarily her purity.

However, for the bride to wear white at her wedding is a recent tradition. According to most sources, it was not until the late nineteenth century that brides began wearing white wedding gowns in Europe. This tradition became very fashionable in Victorian times (circa 1840s– 1900). Amongst upper-class Victorian ladies, the white dress showed off wealth socially. After all, as a white dress is very impractical, it was its own advertisement that it would only be worn once, on that very special occasion. These were, of course, times when most people only owned two outfits: working clothes and Sunday best. Hence, the wealthy alone could afford a creation that would only be worn on one special day. Slowly, however, despite its ostentatious beginnings, the white wedding dress gained in popularity and is today a firmly established tradition.

Before the white wedding gown, new brides were free to select any colour except red and black, traditionally linked with witchcraft and the devil. However, a widow marrying for the second time could choose to wear black at her wedding, provided she also wore a rose in her hair. Prospective brides did not rush out to buy something new for the occasion, but simply decked themselves out in their best finery. The following English rhyme advises which colours were considered suitable for the wedding gown:

> Married in blue, love ever true,
> Married in white, you've chosen right,
> Married in red, you'll wish yourself dead,
> Married in black, you'll wish yourself back
> Married in brown, you'll live out of town,
> Married in yellow, jealous of your fellow,
> Married in pink, of you only he'll think,
> Married in green, sorrow is soon seen.

In many parts of England, green was regarded as an unlucky colour, especially for a bride to wear. Green was seen as the colour of mean-spirited fairies, pixies, and malicious wood spirits and, therefore, was to be avoided at all cost. It was believed that these spiteful little beings resented anyone else wearing their colour and, therefore, take revenge. Already in ancient times, it was believed in many northern European countries that a bride wearing green was liable to be carried off by the 'little people' to their underground abodes.

Apart from the colour chosen, various traditions are also linked with the making of the wedding dress and the choice of material. Superstition dictates that the bride making her own wedding dress is most unlucky, as this presages a life of tribulations and nothing but hard work ahead. Similarly, a bride was not to try on the completed bridal ensemble before the wedding day. Should this, however, prove unavoidable, she was, on no account, to look at herself in a full-length mirror. This superstition stems from the belief that a part of oneself is caught up in the reflected image. Therefore, she would not be presenting her whole self to her new husband. Alternatively, to avoid the ill luck associated with looking at herself in a full-length mirror completely dressed for the ceremony, the bride could do so by not wearing one of her gloves.

It was considered important that the wedding dress, on no account should be finished until just before the ceremony or she would incur bad luck in the future. Hence, a short length of hem could be left unfinished until the very last moment; a last stitch added to the bride's dress just before she left for church was thought to bring her luck in the future. It was also universally acknowledged that the groom, under no circumstances, should see the wedding dress before his bride joined him at the altar. It was equally unlucky for bride and groom to see each other on the morning before meeting at church. The seriously superstitious even warned that the groom should resist the temptation of seeing his bride-to-be come down the aisle.

Silk was the preferred material for bridal gowns in the past, whereas satin was considered unlucky. A velvet gown was considered too ostentatious for ordinary folk and, therefore, thought to lead the couple to poverty later in life. Some brides sewed a hair or a silver coin into their dress for good luck. Pearls, considered symbolic of tears, were not to be featured on any part of the dress and not worn at all by the bride. It was thought that for each pearl the bride wore, her husband would cause her weeping. Finally, a bride should always have her hair dressed and her veil adjusted by a happily married woman, as this happiness would transmit to the future wife.

In modern times, most of these traditions have been forgotten or are purposefully ignored. Grooms select the dress with their young brides; the dress can be of any fabric and any style; and red, and even black, have become favoured colours at weddings for the mother of the bride, the guests, and even for bridesmaids to wear. Similarly, in bridal bouquets, most flowers are considered acceptable and depend on individual preferences and coordination with the bride's ensemble – all symbolic meaning once attached to the various flowers a young bride held, lost and forgotten.

The Virtuous Bouquet

The bridal bouquet once symbolised sexuality and fertility and was traditionally bound with luck-bringing ribbons. Originally, these adornments were partly made of herbs, all believed endowed with magical properties and, hence, thought to have an impact on the couple's future life together. Long ago, the bride carried strong and potent herbs such as garlic, chives, bay leaves, rosemary, and others, all selected for their special protective powers, to ward off evil. To symbolise fruitfulness, a bride often carried stalks of wheat and corn or wore a wreath of these entwined with leaves in her hair. Herbs were not only believed to have protective powers, but also symbolised certain virtues. Sage was the herb of wisdom, and ivy stood for fidelity. Dill and marigold, both symbolising sexual energy, were included in the bouquet and served at the wedding feast – marigold being an edible flower. Together in a bouquet, all the various herbs assured the bride of their symbolic virtues in her married life. Later, flowers replaced herbs and took on their own meaning.

The flower world is linked with all the finer sympathies and feelings of human nature. Flowers are the delight of our childhood, bouquets are the offerings of love and courtship, and wreaths are the last gift of sorrow and love to the deceased. Flowers have always held a prominent place in wedding ceremonies. It would be almost impossible to name all the flowers used in the many various marriage customs of different countries. Considered a symbol of happiness, nuptial garlands and crowns of flowers go back to remote antiquity and once decorated both bride and groom.

According to a very early Grecian custom, Athenian brides used hawthorn blossoms to decorate their attendants; the bridal wreath was made of hawthorn and the altar decked with its blossoms. Dedicated to Hymen, the Greek god of marriage, his altar was lighted with torches made from the wood of the hawthorn, a small tree belonging to the rose family. Hawthorn was probably used during marriage ceremonies because of its protective qualities, as thorn trees have, throughout history, been regarded as powerful protectors against evil forces.

In ancient Rome, newly married couples were often crowned with marjoram. The hazel, above many other trees and plants, also held a prominent position in the marriage ceremony, with hazel torches burned on the wedding evening to ensure prosperity for the newly married couple. Oaken boughs were carried at Roman weddings as a token of fertility, and a bridal wreath of verbena had to be plucked by the bride herself. The verbena, called the sacra herba, 'sacred herb', by Pliny the Elder, was well-known throughout the ages for its protective qualities. In Germany, it was customary to give a verbena wreath to the bride, besides a wreath of myrtle, which she wore on her head because of the mystic virtues with which the myrtle plant was credited.

Orange blossoms, symbolising innocence, purity, and fertility were used in the East for centuries to decorate brides. Brought to Europe by the Crusaders during the Middle Ages, the custom of including orange blossoms in the bridal bouquet was soon adopted. However, because of their rarity, they were very expensive and, hence, worn only by the noble and wealthy. Because the orange tree bears flowers and fruit at the same time, it symbolises the innocence and purity of youth in its delicate blossoms, and the promise of fertility and offspring in its fruit. Hence, the saying that a bride wearing orange blossoms will have good luck – the luck, of course, referring to the blessing of many children.

White flowers have traditionally always been avoided because of their association with death. The lily especially is commonly regarded as the flower of death, used at funerals in wreaths and sprays. Similarly, the white rose is linked with death in northern European countries. Therefore, if white blossoms are used in bridal bouquets, they should never appear on their own, but always be mixed with other colours.

The widespread custom of throwing the bride's bouquet is relatively recent and originated in the U.S., replacing the – perhaps often painful – European tradition of throwing the bride's shoe.

Circle of Love and Power

The ring, a circle with neither beginning nor end, symbolises eternity, unity, and perfection. In modern times, a ritual most crucial for all couples committed to matrimony is the purchase of the engagement ring. Generally, the engagement ring is somewhat more ornate than the plain wedding ring and is traditionally worn only by the bride, depending on cultural background. In some countries, especially in the East, both the woman and the man wear an ornate engagement ring.

It is widely accepted that a ring first signifying engagement can be roughly linked to the Fourth Lateran Council held by the Church in 1215, when it was declared that a longer waiting period between betrothal and marriage was appropriate. Plain rings of gold, silver, and iron were at first used to indicate betrothal. But a betrothal was also considered official if the couple simply drank a toast together, linking their little fingers while drinking, if this was done in front of witnesses.

The origin of the ornate engagement ring set with precious stones, particularly diamonds, is obscure. But the choice of precious stones for an engagement ring was once considered of utmost importance, as every month was believed to be under the influence of a specific stone, and each stone came attached with its distinctive wisdom and lore. Historically, the first recorded diamond engagement ring was presented to Mary of Burgundy as a betrothal gift by Archduke Maximillian of Austria in 1477.

In the past, florid gems were an important status symbol for the aristocracy, and laws were in place to ensure that only the privileged class wore gemstones, thereby preserving a visible division of social rank. Once, a popular concept was to represent and celebrate the joining of two families by mounting the engagement ring with the birthstones of the bride and her parents on the left side of the ring and the birthstones of the groom and his parents on the right side.

During the sixteenth century, joint rings, made with two or more hoops, were common between lovers. Each ring was engraved with a portion of a specific design, so that the complete figure was only formed when all the rings were in position. The hoops of the so-called gimmal ring turned on a hinge, and on betrothal the groom's fingers were placed in two of the hoops while the third hoop was on the bride's finger, to indicate to everyone that the bond or union was a mutual one. During the marriage ceremony, the separate rings were then fastened together to form the wedding ring for the bride. This custom died out, however, and for several centuries now, it has been customary, especially in English-speaking countries, for the man to present an engagement ring to his fiancée on their betrothal.

The luckiest stones set in an engagement ring are emeralds, rubies, sapphires, and of course, diamonds. The diamond symbolises conjugal love and is therefore every girl's dream and 'every girl's friend'. However, pearls are seldom found in engagement rings, as they resemble tears and are said to bring tears to the marriage. Opals, regarded as ill-omened, should also be avoided unless they represent the wearer's birthstone. In some European countries, such as Germany, Denmark, Sweden, and the Netherlands, plain gold bands are still worn to signify engagement, whereas in other countries such as France, coloured gems instead of diamonds are preferred.

Exactly when the wedding ring became an established social custom is difficult to ascertain, and many theories abound about its origin, but rings have certainly been an outward sign of marriage since antiquity. As a symbol of marriage, the wedding ring might even be a memento of the days when a man customarily stole his bride. If the lady objected to being dragged away, she would be fettered at the wrists and ankles. This is not as far-fetched as it sounds. Amongst the Venda of Southern Africa, for instance, it is still customary for married women living in rural areas to wear many heavy metal rings on their legs. The rings stretch from the ankles to just below the knees and are traditionally regarded as a sign of beauty. They are never removed, greatly impede walking, and leave out any possibility of washing the skin underneath. Originally, their purpose was to prevent the woman from running away, but over time, they have become a symbol of matrimony within the tribe.

The Bible does not mention wedding rings, but ring ceremonies, symbolising the eternal bond between two people, existed during Talmudic times. Wedding bands were found in Egyptian tombs, were worn by Greek and Roman ladies, and seem to have been a part of nuptial customs among the earliest civilisations. The early church leader and prolific writer, Tertullian, tells us that it was customary for the groom to send a gold ring to his intended bride; hence, the custom seems to have been well-established in the second century CE. It was also customary among the Anglo-Saxon tribes of northern Europe to give rings as pledges before a wedding. The word 'wed', from which is derived 'wedding', is of Anglo-Saxon origin and means 'pledge'.

During Roman times, throughout the Middle Ages and into the Renaissance period, only the wealthy wore rings, as it was a sign of nobility and rank to possess such an ornament. It was not tolerated for single or unmarried persons to wear rings unless they were judges, doctors, or other honourable persons. The one single exception allowed the lower classes was the wedding band, an indication in itself of the esteem in which it was held. So it was with great pride and vanity that those intent upon marriage, and thus permitted to wear this honourable adornment, hastened to do so.

Before the advent of a church ceremony, it sufficed for the betrothed couple to exchange rings, sealing their contract in front of a gathering with a kiss. Usually, these rings took the form of a plain band, generally made of iron, as only the wealthy could afford gold. The ring, however, is unnecessary to constitute a legal marriage. For those who could not afford any ring, a ring could be borrowed for the ceremony, and often, the priest lent the couple a golden wedding band during the ceremony at a small fee, or else, the bride could slip her finger into the loop of the church key as a substitute. Alternatively, for those who could not afford wedding rings, it was enough to bend a coin with promises of love. Such bent coins, with oaths sworn and prayers breathed over them, could be used as a bond of union. These crooked pieces of metal were believed to be endowed with mystic properties and curative virtues and were, therefore, carefully kept by the couple.

In England during the thirteenth century, rings made of rushes were sometimes used among the poorer classes. Shakespeare mentions rings of rushes in The Two Noble Kinsmen, and Edmund Spenser refers to them in Faerie Queene. In William D'Avenant's work, The Rivals, the following lines appear: 'I'll crown thee with a garland of straw, and I'll marry thee with a rush ring'.[13] Rush rings, however, were predominantly used for fake or pretend marriages, and ecclesiastical authorities warned that no young girl should let a man put a ring of rushes on her hand, as this was only done expressly to seduce her.

Many superstitious speculations, of course, are centred on the ring as a pledge of matrimony. The ring should never be dropped during the wedding ceremony, because whoever dropped it would be first to die; to take the ring off at any time could jeopardise the marriage; to lose it meant losing the husband's affection; to break the ring or to part with it at any time was considered ominous; and to remove the ring permanently meant seriously tempting fate. A variation on this superstition, however, allowed the removal of the wedding ring once the couple had been blessed with their first child. If, however, the wedding ring had worn so thin as to break, either the wife or the husband would soon die. Wedding rings were also often used for divination. By suspending the wedding ring on a string over a pregnant woman's belly, it was believed that the unborn child's sex could be determined by interpreting the ring's swing.

The swearing of oaths on rings is a practice dating from ancient times and is reflected in the exchange of rings during the marriage ceremony. In the past, rings were regarded as symbols of power. Amongst Romans, it was customary to wear an iron ring on the left hand as a symbol of bravery. The Roman historian, Pliny the Elder, relates how a law concerning the right to wear rings was passed by the Senate in 22 CE: 'A rule was [...] imposed, that no one should have the right to wear a ring, unless he himself as well as his father and grandfather, were free born, had capital assets amounting to 400,000 sesterces, and under the Julian law relating to the theatre, possessed a seat in the first fourteen rows'.[14]

As emblems of power, rings were traditionally used as seals by which orders were signed and objects of value secured, as the following passages from the Old Testament attest: 'And he said: What pledge shall I give thee? And she said: Thy signet and thy bracelets....'.[15] From ancient times, throughout the Middle Ages, and beyond, the delivery of a seal ring represented the assurance that the person to whom it was given could be admitted the highest friendship and trust. A woman, having her husband's seal ring in her possession, could issue commands on his behalf and was considered his representative in every respect.

Depending on their design and composition, rings were once widely credited with supernatural powers, including healing properties. It was also thought that through their shine and gloss, rings conveyed their owner's well-being. Strengthened through mystical inscriptions and magical stones, rings were believed to have the power to make humans invisible, fireproof, and invulnerable. Popular legend partly ascribed the military prowess of Joan of Arc and the meteoric careers of Thomas Cromwell and Cardinal Wolsey to the powers of magic rings in their possession. Biblical leaders such as Moses and Solomon were believed to be skilled in the art of fashioning magic rings. Solomon is reputed to have used a magic ring in making the stones for building the Temple in Jerusalem, as the use of iron tools was forbidden.

Rings were also thought to possess medicinal properties and were used to cure rheumatism, paralysis, and other cramping disorders. In European countries, so-called cramp-rings were often made from the metal attachments, such as the handles, hinges, nails, or screws, obtained from coffins. Alternatively, rheumatism sufferers could quietly stand at a church entrance and wait to receive many pennies from parish bachelors. After receiving the pennies, three circuits of the communion table had to be completed. If the priest was obliging, he then exchanged the pennies for a silver coin, which, when made into a ring, was believed to be a definite cure for the ailment – woe to those unable to find a bachelor!

Inscriptions on rings, ranging from magic formulas to the names of loved ones, were once considered effective in warding off evil, hence, worn solely for protection. So-called charm rings, engraved with words of power and made from suitable protective material such as silver, could be used to ward off the evil eye. Belief in the protective power of rings even extended to warding off the dreaded plague by using rings on which the names of the Holy Family and the three Magi were inscribed.

Which Finger?

The circle represents eternity and symbolically unites the couple. Generally unknown is that marriage rings were formerly only worn by the bride, not the groom. This custom continued until the beginning of the nineteenth century. But on which finger and which hand the bride wore the symbol of matrimony varied with the period and the country.

Thirteenth-century illuminations show wedding rings on either the index or third finger. There was a period during the late sixteenth and early seventeenth centuries when some women even wore their wedding rings on their thumbs. Engagement and wedding rings were worn on the right hand in Catholic Europe. It was only during the Reformation in the sixteenth century that the custom of wearing the wedding ring on the left hand was introduced.

Today, the wedding ring is worn on the right or left hand, depending on the couple's nationality. It is worn on the right hand in Germany, France, and other European countries to indicate marriage. In all English-speaking cultures, though, it has become customary for the wedding ring to be worn on the left hand.

There are several reasons for the wedding ring to be worn on the hand's fourth finger. The fourth finger, called annularis or 'ring finger' by the Romans and 'gold finger' by the Anglo-Saxons, was also known as the 'heart finger'. This finger was believed to connect directly to the heart, which in ancient times was considered not only the seat of the soul, but also the organ from which all feeling emanated. Therefore, this finger was the most suited to carry a symbol of love. On the authority of the Greek historian, Appian (95–165 CE), it was believed that a small vein, the 'vein of love', known as vena amoris by the Romans, runs from this finger directly to the heart – a belief popular throughout Europe for centuries.[16]

Another reason for choosing the fourth finger as the ring finger might have originated from the Christian Church. According to Church doctrine, the thumb, index, and middle fingers stood respectively for the Father, the Son, and the Holy Ghost, whereas the fourth finger, which is commonly called the ring finger, stood for earthly love between a man and a woman. However, there is also an explanation based on practicality put forward by the Romans. The fourth finger is not easily extended without moving all the others; in other words, it is the finger best protected, and hence, the ring's safety is ensured.

The Grim Reaper

Death is universally regarded as a rite of passage because it is the supreme initiation – the beginning of a new spiritual existence.

Superstitious fear has always dictated that everything possible be done to ensure the safe passage of the deceased's soul into the afterlife, particularly because the dead were considered far more powerful in that state than they ever were during their lifetimes. Consequently, complex and universally extensive customs have evolved in all cultures around the dying and dead to gratify and appease their spirits. Ancestor veneration, therefore, has become an important cultural characteristic in many varied communities worldwide.

In some African and Asian cultures, a family member's death is not seen as destroying the important solidarity of a family. The 'living dead' are still looked on as elders of the family and are seen as maintaining an interest in their daily affairs, therefore respected and consulted in all matters. Ancestors are thought to wield power beyond the grave for about three to five generations, and then be replaced by more recently dead family members within the living's memory span. Neglect of family's ancestors is thus perceived as bringing illness and misfortune to the living. Conversely, unworthy people in the community or those who do not have children are not accorded the benefits of ancestor veneration, this being one reason, why childlessness is considered a great tragedy in these cultures. In turn, the dead soul is given strength in the afterlife through offerings and prayers from the living.

In many societies, only prescribed ritual burial, which formally conducts the dead person's soul to the other world, confirms death, and he who is not buried according to the people's custom is not regarded as dead. Most Australian Aborigines believed that the deceased's spirit lingered around the living, especially those close to the person in life. Relatives, therefore, flagellated themselves and cut their flesh to clearly indicate their grief to the dead. It was firmly believed that unless the dead were properly put to rest, they continued to bother the living, going so far as to steal them. Similarly, on the European continent, it was believed that those dying without the relevant and appropriate rites were not properly dead. Hence, they were greatly feared by the living because they were thought likely to return as vengeful ghosts.

The time before death and the moments of dying were once surrounded with numerous superstitious beliefs and, therefore, over time in different cultures, various ritual tasks to be carried out evolved.

A widely held superstition in Europe was that the dying person's soul could not easily pass out of the body if he or she was lying across the direction of the floorboards. If the person was lingering, the bed was moved around until it lined up with the boards' direction. Another belief related to dying was that a pillow stuffed with pigeon or dove feathers caused untold agonies to the dying person, which is why pillows were often taken from someone struggling with death. It was also considered important that nobody should stand at the foot of the bed when a person was dying, as it greatly hindered the spirit in its departure.

Similarly, a notion prevailing for centuries in most coastal towns throughout England and Europe was that deaths occurred during the ebbing of the tide. Charles Dickens referred to this tradition in his novel, David Copperfield, when Mr. Peggotty remarks about the dying Barkis: 'He's a going out with the tide', and then explains: 'People can't die along the coast, except when the tide's pretty nigh out. They can't be born, unless it's pretty nigh in – not properly born, till flood'.[17] Hence, we have the common phrase: 'To go out with the tide', a euphemism for death. Interestingly, we come across exactly the same belief on the other side of the world in Australia. In Healers of Arnhem Land, John Cawte recounts the various prophetic dreams experienced and told to him by a Yolngu woman in Arnhem Land. She explained to him that whenever she dreamt of the tide going out, it signified someone's death according to her people's tradition.[18]

In many European countries, it was traditional until well into the nineteenth century for a close relative to be given the honour of inhaling the last breath of the dying person, as this was believed to imbue the living person with great spiritual strength. The same custom was already observed two thousand years earlier in ancient Rome, where the closest relative was permitted to inhale the last breath of a dying person and thus benefit from its perceived spiritually nourishing qualities.

In Europe and Asia, the belief was widely disseminated that a dead person's soul departed through the chimney, the smoke hole, or the roof. Therefore, German superstition advised taking three tiles off the roof if someone in that house was labouring with death. Similar beliefs prevailed in the East. The Chinese made a hole in the home's roof wherein someone lay dying to give the soul an easy exit. In prolonged death agony, one or more boards or tiles were removed or the roof even broken.

A widely prevalent belief propagated that locked doors, knots, or bolts hindered the soul from leaving the body when the person was at the point of death. Hence, it was customary to throw doors and windows wide open and to undo all knots and bolts, thereby making the struggle between life and death easier. A German belief intones: 'When a person dies, set the windows open, and the soul can get out'. In his Encyclopaedia of Superstitions, Edwin Radford writes that this superstition was still prevalent in the rural areas of northern Europe in the 1950s.[19] Knots were especially believed to interfere with the process of dying, and it was firmly believed that someone could not die while any knots were around or on the person.

The curious notion that a person's favourite clock stops at the time of their death is widely known and still believed by many in rural Europe and America. The explanation for this belief is most likely because clocks in the past were so temperamental that only their owners knew precisely how to operate them. Hence, if the owner was confined to bed for a lengthy period, the clock most likely wound down and, after a while, expired altogether, perhaps even coinciding with the time when the unfortunate owner took his last breath. In some households, clocks were deliberately stopped and shrouded when someone died to signify that time had stopped with the death. This was also often done to indicate to the 'angel of death' that his work there had been completed and that he should leave. After the funeral, all clocks in the household were started up again.

Another widespread tradition concerns prophetic powers attributed to the dying during the period immediately preceding their deaths. This idea probably originated from the belief that when the soul was detaching itself from the body, it had already partly entered the spirit world. It was therefore, so to speak, in the confines of two worlds and consequently perceived to possess great supernatural powers. This tradition is well documented in literature. Shakespeare refers to it in Richard II: 'Methinks I am a prophet new inspired, and thus expiring do foretell of him'.[20] A similar reference is made in Richard III when

Hastings exclaims minutes before being led to his execution: 'I prophesy the fearfull'st time to thee that ever wretched age hath look'd upon. Come, lead me to the block; [...]. They smile at me who shortly shall be dead'.[21] This belief is also reflected in the Old Testament when Jacob gathers his sons and says: 'Gather yourselves together that I may tell you, that which shall befall you in the last days. [...] And when Jacob had made an end of commanding his sons, he gathered up his feet into the bed and yielded up the ghost [...]'.[22]

It was regarded as a good sign if the eyes of the dying person shut on their own at the moment of death. If this had not naturally taken place, attending relatives immediately hastened to close them because a corpse whose eyes remained open was said to be 'waiting for the next' – in other words, searching for the next person to die. In modern times, this custom is observed, although the reasons for doing so have become unclear.

Another important observation to be considered was for the corpse to always be placed with feet facing the door. This, of course, gave rise to the saying, 'They carried him out feet first'. As only corpses were said to lie with their feet facing the door, orienting a bed normally in that direction in the bedroom was viewed with great apprehension and dire superstition.

Mourning the Dead

Specific traditions and customs govern the post mortem period, as with all other death rites. From the moment of death, ceremonial weeping was customary in different cultures. Expressions of grief once widespread, especially in Middle Eastern countries, included fasting, the wearing of sackcloth, the tearing of one's clothes, the pulling and tearing out of one's hair, and of course, extensive wailing and weeping. In Biblical times, these practices were carried out so vigorously that a clear ban against excessive rites of mourning, such as cutting one's hair or mutilating one's flesh, was laid down in various Old Testament books.[23]

In European countries, mourning was, and in many cases still is, signified by the wake, the wearing of black clothes, and various other traditions, such as the custom of covering mirrors or turning them to the wall in houses where a death has taken place. This practice is almost universal and found in countries as far apart as England, India, Germany, Greece, and Madagascar. Behind the tradition lurks the superstitious belief that in a house where someone had recently died, the ghost of the deceased would carry off one's soul projected in the mirror-reflection, as any reflection of oneself was thought to contain one's soul. Therefore, once a death had occurred, it was of utmost importance for the living to do everything in their power to help safely convey the soul as far away as possible into the other world. Nobody wanted the deceased to be detained and remain as a bothersome ghost in the house, perhaps appearing behind someone looking in a mirror. For this reason, it was customary in some countries to cover not only mirrors, but also all shiny things in the house, such as brass, copper, silver, and gold.

Besides mirrors, portraits were also thought to contain the soul of the person portrayed, hence, the superstition about misfortune befalling someone whose picture falls off a wall for no apparent reason. There are still people today, who hold the belief that to capture their likeness robs them of their soul, and consequently, they are aghast at seeing their image in a photo. In rural parts of Turkey, Morocco, and various Asian countries, this notion lingers.

Another important aspect to be considered when someone has died is Mortuis nil nisi bonum, meaning 'Never speak ill of the dead'. As early as 77 CE, Pliny wondered: 'Why, at any mention of the dead do we protest that we do not attack their memory?'.[24] This superstition is still widely observed. The dislike of speaking ill of the dead has been proverbial throughout the ages. To speak of the dead at all has always been viewed with great disquietude and is usually accompanied with the apologetic statement, 'God bless his soul'. Furthermore, if anything disparaging and negative is said of the dead, it is common to qualify such a statement by adding a phrase of regard or sympathy, such as 'poor man', or 'honest man', however, often in direct contradiction to the deceased's character.

Formerly, to speak of the dead, that is, mention their names, was greatly feared, the reason being the firm belief that should the name be mentioned, the spirit of the dead appeared immediately. This reminds us of a quote from the ancient Egyptian Book of the Dead: 'To speak the name of the dead makes them live again, brings them back to life'.[25] In European countries, the topic of death is still avoided, and we say that a friend or relative has 'passed away', 'passed on', 'taken the road of no return' or that the 'thread of life has been severed'. A direct referral to the unpleasant topic of death is thereby avoided, the evocative power of speech vaguely lingering as a fearful superstition. However, in many traditional societies, this belief prevails. Among Australian Aborigines the name of a deceased person is not mentioned for some time following a death.

Another important death rite is the custom of touching the dead as a final courtesy or gesture of farewell. This tradition is widespread and is found in many parts of Europe and America. It demonstrates a lack of ill feeling towards the dead person. Superstitious belief once held that touching a corpse prevented its spirit from inducing any visitations or troubling dreams. In Scotland, it was once firmly held that a murdered man's corpse would not decay if all mourners had not ceremoniously touched it. The tradition of touching a corpse as a gesture of goodwill might be a relic of the medieval trial by ordeal, in which someone accused of murder was taken to the dead body and made to touch it with his hands. Should blood ooze from any wounds or any change occur in the colouring of the corpse's feet or hands, the person was judged guilty.

Often, the implicit belief in this form of justice resulted in the accused displaying great fear, then considered to indicate guilt, whether the person was guilty of the crime or not. Such trials by ordeal are mentioned in the Daemonologie (1597) of King James I: 'In a secret murther, if the dead carkasse be at any time thereafter handled by the murtherer, it will gush out of blood, as if the blood were crying to heaven for revenge of the murtherer'.[26]

In many Asian and African countries however, taboos are still in place against touching the dead and everything associated with them. According to Hindu belief anyone touching a corpse becomes polluted and must undergo ritual cleansing, which is why the burning of corpses is traditionally carried out by Sudras, adherents of the lowest Hindu class. Similarly, the Old Testament intones: 'He who touches the dead body of anyone shall be unclean seven days. He shall purify himself with water on the third day and on the seventh day; then he will be clean'.[27]

Apart from touching the dead it was once also considered a pious necessity, according to European tradition, to kiss the deceased to bid them farewell. An old English belief firmly stipulated that children especially should be made to kiss the dead and, by so doing, receive the gift of long life and physical strength from the newly dead. Needless to say, many a child must have been terrified and severely traumatised by being forced into this ritual.

In many cultures, it was also customary to exhibit an exaggerated, melodramatic show of grief by hiring professional wailers. According to Western cultural observances, the correct deportment for mourners of rank has always been one of controlled repression. Professional wailers, therefore, were employed by the well-to-do to dispel an impression of indifference on the part of those left behind. Women, traditionally more inclined than men to displays of emotional sorrow, have always been in great demand as professional wailers. For suitable remuneration, they followed ancient Greeks and Romans to their tombs, loudly weeping, flaying their arms, and beating their breasts. Such wailers were still employed in various European countries in the early 1900s.

On the other hand it was thought that too much mourning and crying was very disturbing to the ghosts of the dead. In countries such as England and Germany, it was regarded as wrong to weep inconsolably at a funeral, as this was thought to hinder the departing spirit. Crying was considered to hold the dying person back and was commonly referred to as 'crying back the dead', therefore, not acquiescing to Divine Will. On the islands off the west coast of Ireland, no funeral wail was permitted until three hours after someone's death so that the sound of lamenting would not hinder the soul from leaving the body.

A morbidly fascinating custom is that of post-mortem photography, which evolved as a direct result of the invention of photography in 1839. Up until this time only the wealthy possessed portraits of themselves. However, photography suddenly enabled those, who would never have been able to afford to sit for a painted portrait, to have their picture taken. For all those who had missed out on a photographic likeness during their lifetime and to help families in the grieving process, photographers offered 'last look' photographic portraits, taken either in a studio or in the home of the deceased. To our modern-day sensibilities the custom of the proverbial 'last look' may seem somewhat morbid, but during the nineteenth century the practice was widespread and formed a vital part of the mourning process in European and American culture. Death was a common occurrence: life expectancy was low and infant mortality especially high. When post-mortem photography was in vogue, it was customary to make the deceased appear to be merely sleeping or resting, which is why the deceased was often propped upright in bed or in a chair or settee. Sometimes the eyes were left open to give the corpse a more life-like appearance. Parents posed with dead infants in their arms and various props such as flowers or a cross were added to the scene in order to give an indication of the post-mortem nature of the photo. With the passage of time however, post-mortem photography slowly changed to focus on a draped coffin adorned with flowers, with a photograph of the deceased placed on top.

Black — The Colour of Death

In most Western countries, black is worn as a sign of mourning, but different cultures have varying ideas about the correct and sincerest method of expressing grief, hence, various colours of mourning are found around the globe. However, black is considered the most befitting for sorrow and grief, as blackness and bleakness symbolise the deprivation of life in nature. Therefore this colour, since ancient times, has been preferred in most countries as an outward indication of mourning.

The Greek philosopher, Plutarch, considered white fitting for the dead, as it is pure and least defiled; hence, in ancient Greece, matrons attired themselves in white on the death of their husbands. In ancient Rome, both black and white signified mourning. Roman widows used to wear white to mourn their husbands, and throughout Italy, a white band worn around the head was the sign of widowhood. White as a colour of mourning was also known in England and other European countries, where it was customary in olden times for all mourners to dress in white if the deceased was a virgin. A pair of white gloves was carried at the head of the funeral procession, the white gloves considered symbols of love and purity. At the turn of the century, it was still traditional in rural England to hang a garland of white paper roses over the pew of unmarried villagers who had died in the flower of their age.

In certain Asian countries such as China, Vietnam, and India, white is regarded as the colour of purity and holiness. It is therefore regarded as the appropriate colour of mourning and worn by those attending funerals. Other cultures express grief by wearing yellow or blue. The ancient Egyptians regarded yellow as the colour denoting death, as nature in the Nile Valley typically faded to yellow, indicating transience. Syrians and Armenians wear sky blue and Ethiopians, grey, the colour of their native earth, which receives the dead, symbolically typifying human mortality.

Black is the commonest indication of mourning, particularly in Europe, apparently originating from ancient Roman tradition. However, throughout the centuries, many varied explanations for this custom have arisen through superstitious speculation. Some contend that wearing black, as a colour of mourning is not done as a mark of respect for the dead, but to acknowledge humankind's inferiority in the face of the Grim Reaper. Alternatively, the custom is attributed to the belief that the devil cannot see or discern black; hence, anyone wearing this colour is invisible to him. Thus, black mourning clothes were worn in an attempt to trick the devil, always on the lookout to snatch newly departed souls and, therefore, considered ever-present at funerals. Another belief about black mourning clothes was that everyone dressed in black looked the same; hence, the ghost of the deceased was unable to recognise anyone, especially women, as they also wore veils. Therefore, the dead could not linger with those attending the funeral.

In the past, periods of mourning for different degrees of blood relationship were exactly laid down and strictly followed. Depending on the closeness of the relationship, it was almost compulsory to wear black. A widow even continued donning this colour for the rest of her life, a custom still found in many Catholic countries, especially in rural areas. Now, except in Roman Catholic and South American countries, the outward formalities of grief and mourning have been largely dispensed with.

Watching the Dead

During the days between death and burial, many customs are observed in all cultures. In Western countries, most traditional rituals surrounding death are not adhered to anymore, although some folk customs persist. An old and deep-rooted notion is that the corpse should never be left alone between death and burial. All societies, especially in earlier times, tended to fear the dead and to wish them safely gone. Some customs, such as the wake, might have originated to appease the dead by honouring them with a farewell occasion.

In the past, when a death had occurred, it was not customary to have an undertaker whisk away the dead, as it is done today. Instead, the corpse was cleaned; ceremoniously laid out with hands folded across the chest, surrounded by lighted wake candles; and kept watch over until the funeral. The death-watch-watch or wake, as it is known now, was originally taken literally, the corpse carefully watched until its burial. There was always the very real possibility that the person considered dead could be in a swoon and wake up at any time! Because evil spirits and demons were considered creatures of darkness fearing the light, wake candles were often also lit in all other rooms of the house, thereby keeping evil spirits away from the dying and dead. Thus, candles were often left to burn in a room for days after someone had died there.

Besides lighting candles at the head, feet, and sides of the corpse, other rites were performed during the death-watch or wake. Throughout Europe, the belief persisted that a saucer of salt placed on a corpse's chest before burial served to keep the devil at bay. Because of its qualities of preservation, salt was universally regarded as a symbol of eternity and immortality. Salt, an emblem of the immortal spirit, was apparently hated by the devil and was believed to keep the deceased's ghost from walking about or 'rising', as a popular saying in the British Isles verifies: 'There is no weight so heavy, as salt gets, when it is on the dead'. This custom was widespread in Europe, and according to the Dictionary of Superstition by Iona Opie, recorded as late as the 1950s.[28]

During the wake, a coin known in England as Charon's fee or Charon's toll was often placed on the corpse's closed eyelids. This custom stemmed from ancient Greece, where it was customary to place a coin in the mouth or hand of the deceased as a payment to Charon. He was believed to be a hideous old man ferrying the dead across the Underworld rivers of Acheron and Styx for the fare of an obolus. Curiously, this tradition is not only found in European countries. Ancient Inca mummies, when unwrapped, were found to have thin copper discs placed in their mouths. These discs constituted the fare to Xolotl, god of the Underworld, who guided the dead over the River Chicunauictlan. In Europe, providing for the deceased's future needs is not common any more, although the Charon penny still accompanied the dead as recently as the late nineteenth century.

In the past, among the common people, wakes were often get-togethers with much feasting and drinking. They were inducements for out-of-control debauchery and licentious behaviour, where no opportunity was neglected to make up for the loss and death of one human by trying at all costs to conceive another!

The once traditional wake, or sitting-up with the corpse, has now become rare, with most people preferring not to keep the body in the house. Instead, an undertaker collects and ceremoniously lays out the deceased, thus making the loved one available for viewing and visitation by relatives and friends at the undertaker's premises.

The Funeral

Funeral rites have always played an important part in humankind's social behaviour. The Latin word funus means 'funeral'. It is closely connected to the term fumus for 'smoke', indicating ancient disposal of the dead by cremation. Although funerary practices vary worldwide, they all seem to reflect belief in the afterlife and, originally, were attempts to protect the living from the powers of the dead. Egyptian funerary practices were based on the belief that the afterlife was very similar to earthly life, entered only if the body was properly preserved, hence, the custom of mummification in ancient Egypt. However, Chinese funerary rites were designed to let the spirit safely traverse the Underworld and arrive at the spirit tablet in the ancestral shrine of the family. Hence, the ancestral shrine is regularly honoured to keep alive the dead person's memory.

Burial rites of different countries and cultures evolved not only according to the customs of the people, but also the nature of the country and circumstances of the times. In hot climates, for example, it was of utmost importance to bury the dead as soon as possible. There has always been a widespread fear of lying unburied after death because it was believed that after death the soul continued to feel what was done to the body, prompting an urgent need to provide the dead with a proper grave – only then could the soul move on to the next life. The requirement for proper burial is reflected in the Old Testament in which a curse expressed against those who disobeyed the commandments intoned: '...your dead body shall be food for all the birds in the air and for the beasts of the earth [...]'.[29]

Around the world, the omission of funeral rites was regarded as the main reason ghosts returned to the physical plane. Everything possible, therefore, was done to prevent this. Many of our funeral customs now derive from the Greeks and Romans, such as wearing black to indicate mourning, walking in a funeral procession, raising a mound (Latin tumulus, or 'tomb') on the grave, decorating graves with flowers, and feasting with relatives and friends after the funeral.

In many cultures, it was believed that the sins of the deceased could be transferred after death to another person to make the afterlife easier for the departed soul. In Europe it was customary to hire poor people, so-called sin-eaters, for small amounts of money to attend funerals and to take on the sins of the deceased. (See Chapter I, The Scapegoat).

Another important factor in burial rites of the past was the universal importance accorded the physical body in the afterlife. Therefore, mummification and other preservation methods were based on the concept of the importance of the physical body in its role in the afterlife. Offerings of food, drink, and personal possessions were left in tombs for the dead to use in the hereafter. Fear of the dead often influenced the treatment a corpse was accorded. For example, in ancient Greece, it was customary for murderers to cut off their victims' extremities and to place these neatly beneath the armpits of the slain person to lay the ghost of the victim and prevent all physical revenge – as the ghost of the victim was now imagined without arms and legs and hence unable to come after the murderer. Similarly, Australian Aborigines cut off their dead enemies' thumbs so that their ghosts were too mutilated to throw a ghostly spear.

The notion of keeping the physical body intact was strengthened in Christian Europe by a literal acceptance of the Christian doctrine of the resurrection of the dead and a papal ban specifically on dividing the physical body. At all costs, the body was to be kept whole to await resurrection. For this reason, European anatomists had great difficulty, during the early Middle Ages, obtaining corpses to pursue their anatomical studies. To be buried with any body part missing was thought to incur a risk for the dead of spending all eternity without it. Therefore, many people even went as far as preserving all lost teeth so that these could be buried with the rest of the body. In parts of England, the dead were often interred with their Bible, hymnbook, and Sunday school class ticket to ensure a favourable outcome at the Last Judgment.

Today, when the average Westerner dies, the funeral is comprehensively organised by an undertaker who is called as soon as possible. Coffins supplied by the undertaker are usually made of wood, ranging in workmanship and price to suit the family's financial situation. Predominantly, the American fashion of caskets, instead of traditional tapered coffins, has become popular in Western countries. Death notices are published in newspapers, and once all the arrangements have been made, the corpse is buried. The hearse bearing the casket is usually a black estate wagon, far more expensive than most people could ever afford in their lifetime. Usually, the casket is decorated with flower tributes. In the past, these consisted of wreaths and crosses intricately woven with flowers, but now, simple large flat sheaves are more fashionable. The hearse, followed by the mourners, drives slowly to the church or cemetery chapel for the burial service, after which the coffin is lowered into the already dug grave. Mourners might throw flowers or a little earth on the casket before departing. Cemetery staff fills in the grave, later capped by a tombstone. Interestingly, the first tombstones might have been placed on graves to keep the dead under the ground. Slowly, however, the gravestone evolved into a status symbol indicating just how wealthy and successful one's life has been and to convey certain information about the dead. Great misfortune was believed to follow the desecration of a grave and any disturbance of the dead, which are now looked on as crimes.

Flowers and Trees for the Dead

Traditionally, flowers are strewn over the graves of loved ones and placed in coffins and in the hands of the dead. Flowers have always been considered a suitable emblem of frail human bodies. The dead were seen as sleeping in the earth for a period, only to rise when the 'Son of Righteousness' awakens them at the Day of Judgment. Similarly, flowers were believed to sleep naturally under the frost-bound earth during winter, only to awaken at the first warm touch of the spring sun. This comparison between nature and humankind is alluded to in the Old Testament when the prophet Isaiah proclaimed, 'Arise and sing, ye that dwell in the dust, for thy dew is as the dew of herbs'.[30] It was customary amongst our pagan ancestors since the earliest times to scatter flowers on unburied corpses. Specific flowers and wreaths also accompanied the dead because of the select powers attributed to some plants in warding off evil.

In the past, purple and white flowers were considered especially suitable for the dead, and graves were adorned with various types of these coloured flowers, expressing love and respect for the dead. White lilies are traditionally linked with death, which is why they should never be given to the sick or kept indoors as cut flowers. White snowdrops, thought to look like a corpse in a shroud, are still used in funeral wreaths and placed on graves. Roses are also customarily related to death and were already strewn on graves by the ancient Romans. In Austria, Germany, and Switzerland, cemeteries are still sometimes referred to as 'rose gardens' because of the profusion of these specific flowers. In northern European countries, white roses were placed especially on virgins' graves, and in the funeral procession of unmarried females, garlands of white paper roses were carried before the coffin.

Similarly, the custom of planting certain types of trees in graveyards was prevalent in early times. The Greeks and Romans used the cypress and the yew, which were indicative of mourning, at burials and in graveyards. Because they attained great age and their foliage was virtually evergreen, these trees were specifically regarded as symbols of immortality.

The cypress, proverbial for its durability, has always been linked with funerals and graveyards, probably also because its wood was believed resistant to the attack of worms. This is why most of the chests containing Egyptian mummies were made of cypress wood, why the ancient Athenians used it to make coffins specifically for their heroes, and why the doors of St. Peter's Church in Rome, which have lasted for many hundreds of years, were crafted from cypress wood. Similarly, this wood was also included at English funerals, as expressed by Hilderic Friend in her well-known collection, Flowers and Flower Lore: 'Cypress garlands are of great account at funerals amongst the gentler sort, but Rosemary and Bayes are used by the commons both at funerals and weddings'.[31]

In northern and western Europe, the yew tree's foliage was specifically associated with religious worship and was popular at burials. This is probably because yew trees live longer than any other species of trees in Europe. They grow to enormous size and many are believed to be more than a thousand years old, which is why they were regarded as a symbol of immortality.

However, the yew tree is also linked with death. The tree's association with death is probably because the Greeks and Romans regarded it as highly poisonous. Pliny the Elder tells us the tree is so poisonous that to sleep under it or eat one's food under it is immediately fatal.[32] In Richard II, Shakespeare refers to the yew as 'the double fatal yew',[33] because the leaves of the yew are poisonous and the wood was traditionally used for making instruments of death, that is, bows.

The Druids of ancient Britain, France, and Ireland revered the yew as sacred. Therefore, it is likely that the early Christian missionaries preached in the shelter of these trees before the first churches were built next to them. This assumption is based on the fact that many yew trees are much older than the churches built beside them, suggesting that these churches were built in places already devoted to worship near the sacred yew tree. This association continued, and it thus became traditional to plant yew trees in churchyards, so much so, that the yew was considered indispensable in European churchyards.

Under Edward I (1239-1307), when permission was first given to fell trees in churchyards for building and repairs, yew trees were the only ones left standing because of the superstitious beliefs attached to them. However, because yew trees were popular for making bows, it has also been postulated that they were planted in churchyards specifically because such places were least likely to be desecrated. This created some control in the making of bows, articles of importance to our ancestors before the introduction of gunpowder. The old English yeomanry, regarded as the best and most dreaded archers in Europe, were supplied from the yew tree. Eventually, the constant and universal demand for yew wood caused such a scarcity that under Edward IV (1442-1483), an express act of Parliament directed bowers to make four bows – one each of hazel, ash, and elm and only one of yew wood.

In modern times, funeral flowers can be selected from any colour or type, just as bridal bouquets consisting of white lilies or pure white roses – traditionally flowers of death – are considered suitable. The wonderfully intricate, traditional knowledge accumulated over many centuries, underlying the lore of various attributes, aspects, and characteristics of flowers and trees has been largely forgotten or lost – and perhaps, we are the poorer for it.

VII

THE HUMAN BODY

The Soul in Animal Form

O ur distant ancestors believed that the life force animating humans came from the soul, imagined as a small being within us all, responsible for physical and mental actions. As the activities of animals or humans were explained through the presence of a soul, it was thought that in sleep or trance, the soul was temporarily absent, and in death, permanently so. Therefore, to guard against death meant to prevent the soul's exit. However, once the soul had been perceived as having departed for good, it was of the utmost importance to prevent its re-entry. To secure either of these ends, our ancestors adopted many precautions, taking on the form of various rituals and taboos and the wearing of ornaments around the nose, ears, and mouth, ensuring that the soul could not leave and unwelcome forces could not enter.

Among most cultures, the belief at some time persisted that the soul could temporarily leave the body without causing death to the person concerned. However, such temporary absence of the soul was thought to involve considerable risk, because the wandering soul could be subjected to various mishaps, be hurt, or even fall into enemy hands. It must be remembered that in the past, the soul was not perceived as an abstract concept, but thought to represent a concrete material thing, which could be seen and handled. Therefore, it could be kept in a box or a container and could be smashed, injured, or destroyed. We only have to think of the countless fairy tales, where the soul of the villain or magician is contained in a particular object that first has to be destroyed to break his power and magic.

During sleep, the soul was thought to wander away and visit the very places of which the sleeper dreamt. The danger was ever-present that it would be deprived of finding its way back. Hence, it was formerly a common rule never to wake a sleeper, lest the soul had not yet returned, in which case, the person concerned fell ill. The wandering soul, however far it roamed, was always believed to return in the end. As long as it remained unharmed, even when it was outside the body, it would continue to animate the body it had left behind, and the person to whom it belonged would be safe.

In myths and tales from around the world, the souls of the dead or those under a spell are often housed, if only temporarily, in the bodies of birds, butterflies, lizards, serpents, mice, frogs, and toads. Therefore these animals were never to be killed.

Birds were especially thought to shelter the souls of the dead or those under a spell, a belief not only commonly Indo-European, but also found in China, Indonesia, Melanesia, Africa, and the Americas. In the lore of all nations, birds function as prophetic beings, messengers of death, or as housing those already passed into the netherworld and come to guide a newly released soul. In Greek myths, the souls of the dead are contained in birds, the soul of Alexander the Great reputedly flying to heaven as an eagle.

Early Christian art took over this symbolism, depicting the souls of the dead in the hereafter as birds nesting in trees. In the catacombs around Rome, countless depictions of birds bearing the name of a dead person, or with inscriptions such as anima innocens, meaning 'innocent soul' and anima simplex, meaning 'sincere soul', can be found. These depictions clearly picture the birds as emblems of departed souls. According to Slavic lore, a soul leaves the body through the mouth as a bird. Silesian folklore contends that dead children's souls are housed in birds fluttering over graves and gravestones. Around the coasts of the British Isles, it was said that seagulls are the souls of drowned seamen, and in Germany, ravens were believed to house the souls of the damned.

In myths and fairy tales from around the world, there are countless examples of the souls of those under a magic spell or merely asleep, housed in animal form. The Nordic saga, The Song of Wolund, tells the sad tale of beautiful women turned into swans. In the well-known fairy tale, The Princess and the Frog, the frog can only be turned back into a prince through the love of a beautiful maiden. Often, tales relate how the soul leaves the body as a small animal or bird.

This recalls the story of the Frankish king Gunthram (circa 600 CE). One day, while on a campaign, he lay sleeping in his servant's lap. Suddenly, the man saw a small snake-like animal, perceived as the king's soul, exit the monarch's mouth. As the servant was observing the little creature, he realised that it seemed to want to cross the small stream next to which he and his master were resting. Carefully, he placed his sword across the narrow flow of water, and using this as a bridge, the small creature disappeared into the dense bushes, much to the manservant's apprehension. After a few hours, however, it returned safely into the mouth of the sleeping king. Shortly thereafter, the king awoke and related the wonderful dream he had. In his dream, he had crossed an iron bridge spanning a large river. On the other side, he had found a cave filled with fabulous treasure. When the king and his men explored the dense bushes, they found a cave, exactly as in the dream, and claimed the treasure.

Ablation of the Heart

On December 8, 2003, a BBC News broadcast reported: 'The heart of the son of French King Louis XVI and Marie-Antoinette is to be laid to rest in the family crypt after 200 years of controversy'. Not long after the execution of his parents, the child, believed to be the dauphin, died in prison in 1795. A doctor by the name of Pelletan removed and conserved the boy's heart, under the assumption that he was indeed the young dauphin. Legend and myth has surrounded the death of the 10-year-old, some believing he died in prison, and others speculating that an impostor had replaced him. However, DNA tests have since conclusively proved that the preserved heart belonged to a member of the House of Habsburg, from which Marie-Antoinette, the dauphin's mother, originated.

In the ancient world, it was thought that human emotions were linked to specific organs. The Greek physician Galen located the seat of reason in the brain, the seat of passion in the liver, and the seat of emotion in the heart. Our ancestors also attributed special magic properties to particular parts of the body. Although the soul was thought to reside partly in all body parts and fluids, the heart was specifically regarded as the domus anima or 'abode of the soul'.

During the Middle Ages in Europe, the heart symbolised a wide range of meanings. Medieval Christians regarded the heart as the moral, emotional, and intellectual centre, representing the whole body. The heart was thought to contain a person's beliefs, thoughts, feelings, and memories – a 'book of self' as it were, and a receptacle where a record of each person's life was kept. God was thought to have a copy of each 'record' and occasionally made His own 'entries' in the hearts of saints. Numerous legends of saints commemorated martyrs whose hearts, it was believed, contained marks of special divine favour, such as inscriptions or sacred objects. For example, it was documented that the hearts of two Italian abbots contained images of Christ and 'nails from the Cross' [1]. The concept of a 'book of the heart', modelled on the medieval manuscript codex, reached its most expressive representation in literature and art: Beautiful manuscript books were fashioned as heart-shaped, while paintings often portrayed hearts as open books in the chest, recording all deeds, good and evil, for the Final Judgment. Alternatively, paintings represented authors holding a heart and pen. When we still use figures of speech such as 'reading' someone's mind, or we express the need to 'turn over a new leaf' we are in fact using phrases, which inadvertently refer to the 'book of the heart'.

As the heart was seen as representing the moral and spiritual core of a person, this specific notion gave rise to the rite of burying the heart separately. Therefore, in Northern Europe amongst royalty, aristocrats, and ecclesiastics, post-mortem ablation of the heart was a widespread, common funerary practice. This process involved separate, independent burial not only of the body but also the entrails, as well as the excised heart in locations of sacred worship. For example, when King Heinrich III died in October 1056 in Bodfeld, Germany, his heart was buried separately from his body. When Henry I of England died in France in

1135 his entrails, as well as his brain and eyes were buried in Rouen and his body was returned to England for interment in Reading Abbey. The crusading English King Richard I, known as Richard Lionheart, decreed before his death in 1199 that his brain and entrails be buried in Charroux, France, his body in the Abbey of Fontevreau, and his heart in the Cathedral of Rouen. The heart of Frederick Wilhelm IV (1795–1861), King of Prussia, and member of the House of Habsburg, is buried at his parents' feet in the Mausoleum of Charlottenburg, Berlin.[2]

Since the seventeenth century, the hearts of all members of the House of Habsburg have been buried separately from their bodies in the Augustiner Church in Vienna.

The desire to apportion one's remains to various favoured locations was to solicit prayers from the living for salvation of one's soul in more than one place of religious foundation. Sometimes, only the heart was buried, whereas the body was dismembered and boiled to keep only the bones, either reserved as relics in various churches and cathedrals or buried in a specific location. An example is Louis IX of France. After his death during the crusades in 1216, his entrails were entombed in a church in Sicily, while his skeleton – obtained by boiling the dismembered body, and his ablated heart, were returned home to France. Edward I (1239-1307), wished for his heart to be embalmed after death and taken to the Holy Land, whereas his body was to be dismembered, then boiled, and the bones carried into Scotland on his last campaign. Similarly, when Robert the Bruce, King of Scotland, died in 1329, his body was buried in Dunfermline after excision of the heart. In keeping with the king's last request, James Douglas, his comrade-in-arms, took the heart on crusade to the Holy Land. Although Douglas was killed in battle in 1330, Robert's heart was returned and buried at Melrose Abbey in Scotland.

In Europe, separate burial of monarchs' hearts continued throughout the Middle Ages up to the eighteenth century. In France, ablation of the heart persisted until the French Revolution in 1789. Up until then, the hearts of French kings, as well as their family members had been secreted in various cathedrals in Paris. But, after the French Revolution in 1792, the various gold and silver caskets containing these hearts were melted down by revolutionary authorities. The mummified hearts were sold to painters, who at the time customarily added mummified organic matter as a pigment in paints to produce a colour popularly known as 'mummy brown'.[3]

The belief in the heart as the abode of the soul is also confirmed in the tradition of driving a stake into the heart to prevent someone from turning into a vampire after death – by impaling the heart, the soul was destroyed. Before his death in Paris in 1874, Romanian Count Borolajowac requested his heart be torn out immediately after death, as he wanted to prevent his returning as a vampire.[4]

Whereas the heart was seen as the abode of the soul, every person's soul-essence was also thought partly contained in the name, various body fluids, body parts, and the shadow.

To Walk in Someone's Shadow

In all cultures around the world, the belief has once persisted that a man's shadow was an integral part of himself. This belief was strengthened by the strange image that followed its owner around everywhere, copying all movements. At certain times of the day, this image grew longer, and at other times, it totally disappeared, giving rise to the belief that the strength of a warrior waxed and waned with his shadow. In the morning, when his shadow was at its longest, his strength was presumed greatest. As his shadow diminished, so his strength decreased, only to return in the afternoon as his shadow again stretched. This belief is also recorded in countries outside the tropics. The diminished shadow at noontime might have caused superstitions in Europe regarding noon as the most dreaded hour during daylight – an hour when it was advisable to stay indoors and rest.

The link between soul and shadow is found universally. In the ancient Egyptian text of Unas, the shadow is mentioned in unison with the soul of the deceased. It is evident throughout the text that to the ancient Egyptians, the shadow was inextricably linked to the soul and was believed to be always near it. The Egyptian Book of the Dead states: 'Let not be shut in my soul, let not be fettered my shadow, let be opened the way for my soul and for my shadow, may it see the great god'.⁵ The Egyptian Book of the Dead contains a specific chapter titled 'Chapter of opening the tomb to the soul and to the shadow'.⁶ With reference to the afterlife, it is clearly stated, 'Not shut ye in my soul, not fetter ye my shade, be there open a way for my soul, and for my shade'.⁷

So inextricably linked are the concepts of shadow and soul that many languages have only one word to express both 'shadow' and 'soul'. For example, the Zulus in Southern Africa use the word tunzi to describe a man's shadow and his soul. Among the Algonquian Indians, the word otahchuk has the same double meaning. As the soul was thought to physically and mentally animate the body, the shadow, closely coupled to its owner's body, was seen as containing the soul. Hence, all injury done to the shadow or the reflection of someone was thought to harm that person physically, and if anything happened to the shadow, it would be physically felt. Therefore, Australian Aborigines believed that an injury to a man's shadow, such as stabbing, beating, or cutting, injured his person to the same degree. Hindus are expressly forbidden to urinate on anyone's shadow lest they harm the person. The same belief was extant in ancient Rom and is referred to in Pliny's Natural History.⁸ Similarly, a very specific belief in places as far apart as India, ancient Greece, and Rome, was that an animal stepping on one's shadow resulted in a loss of speech and movement.⁹ In Germany and Italy, a notion taken very seriously in the past was that stepping on someone's shadow stunted the person's growth. Now, remnants of the fearful beliefs surrounding the shadow are evident in the prevalent superstition that stepping on someone's shadow is 'unlucky' – customs remain, but with time, the reasons behind them change.

An old belief in England was that if anyone sold his soul to the devil, he would lose his shadow, reaffirming the universal belief that the soul was contained in the shadow. This idea lies at the root of the legends surrounding mythical heroes killing their enemies by stabbing their shadows. Moses reassured his people not to fear their enemies, the Canaanites, as these have 'lost their shadows'.¹⁰ An evil spell uttered in Turkey intones: 'May you cease to cast a shadow'– in other words, lose your soul.

A belief prevalent in tribal societies concerned the shadows of persons regarded as taboo in those societies.[11] Such restrictions applied to the shadows of enemies, warriors fresh from battle, mourners, and the shadows of mothers-in-law, menstruating women, or women in confinement. All these personages were regarded as unclean, and until ritual cleansing had taken place, their shadows were thought to endanger those on whom they fell. In some African societies, letting one's shadow fall on the king, in other words, overshadowing him, was a crime punishable by death. Now, the term to overshadow someone, meaning to 'render insignificant by comparison', has lost its literal meaning, although the disparaging association remains.

For thousands of years, humans, especially farmers and fieldworkers, used the lengthening of the shadow to indicate time. This is still general practice, just as it was in biblical times: '... are not his days like those of a hireling? As a servant earnestly desireth the shadow....'.[12]

In Europe, it was customary in places as far apart as Greece, Rumania, Bulgaria, and the British Isles to 'bury' someone's shadow, once the traditional human sacrifice committed to building foundations had been abolished. A person was unwittingly enticed to a building site to let his shadow fall on the foundations. Another option was for a shadow-trader to measure a man's shadow with a piece of string unbeknown to him, then put the string in a box and bury it under the foundation of a building, thus symbolically burying the shadow. It was thought that the man whose shadow had been buried would soon die. The shadow containing the life force or soul, once buried, was believed to equate a living sacrifice, substituting the old custom of immuring living people in the walls of buildings.

The strength and clarity of the shadow was held to indicate physical well-being. Therefore, someone dying or close to death was thought to have a diminishing shadow, whereas a detached shadow meant death had already occurred. However, a sick person whose shadow was observed as clearly outlined and strong could expect rapid recuperation.

Not only the shadow, but any reflection of a person was thought to contain their soul. This explains why in ancient times, it was regarded as positively dangerous to see one's reflection in water – in case the denizens of the deep, pulled the reflection and hence one's soul into the unknown depths. Similarly, it clarifies the notion that a terrible calamity awaited the person destroying his own image by breaking a mirror. (See Chapter IV Seven Years of Bad Luck).

Healing, Magical Blood

Numerous and varied are the beliefs surrounding this vital body fluid. Believed to contain the life force and essence of humans and animals, as well as the soul, blood has for thousands of years been used in all major religious rites for sacrificial purposes. It has also been used in magic, witchcraft, and folk medicine.

Bloodshed in sacrifice symbolises human or animal life being given back to God its creator. In ancient times, the offering of sacrificial blood was the most holy covenant between man and God, which is why Moses ritually purified his people by sprinkling them with the blood of sacrificed animals.[13] The tradition of pouring sacrificial blood directly on the ground, so that the Earth Mother could reabsorb the life force, or of sprinkling blood on an altar, was once common to all cultures.

The many beliefs linked with blood centre on the idea that it was the seat of the life-essence containing the soul. Therefore, blood loss was considered doubly serious; to be staunched at all costs. Our ancestors must have observed thousands of years ago that bodily death involves the cessation of blood flow because when a person is wounded, he or she loses blood, weakens, and eventually dies. This gave rise to the belief that a creature's blood constitutes its life force and ultimately contains the soul. Hence, blood has always been an essential part of human sacrificial rites the world over. The Aztec Indians, in many other respects an enlightened people, offered copious amounts of blood sacrifice to their gods in exchange for divine favour. In ancient Central and South America, many thousands were killed to appease the gods and to ensure bountiful harvests, nourishing the soil, as it were, with the strength of human blood.

During the Middle Ages, the magic power of witches was believed to reside in their blood. It was, therefore, important and standard practice by the Inquisition to order that their bodies be totally consumed by fire;

hence, they were usually burned at the stake. It was also thought that a witch's magical power to harm could be wiped out by drawing a few drops of her blood from the upper part of her face. During the times of the witch-hunts, this became known as 'scoring above the breath'. Witches reputedly used blood as a powerful ingredient in spell making to subdue demons and control certain people. Blood could also be used as a love-charm to bind the lover to oneself. For example, Hungarian girls, on occasion, rubbed some of their blood in their lover's hair to ensure his everlasting affection.

On the other hand, blood was valued for its healing and restorative qualities. Children's blood was especially credited with special healing powers. In Natural History, Pliny the Elder describes blood as a well-known cure for leprosy in Egypt: 'Leprosy is endemic in Egypt. When kings contracted the disease it had deadly consequences for the people because the tubs in the baths were prepared with warm human blood for its treatment'.[14] The belief that human blood cured this dreaded disease was most certainly also prevalent in ancient Greece and Rome. During the Middle Ages, a virgin's blood was regarded as a certain cure for leprosy, a theme central to the Middle-High-German epic Der arme Heinrich (written circa 1195). Alternatively, the sufferers of this terrible malady were advised to bathe in the blood of children. The tradition of healing leprosy with the blood of innocent children is seen in many texts of the Middle Ages, as well as in early Hebrew biblical commentary. As leprosy was thought to stem from moral impurity and sin, it was perceived that the antidote or cure could only be one of high moral purity – to bathe in the blood of a virgin or young child. Using blood for healing purposes was still recorded in many parts of Europe as late as 1891.[15]

Similarly, the blood from an executed man or for that matter, anyone who had died violently was believed to cure many ailments. The famous writer of fairy tales, Hans Andersen, witnessing a public execution in 1823, saw the father of an epileptic child collect a cup of the dead man's blood and administer it to his child as a potential cure.[16] The blood of an executed man, as a cure for epilepsy, is also mentioned by Jacob Grimm in his collection of German folklore: 'It is good for epilepsy to drink the blood of a beheaded man'.[17]

Because blood was thought to contain the soul-essence of the being it came from, the drinking of blood has for thousands of years been regarded as an elixir to imbue with strength and vigour. Known during the Middle Ages as elixir vitae, the 'elixir of life', blood was thought to rejuvenate the old and decrepit. For Moses to explicitly forbid the drinking of blood, [18] for the Koran to disallow the practice, and for the Church to vehemently object to it during the Middle Ages, proves how prevalent and ingrained this tradition was in the past. In ancient Europe and elsewhere, a common feature of tribal life was once the drinking of blood-brotherhood. This ritual involved the mutual drinking of blood by two unrelated people to create kinship, or brotherhood, between them.

The notion that by eating the flesh or drinking the blood of another human, one may absorb that person's nature into one's own is one, which appears among various cultures in many forms. (See Chapter I – Magic Practices). Among tribal societies, it was also customary to ingest the flesh and blood of brave men to inspire courage. Similarly, Norwegian hunters once drank bear blood to acquire the bear's formidable strength. African Masai warriors invigorated themselves with the blood of various animals, especially lions, to gain strength and courage. In England, the blooding ceremony held before the foxhunt, which in modern times has been reduced to turning out a decrepit animal for the hounds to pull down to stimulate their bloodlust, is a disguised remnant of an ancient custom, according to which hunters around the world smeared themselves with their prey's blood to prevent revenge from the dead animal's soul.

The notion of absorbing the animal's soul or nature contained in its blood into one's own led to certain food taboos amongst various cultures. The prohibition against consuming blood and flesh from specific animals, among Jews and other communities, attests to the undying strength of this ancient belief.

Worldwide, throughout history, a reluctance to spill blood on the ground has been recorded. Again, the explanation behind this universal fear can be found in the belief that the soul is contained in someone's blood. Therefore, any ground stained with blood becomes taboo or sacred. By impregnating the earth with the soul-power of its owner, the blood is thought to threaten anyone treading on it. Especially the shedding of innocent blood on the ground can make the spot accursed forever, as the outraged soul contained in the blood eternally cries out for vengeance. Hence, the belief that the soil remains barren where a foul and bloody murder has been committed is very common. A curse was said to spread on the ground where human blood had been shed, and nothing would grow there again. This superstition is reaffirmed in Genesis 4:9–11: 'And the Lord said unto Cain: The voice of thy brother's blood crieth unto me from the ground. And now art thou cursed from the earth, which hath opened her mouth to receive thy brother's blood from thy hand; when thou tillest the ground, it shall not henceforth yield unto thee her strength'.

Another ancient belief connected with murder was that the victim's wounds began bleeding every time the murderer was present, even many days after the terrible event had occurred. During the Middle Ages, the method of 'trial by ordeal' was a popular way of discerning the guilty party in a homicide. Those accused of murder would be forced to touch the corpse with their hands. Should blood ooze from any wounds the person would be judged as guilty. Shakespeare refers to this belief in Richard III, when the murdering Duke comes near the corpse of the one he killed: 'See, see! Dead Henry's wounds open their congeal'd mouths, and bleed afresh. [...] tis thy presence that exhales this blood, from cold and empty veins, where no blood dwells'.[19] In all likelihood, the extreme psychological pressure of such a trauma elicited a confession of sorts, whether the person accused was guilty or not.

Over millennia, the concept of blood has become incorporated in our social attitudes, our language, and especially in common phrases. Hence, we speak of 'cold-blooded' murder, 'bad blood' as the result of quarrels and feuds, anger making a man's 'blood boil', a particularly amorous person being 'hot-blooded', aristocracy as 'blue-blooded' and inherited characteristics as 'running in the blood'.

Dangerous Menstrual Blood

Throughout the ages, societies around the world, at some stage in their history, have secluded menstrual women and those in confinement as dangerous pollutants to be cautiously avoided. Universally, many beliefs regarding the harmful, loathsome, even dangerous potency of menstruating women were common. In Natural History, Pliny the Elder implicitly warns that the touch of a menstruating woman blights crops, kills seedlings, rusts iron, turns wine to vinegar, dims mirrors, blunts razors, kills bees, and generally causes misfortune in all ventures.

The fear of menstrual blood was deeply ingrained in early societies. Menstrual blood was believed to have a disastrous effect on the entire male population. In many cultures, therefore, women were forbidden during these times, under pain of death, to touch any utensils belonging to men. It was earnestly believed that their touch so defiled everything that later use of the utensils would be accompanied by certain misfortune. Such notions excluded menstruating women or those in confinement from being present at important ritual events, from participating in various religious acts, and from carrying out mundane everyday tasks, especially those related to gathering and preparing food. In various societies, contact with women during this time was limited, if not strictly forbidden, and often, they were expected to live secluded. Among North American Indians, Australian Aborigines, Indian, and East Indian tribes, a woman was not allowed any contact with food during her time of the month or during confinement. Similarly, it was firmly believed in many rural parts of Europe, that a woman in her courses or one about to become a mother should not salt pork as it would turn the meat bad; nor was she to make jam or butter; similarly, she was to abstain from bottling fruit, as all would not keep. Such notions were still recorded in Worcestershire, England, in 1945.[20]

Much of this superstitious fear and mistrust can be attributed to the ignorance that has always surrounded female physiology, which is only now fully understood and accepted by most civilised societies. In the Old Testament Book of Leviticus, it is stated: 'If a woman have.... born a.... child: she shall be unclean.... She shall touch no hallowed thing, nor come into the sanctuary, until the days of her purifying be fulfilled....'.[21] In Islamic societies, a menstruating woman is excused from the obligatory daily prayers and is required to cleanse herself ritually before resuming her religious duties. Orthodox Jews adhering to the laws on menstrual impurity, as laid down in the Talmud, must avoid all contact with a spouse during this time of the month.

In Europe, the internal workings of women's sexual organs were governed by numerous misconceptions, still firmly held by the orthodox medical establishment and the general populace until the late eighteenth century. In ancient times, the Greek philosopher, Plato (428–348 BCE), originally put forward the idea that the womb was an animal in its own right, existing independently inside a woman's body, while medieval anatomical drawings depicted the womb as a mysterious organ with seven chambers. Because of gross ignorance, the regular, monthly discharge of blood from a perfectly healthy woman's womb was widely regarded by most cultures as pollution, second only in severity to having contact with a dead person.

Interestingly, it was not until 1831 that French physician Charles Négrier suggested that menstruation controlled ovulation. The realisation that woman menstruated because they had failed to conceive took hold some years later around 1877. Before this finding, physicians wrestling with the question of menses postulated that it had something to do with the disposal of superfluous blood or a cooling of the heightened emotions only women were prone to and that both processes were controlled by the phases of the moon.

The stigma of uncleanness surrounding menstrual flow, pregnancy, and childbirth, was strengthened in Europe by the teachings of the Church. Archbishop Theodore's seventh century Penitential forbade women to enter a church or receive communion during their monthly periods. The same ruling applied to pregnant women until forty days after childbirth Christian churching, therefore, was to purify and reintegrate the new mother into the religious community. Until the church ceremony of churching, or kirking, as it is referred to in Scotland, had been carried out, a woman after childbirth was looked upon as being unclean and believed to be a danger to her neighbours and the community. In Germany, it was believed that if a woman spun wool, hemp, or flax before having been churched, her child would one day be hanged. It was also thought that 'if a woman within six weeks after confinement walks a field or flower bed, nothing grows on it for some years, or everything spoils'.[22] In Scotland, she was not permitted to enter any house but her own, as she brought evil and misfortune with her. In Ireland, the belief was that should she appear out of doors and any harm, injury, or insult should come to her, she would have no recourse through the law. To deal with this situation, women were known to fasten a piece of thatch or slate to their bonnets when going out so that they could rightfully claim never to have left the shelter of their own roof.

Such beliefs continued for centuries, throughout the Middle Ages and beyond.

To Spit for Luck and Health

In the past, breath and spittle were thought to contain soul-substance. Hence, to breathe or to spit on someone or something conveyed a magical effect. In various European cultures, spitting when making an oath was in the past considered as binding as swearing on the Bible. Ritual spitting is one of the most ancient creative actions, which is why spittle was once traditionally used in religious ceremonies, in exorcism rites, and for curing the sick. Because spitting was equated in indigenous societies with the ejaculation of semen, women were disallowed this practice.

In modern Western societies, spitting is perceived as an offensive, dirty habit. However, universally, it was once regarded as a charm against enchantment – a trusted safeguard, offering protection against fascination and evil. Pliny the Elder recommends: 'It acts as a charm if a man spits in his urine; similarly if he spits in his right shoe before putting it on, or when passing a place where he has encountered some danger'.[23] During the name-giving ceremony in ancient Rome, it was customary not only to sprinkle the child's head with water, but also to wet it with spittle. This was believed to avert evil. Similarly, in Scotland it was once deemed necessary that a priest also use spittle when christening a child. Amongst many African tribes the custom prevailed that a child to be named be spat three times in the face to protect it in later life. Some Turkish mothers still believe in the efficacy of spitting in their infants' faces to avert the influence of the evil eye.

Celtic and African kings were known to spit ritually towards the four cardinal points during annual mid-summer cleansing celebrations, thereby raising the protective Earth forces and creative energies over their land for the new season. Today, various African, Asian, and Middle Eastern societies, still harness the power attributed to spittle. The African Swazi peoples observe this practice annually during the sacred rite of Incwala, the mid-summer festival of regeneration.[24] The South African Zulu spit on the ground during an electric storm to avert being struck by lightning. They also spit to expel evil and anger and at funerals to say farewell to the departed without bitterness.

In Islamic North Africa, spitting is used for ritually transmitting virtue or the passing of baraka, meaning 'blessing'. As spittle was believed worldwide to partly contain one's soul, spitting out propitiated the forces governing fate. In spitting, a person was believed to release a little essence of their soul, which then became a sacrifice to the deities, guaranteed to attract divine favour. Hence, one could spit out for luck or in defiance and as a challenge. Spitting could be an injurious act, and to spit behind someone's back was believed to bring that person bad luck, a custom prevalent amongst many European people and other parts of the world. In Africa, to spit deliberately over the left shoulder in anger is to invoke a curse. Another custom we are still familiar with is spitting for luck. For this reason, it is still customary amongst Greeks and Turks to spit at the bride and groom after a marriage ceremony.

It is a very curious habit that when working men prepare to do something requiring great strength or fight, they invariably begin by spitting in their hands. Spitting on the hands seems to give the idea of courage, although to spit on the fist before a fight, on a coin or a dice, even on the right shoe when setting out for a journey, is an ancient notion meant to bring luck by warding off evil.

Spitting out was thought to protect not only against evil forces, but also against contagious sicknesses. This is confirmed in Natural History by Pliny the Elder: 'We are in the habit of spitting to repel contagion'.[25] Similarly, the ancient Greeks spat three times into their bosoms at the sight of a madman. Spittle was also considered effective in the healing process, and the curative powers of spittle have been advocated throughout the ages. The most well-known examples come from the

New Testament: 'And they brought unto Him one that was deaf, and had an impediment in his speech [...] And he took him aside from the multitude, and put His fingers into his ears, and He spit, and touched His tongue; [...] and saith unto him Ephatha, that is, Be opened'.[26] Fasting spittle was especially considered efficacious in curing various eye diseases, preventing scarring, curing rashes, and removing warts. The Roman historian Tacitus attributed to the Emperor Vespasian the act of restoring sight to a blind man with fasting spittle.

Many people will automatically spit on an insect bite to obtain relief. In her book, Africa through the Mists of Time, Brenda Sullivan relates that African herbalists and diviners still customarily spit medicines over their patients in the belief of hastening a cure.[27]

God Bless You

On a day-to-day basis we carry out and adhere to numerous gestures, actions and codes of etiquette, without the awareness that they are based on relics of long forgotten ancient beliefs. We coverer our mouths when yawning and coughing, and when someone sneezes we immediately respond with a 'bless you'.

In the past, it was thought that the soul escaped during a cough, yawn, or sneeze. All natural openings of the body, especially the mouth and the nose, were thought not only to release the soul but also to let unwanted forces enter, hence they had to be carefully guarded. In certain tribal societies, it was customary to fasten fishhooks to the nose and navel to hook and hold fast the soul, should it escape.[28] Kohl on the eyelids, earrings, nose-rings, and lip-plugs served the same purpose. Similarly, penis sheaths among African and Polynesian tribes prevented the soul's escape, but at the same time also hindered the entry of evil forces, ever ready to slip into all orifices. For this reason, the Chinese were known to plug their nostrils with pieces of jade; a Brahmin traditionally touched his ears when sneezing, as spirits were wont to enter the body through the ears at this time. Amongst various peoples in Africa, Asia, and the Middle East, the custom of covering the mouth can still be observed, not only when sneezing, but also when smiling or laughing.

In Europe during the late 1800s, the sign of the cross was still made instantly over the mouth when yawning to prevent the devil from rushing down the throat and taking up abode. As evil spirits were thought to enter and depart through the natural openings of the body, medieval art often shows black demons escaping the mouths of the possessed during exorcism. Hence, the custom we now observe as etiquette and courtesy, to cover the mouth when coughing, yawning, or sneezing, once had a very different purpose, namely to keep evil spirits out and the soul inside.

According to European folklore, a child was believed to be under the spell of fairies until it sneezed for the first time. Traditionally, considerable importance was therefore attached to a baby's first sneeze. Yet, another notion was linked to the first sneeze. It indicated to concerned parents that the child was mentally normal, based on the widespread belief that idiots never sneezed – strange indeed.

When someone is heard sneezing, we automatically say 'bless you', although the reason for doing so is now generally unknown. Formerly, these words were said to people who, when heard sneezing, were thought to have the first signs of the dreaded plague. The blessing was then meant as an expression of sympathy and distress as bystanders hurried away. The custom of saying 'God bless you' has been attributed to Pope Gregory I, also known as Gregory the Great (540–604 CE), who recommended its use, besides prayers, to protect against infection during an outbreak of the plague.

The Greek historian Thucydides (circa 471–399 BCE) is the first to tell us that sneezing was a mortal symptom of the plague. He writes about the Athenian plague that killed a third of the population of Athens in 429 BCE. This terrible epidemic strengthened the feeling that there was a heightened need for supernatural protection when someone was heard sneezing, as the plague was known to be a mortal disease. For the same reason, the Romans exclaimed absit omen, 'banish the omen', when someone was heard sneezing. The notion that sneezing is an omen, which requires averting, is very ancient and widely diffused. This idea prevailed not only in ancient Greece and Rome, but is also found in Persia, Africa, and the New World.

It has been suggested that the familiar nursery rhyme 'Ring a Ring o' Roses' refers to the Great Plague. The famous refrain 'Atishoo, atishoo, we all fall down' is thought to allude to the fatal symptom of sneezing, an indication of the onset of the dreaded disease.

Various eruptions of the plague over past centuries killed thousands of people on the European continent, the most severe outbreak known as the Black Death wiping out close to a quarter of Europe's population during the fourteenth century – its impact 'not to be sneezed at', which casts the words 'God bless you' in a new light.

Make No Bones About It!

An article published in Time Magazine on November 10, 1952, reported on the Witchdoctor Convention held in Pretoria, South Africa. Attending witchdoctors voted to set up a school in Johannesburg, with a course in 'throwing the bones' as part of the curriculum. Although a dim view was taken of prescriptions that used charred and powdered parts of the human skeleton, at the convention, dozens of ritual murders had taken place that year in South Africa to obtain bones and other body parts for magical purposes. Six decades later on 7 May 2013, a report about traditional South African healers or 'sangomas' by BBC news, alleged that up to eighty percent of South Africans firmly believed that sangomas were able to access advice and guidance through possession by an ancestor or by 'throwing the bones'; tossing the bones like dice, and then reading or interpreting the messages of spirit entities according to how the bones have fallen. This practice is still in widespread use by witchdoctors on the African continent.

Human and animal bones, have been used in divination by the ancient Chinese, and other Asian cultures, as well as in Africa and North America, for thousands of years. Although throwing the bones is seen as a pagan practice, it does not differ in principle from the casting of lots. The casting of lots is frequently mentioned in the Scriptures, serving as a method for choice or selection. For instance, Israel's king was chosen by lot,[29] warriors were chosen by lot,[30] priests offering incense to God in the Temple were chosen by lot,[31] and while Jesus was on the Cross, the soldiers cast lots for his seamless robe.[32] The examples are too many to list but indicate by their frequency how important the casting of lots was considered. To cast lots is an ancient way of making decisions, founded on the firm belief of divine intervention in the outcome. A lot could denote the flip of a coin, a set of specially marked stones (from which dice originated), pieces of bone or knucklebones, sticks with symbols carved into them, or slips of paper mixed up in a hat – the modern version of casting lots. The stones, sticks, or bones were thrown on the ground and then 'read' according to pre-determined rules.

Amongst Pacific Islanders and Australian Aborigines, it was once customary to use a pointing bone as a potent form of sorcery. In Aboriginal tradition, being pointed was a terrifying thought. Once the intended victim knew he had been pointed, he would sicken and die, unless the process was reversed by a medicine man, thereby curing the person.

As with all body parts, bones were universally thought to contain soul-essence and, therefore, were surrounded with many superstitious beliefs. Because bones constitute the longest-lasting parts of the body, they were seen by many societies as the root of life. Interred bones were reverently left undisturbed, as any disturbance of the dead was connected with dire consequences.

In Christian religious tradition, bones in the form of relics were an important focus of worship for hundreds of years. The bones of martyrs, monks, saints, and popes are housed in crypts, chapels, churches, and cathedrals scattered throughout Europe. During medieval times, the acquisition of relics by churches made good business sense. In the same way that oracular sites in ancient times became important and powerful religious destinations, attracting pilgrims and their money, so the bones of famous personages acted as magnets to the Christian faithful. Strictly speaking, the word relic, from Lat. reliquiae, refers to some part of the body or clothing remaining as a memorial of a holy or revered person, but generally, such relics constitute mainly bones and ashes – various martyrs, such as St. Polycarp (circa 156 CE), having been burned at the stake.

The period when it first became common practice to venerate bits of bone, cloth, or parcels of dust housed in religious centres around Europe is difficult to determine. The custom, however, was already widespread amongst Christians during the fourth century. Although the dismemberment and division of the remains of holy personages and martyrs and the sale of relics was expressly forbidden by the Theodosian Code, and later again by Pope Gregory the Great, relics formed an essential part of consecrating churches. During the seventh and eighth centuries, the need for them further increased rather than diminished. This inevitably led to many frauds and abuses perpetrated through motives of greed. The fraudulent aspect surrounding relics was spurned on by the rivalry among religious centres, each keen to possess an especially unusual object to attract the masses. Hence, more and more doubtful relics came to abound, with a tendency to declare any remains accidentally discovered near religious sites as sacred.

As the bones of monks were also revered in the past, various crypts in Europe will delight visiting osteophiles. An example is the macabre Chapel of Bones at the Church of St. Francis in Évora, Portugal, lined with the bones of thousands of monks. Similarly, Rome's Cappuccin Crypt houses hundreds of skeletal remains for the curious tourist to ogle. In the small Austrian town of Hallstadt, limited burial space resulted in the Chapel of Bones at the local cemetery. After spending only twelve years in the ground, bones were exhumed, cleaned, and then made their way into the cemetery chapel. Before being artistically stacked and displayed, all skulls were inscribed with a name, dated, and then beautifully decorated with floral symbols – female skulls with roses, male skulls with ivy.

Bones used in spells, charms, and as medicinal cures were also once popular on the European continent. Obtaining bits of bone for spells and charms was believed of primary importance to witches during the Middle Ages. As late as the nineteenth century, powdered bone was still considered effective for treating assorted physical ailments affecting the skeletal system. To achieve a successful outcome for the patient, it was preferable that the bone particles or pieces had belonged to someone who had died violently. Therefore, the bones of executed persons were often obtained, usually at high prices. (See Chapter I, Curative Powers Associated With the Dead).

In American folk medicine, carrying a piece of bone on one's person was believed to cure backache, toothache, cramps, and fits. However, for children to fall asleep on bones, in other words, on someone's lap, was considered unlucky.

Although most beliefs and superstitions surrounding our bones have been lost in obscurity, bones still play an important role in our language. For example, 'we make no bones' about a topic, by being direct and without scruples; we 'have a bone to pick' when an unpleasant matter needs settling, and we refer to a 'bone of contention', when meaning a point of dispute.

All Thumbs and Poison Fingers

Superstition has always attributed numerous different qualities to the fingers. Many of these beliefs are still commonly held or referred to in jest. Long fingers were thought to predestine a child not only to artistic pursuits, but also to being a spendthrift; a forefinger longer than the middle finger was believed to point to dishonesty; a crooked little finger was seen as a sign of wealth to come, whereas those with bent fingers were thought burdened with an ill-tempered nature; anyone born with extra fingers was believed predetermined for a life of good luck.

In various cultures, the fingers are decorated, a practice traditionally carried out for auspicious, magical, and medical purposes. The ancient Egyptians used henna more than 5,000 years ago to stain the fingers and toes of pharaohs before mummification as protection aiding the soul in the afterlife. Similarly, fingers were tattooed to protect against evil spirits causing diseases such as gout and arthritis, as well as joint sprains. Many mummies found in China, South America, and Egypt attest to this custom.

In the Middle East, India, Pakistan, Indonesia, and other Southeast Asian countries, a temporary art form called mehendi is still practised. Mehendi constitutes intricate designs made with henna on women's fingers and hands. The fingers of traditional brides in these countries are beautifully decorated, and the bride has good reason to look after her henna artwork, as she is not expected to partake in any housework until the colour has worn off.

Various gestures can be made with the fingers to avoid bad luck and protect against evil. People still 'cross fingers' for luck; 'point a finger' to accuse, 'hold thumbs' to ensure good fortune, form a pair of 'horns' with the forefingers to ward off bad luck, 'give the two's-up' or make a 'fig' to show contempt. These are all examples of magic gestures that once had the same function as magic words and magic objects. Many such curious finger signs are still observed, although the original meaning behind these observances has been lost.

Each finger of the hand is held to have specific functions and characteristics. The forefinger or second finger is generally known as the index finger because it is used for pointing. In the past, this finger was referred to as the 'witch's finger', as it was used to cast spells when pointing at unfortunates. Because this finger was considered venomous, it was also known as the 'poison finger'. Therefore, it was never to be used in applying medications and ointments, as this was believed to have unpleasant consequences.

The middle or long-finger was known by several names in the past: medius, medicus, impudicus, and infamis. Popularly, it has always been known as the 'medical finger', and medications were only to be applied with this finger. Although most references collaborate this, it is a contentious issue, as one or two sources specify the fourth or ring finger as the only healing finger and all others as poisonous. Most, however, name the third finger as the medicus and have the physicians of old mixing their potions and medicines only with this finger. It was firmly believed that no venom could stick on the middle finger. Not only was it seen as a healing finger, but also one used for insult. The middle finger when thrust out with the other fingers closed, has always expressed the utmost contempt and derision because of the belief that this finger was connected to the genitals by a specific vein, hence the finger was also called impudicus and infamis, that is, the audacious or detestable.

The fourth finger of the hand, on which the wedding ring is worn, has always been considered lucky. It was believed that a vein, known in Latin as the vena amoris, connected this finger directly to the heart, from where it was thought love emanated. Hence, the fourth finger was generally referred to as the heart finger, but also called annularis or ring finger by the Romans and gold finger by the Anglo-Saxons.

The little finger or 'little man' was also called the 'ear finger' – in many cultures, it is customary to specifically grow the nails on these fingers in order to justify the appellation. Superstitious belief regards this finger as the clever one, hence the saying: 'My little finger told me so', meaning 'I know this, although you did not expect me to'.

The thumb has always been regarded as a symbol of power and is generally known as a luckbringer. The thumb of someone who had died violently was especially a prized object in many European countries. In this context, German philologist and historian Jacob Grimm writes in Teutonic Mythology, his monumental collection of customs and traditions: 'A thief's thumb on your person, or among your wares, makes them go fast'.[33] Similar is this gruesome advice: 'A hanged man's finger hung in the cask makes the beer sell fast'.[34]

The thumb as an emblem of power is clearly indicated by the various gestures made specifically with this digit. By simply holding the thumb towards any suspicious person or object or folding it under the other four fingers, in other words, holding thumbs, it was believed that evil and approaching danger could be averted. To the modern Westerner, the thumb also symbolises clumsiness, hence describing those awkward with their hands as 'all thumbs'. There is another gesture we make with our thumbs. Generally, we interpret the thumbs up sign as upbeat with a distinctly positive connotation. Its origin seems to be from an old English symbol of agreement, dating from medieval times, where a business deal was sealed by the parties involved simply by licking the thumbs, holding them up, and then smudging them together – if only business were that simple in modern times! This custom still resonates when we enthusiastically give a venture the 'thumbs up'. However, curiously, the thumbs up sign has exactly the opposite meaning in the Middle East, West Africa, and some eastern European countries. In these cultures, the gesture is distinctly derogatory, silently voicing great displeasure.

The Magic Power of Hair

Bountiful hair has always been regarded as a mark of beauty in both male and female alike. In the ancient world, hairstyles were indicative of national, religious, tribal, and class differences. Amongst the ancient Egyptians, influential men and women wore decorative wigs – the more elaborate the wig, the more important the wearer – whereas common people favoured shoulder length hair. Their neighbours, the Israelites, traditionally wore their hair long. This changed later when, during New Testament times, they were influenced by the shorter styles of the Romans and Greeks. The Romans regarded long hair as a disgrace, clearly expressed by their disdainful, superior attitude towards the longhaired barbarian Germanic tribes of the north. The Apostle Paul expresses the Romans' contempt for long hair in his letter to the Corinthians: '... if a man have long hair, it is a shame unto him'.[35]

As hair has always been considered one of our most indestructible body parts, numerous beliefs concerning magic properties and the cutting, combing, and disposal of hair abound. In the past, it was firmly held that a person's soul and physical strength were inextricably linked to the hair, therefore, the widespread belief that to cut a man's hair either weakened or killed him – akin to the dying sun losing the strength of its rays. This belief is represented in myths and tales from all parts of the world, the most well-known probably being the story of Samson and Delilah in the Old Testament: 'She [Delilah] made him sleep upon her knees and she called for a man, and she caused him to shave off the seven locks of his head [...] and his strength went from him'.[36]

In ancient times, victorious soldiers sometimes hacked off their enemies' beards to weaken them, as luxuriant facial hair was also regarded as a symbol of strength. One reason behind the supposed connection between bodily strength and hair growth might stem from the observation that boys and eunuchs are beardless. Hence, virility and strength were equated with a profusion of bodily hair, and the simplest way to avoid losing these virtues was not to cut the hair or only on certain occasions. Ancient Egyptian men often left their hair uncut until after an important journey. Frankish kings were not allowed to cut their hair, as this would diminish their power. Similarly, Germanic tribes did not cut their hair or shave until after battle or any other significant expedition, which is probably why the Romans, habitually close-shaven with short hair, thought of them as primitive and barbaric. This is how the Lombards acquired their name. Originally known as Langobardi, meaning 'long-beards', they were a Germanic tribe who, as all Germanic peoples, must have shaved in times of peace, judging from the multitude of razors found in graves and burial sites. Among certain Germanic tribes described by the Roman historian Tacitus, boys in puberty did not shave or cut their hair until after having killed the first enemy in adulthood – the severing of the hair a rite of passage and an indication of bravery and courage.[37]

However, there were also occasions that specifically called for the shaving of hair amongst certain cultures. Throughout history, such hair removal, either from the head or the face, indicated a radical act, marking a time of great suffering or grief. Pliny the Elder tells us that Egyptians shaved their heads to indicate mourning.[38] Similarly, this was customary amongst the Israelites: 'For every head shall be bald, and every beard clipped [...] there shall be lamentations upon all the housetops...'.[39] 'Then Job arose, rent his mantle and shaved his head and fell down upon the ground and worshipped'.[40] The Israelites also performed ritual shavings during certain purification ceremonies.

Amongst early societies, the head was considered universally sacred. According to this viewpoint, hair cutting disturbed the spirit of the head, which could be injured and later seek revenge. Hair cutting, therefore, was considered a delicate, difficult, and dangerous operation. Headhunting amongst these societies was based on the belief that the human head has potential magical powers. These were also thought to be transmitted to the hair, probably because of observations that hair could be cut off without pain or bodily impairment, that it always kept renewing itself and, because of skin shrinkage, even seemed to continue growing after death. Hence, human hair was thought to be endowed with mystical properties.

It was universally believed that hair retained some magical connection with the body even after being shorn off and that the clippings could be used to work contagious magic on the person to whom they belonged. Universally, therefore, various precautions were taken during the cutting or trimming of hair. The Maoris uttered spells when hair was cut, and Brahmins kept up noisy music to drive all evil spirits away. In Japan, 'the hair and nails of the Mikado could only be cut while he was asleep, perhaps because his soul then being absent from his body, there was less chance of injuring it with the shears'.[41]

Whether in New Zealand, the Maldives, ancient Rome, the British Isles, Germany, or Tahiti, the same great care was taken in disposing of hair cuttings. To throw them away was considered imprudent, so they were usually buried or burned, or they could be spat on – spittle being a well-known protective charm. In his book, Healers of Arnhem Land, John Cawte describes how Australian Aborigines, after a haircut at the local barbershop, carefully picked up all their hair clippings off the shop floor and carried them home to store away safely so that nobody could practise borrpoi, or magic, on them.[42]

In Christian countries, the safest method of disposing of hair cuttings was to bury them, which was seen as preferable to burning them, as the person to whom they had belonged was sure to need them on Judgment Day. Further, it was thought that birds might build their nests with discarded or combed out hair, which would be very unpleasant to the person from whose head the hair had come. Jacob Grimm alludes to this in his Teutonic Mythology: 'If a bird carries the hairs to its nest, it gives you headaches or blindness'.[43]

Interestingly, not only the cutting, but also especially the combing of hair seems to be connected worldwide with stormy weather: The ancient Romans believed that one should only cut hair while at sea when a storm was already in progress. Throughout Europe, it was believed that witches could use hair cuttings to raise storms. In the Scottish Highlands, it was believed that any female with a relative at sea should not comb her hair at night, as this would raise storms and imperil the person's life. Curiously, a similar belief is also found amongst the North American Thlinkeet Indians who attributed all stormy weather to a woman having combed her hair outdoors.

Another factor given careful consideration in the past was when and how to cut hair. For the hair to grow back quickly and keep its shine, it was thought that hair should always be trimmed when the moon was waxing. Similarly, some believed that the zodiac was an important consideration when cutting hair. Consequently, it was thought that if hair were cut during the sign of Aries, the sign of the ram, it would grow back very curly or woolly; or if cut during the sign of Leo, an abundant mane of hair would result. Never was hair to be cut on Good Friday or on Saturdays and Sundays, and never was one to attempt cutting one's own hair.

Given the fact that hair is one of the most indestructible parts of the human body and associated with male strength and virility, it was frequently used in magical rites and witchcraft, used as a charm, and used in love potions. During the days of the witch-hunts, it was believed that much of the magical potency ascribed to a witch resided in her hair. At a time, when women covered their heads with hats or scarves, depending on their social standing, and wore their hair modestly pinned up or tied together, shaking the hair loose was seen as a witch casting a spell. Consequently, to meet a woman with her head uncovered was regarded as ominous. This is why depilation of an accused witch frequently preceded torture. Once shorn of all bodily hair, it was believed that the witch became weak and helpless, consequently making the confession required for her execution.

In the past, hair colour was considered important and thought to communicate information about someone's character. Red hair has always been especially regarded with feelings of ambivalence. On the one hand, red hair was associated with a fiery temper, thought to inspire love and passion, and on the other hand, there seems to be a deep-rooted suspicion connected with redheads.

Significantly, some of the most beautiful, passionate, and powerful women in history are said to have had red hair: Helen of Troy, Queen Elizabeth I, Catherine of Russia, and Anne of Austria. But tradition also assigns a reddish tinge to Absalom's hair, and Judas Iscariot is usually depicted with hair of the same colour. As far back as ancient Egypt, red-haired people were regarded with suspicion and dislike. It reminded the ancient Egyptians of the red-haired god Seth, the slayer of Osiris. In honour of Seth, Egyptians customarily sacrificed redheaded people, captives from countries further north, as those with red hair were a rarity in Egypt. In Russia, red-haired people were believed to have more knowledge in magic than others and were not trusted on that account. In Christian countries, it was a common notion, as late as the 1800s, to regard children with red hair as the product of a mother's infidelity.[44] Consequently, these children were considered unlucky and unwelcome in most homes. Regardless of hair colour, however, it was held as unlucky to pluck out any grey hairs, as ten more would grow for every one grey hair forcibly removed.

Of course, in modern Western society where hair colour and texture are habitually changed from one day to the next, where hair is streaked, dyed, bleached, permed, foiled, and straightened according to the dictates of fashion, all these curious beliefs seem as strange as they are obsolete.

While on the subject of hair, it would be remiss not to mention the widow's peak, which refers to a V-shaped descending hairline in the middle of a person's forehead. A widow's peak on a woman was once perceived to mean that she would outlive her husband – in other words, it foretold widowhood. The V-shaped descending hairline was thus named because it was likened to the pointed beak of a specific bonnet worn by widows in various European countries during the sixteenth and seventeenth century to indicate mourning.

The Tooth Fairy

Exactly when the idea of the beautiful tooth fairy fairy leaving coinage for a child's tooth under the pillow emerged in some European countries is unclear, but it seems to have been as late as the 1900s. In the past, the tooth fairy took the shape of a little mouse, which would come and leave some money under a child's pillow in exchange for a milk tooth.

The association of teeth with mice and rats is found in various countries. In Germany, it was believed that a mouse's head hung about a child helped it to teethe. In certain parts of Britain and Germany, if a tooth fell out or was knocked out, it was thrown away with the loud request: 'Rats send me a stronger tooth', as rats' and mice's teeth, able to gnaw through anything, were considered strong. Jewish children in southern Russia practised a similar custom. A tooth that had fallen out was thrown up on the roof with a sincere request to the rats to send a much stronger one. Similarly, thousands of miles away on the island of Rarotonga, part of the Cook Islands in the Pacific Ocean, it is customary for a child whose tooth has fallen out to request another from the rats and mice.

Many strange beliefs concern teething, the teeth, and their disposal, should they fall out. To be born with teeth was looked on as an omen of great misfortune; cutting teeth early was the sign of an early death, as the following saying indicates: 'Soon toothed, soon turfed'; but cutting the lower teeth first, however, was believed to ensure a long life. Milk teeth that fell out had to be burned, for if they should be found and gnawed by an animal, the child's new teeth would be like those of the animal that had gnawed the old ones. When a child's tooth came out of its cavity, the cavity and the tooth should be rubbed with salt to avert any ill luck. Dreaming about one's teeth was seen as an indication of sickness or death in the family. But on a positive note, a gap between the front teeth wide enough to admit a sixpence meant that the child would have riches and prosperity throughout life – a lucrative prospect thoroughly foiled by orthodontists in modern times.

VIII

ANIMALS, PLANTS AND TREES

Birds of a Feather

From ancient times, birds have been regarded as having a close relationship with the various sky-gods dwelling in the heavenly vault and with all heavenly bodies and powers controlling the weather.

Universally, different cultures' mythologies relate how gods appeared in the shape of birds. As symbols of higher powers, birds also became vehicles of humanised representations. Therefore, in Greek art and sculpture, the god Zeus rides an eagle, whereas a swan-drawn chariot drives Apollo, and Aphrodite is borne through the air by a goose. Similarly, Asian divinities are portrayed as mounted on large birds. For instance, the Indo-Chinese warrior god Skanda rides on a peacock and Kama, the Hindu god of love, is appropriately conveyed by a parrot, this bird linked to erotic love in particular.

A widespread belief, common to all myths, legends, and folk tales, is that humans, under certain circumstances, could understand the speech of birds or other animals. Occasionally, people were thought to be born with this gift, but more often, it was believed to be acquired by some mythical feat, such as eating a dragon's flesh. The bird of truth motif is widespread in folk tales and myths, the recurring theme revolving around a bird revealing important information and bearing vital news. Fitting examples are the various flood myths around the globe and fairy tales in which birds deliver intelligible vocal messages. In

Norse mythology, the god Odin had two ravens, Huginn and Muninn, 'Mind' and 'Memory', that roved around the world to gather news. They returned at intervals and, perching on his shoulder, whispered what they had learned into his ear.

Linked to the idea of the bird of truth motif is the widespread belief that birds can serve as guides and oracles in augury. As messengers of higher powers and possessors of secret knowledge, birds have since earliest times been regarded as the harbingers of good and evil. Hence, their behaviour was carefully observed, and auguries drawn from their flight and actions. The ancient Greek and Roman augurs were adept at interpreting the flight of birds, a practice called ornithomancy, which was in fact observed worldwide by differing cultures. Amongst African tribes from the south to the north of the continent, the flight or chirping of birds to the right or left of a specific point was seen as an omen. The same was true of American Indian tribes, indigenous Australians, and on the continents of Asia and Europe.

The direction and manner of flight and calls of birds with sinister associations, such as owls, ravens, or crows, tended to be feared and, hence, considered bad omens. Especially the owl was regarded as an omen of death. Its singular hoots or shrieking, even its appearance alone, had the reputation of heralding horror and disaster. An owl on the roof or flying up against a window augured death inside the house. Shakespeare refers to 'the owl, night's herald' in Venus and Adonis [1] and the owl's role as 'the fatal bellman' in Macbeth. [2] The owl was widely regarded as a demonic bird, housing demons and witches. In the Middle East, it is seen as embodying evil spirits, whereas in China and Japan, the barn owl is believed to be demonic and ill-omened. The bird is also regarded as unlucky by the Maoris and as a messenger of evil entities by Australian Aborigines and African tribes. In Germany, the owl was known as Hexenvogel or 'witch's bird', and in Italy and Sweden, it was believed that owls had the evil eye. Its association with evil forces resulted in its use to ward off these influences; hence, a dead owl nailed to a barn door was thought to prevent fires and other disasters.

While some birds were suspiciously feared, others were eagerly anticipated, as they were the precursors of specific seasonal changes. The annual appearances and disappearances of certain birds must have seriously mystified our forefathers. Their return in spring heralded the rebirth of nature, inspiring general rejoicing, linking some birds, especially the larger species such as the goose, the crane, and the stork with the sun's rays, which would now increase in intensity. The stork, especially, was widely considered a lucky bird, heralding the coming of spring. The word 'stork' comes from the Greek storge, meaning 'strong natural affection'. These birds symbolised filial piety and were credited for their special affection for their young. A factor that might have helped create the myth that the stork delivers babies is the common belief that storks love water and frequent swamps and lakes. Ancient traditions, especially in northern European countries, contended that the souls of unborn children dwelt in these watery places. So, it was easy to link these ancient beliefs to the majestic white birds, known for the tender care of their young, as lovingly delivering a new baby to expectant parents.

Another bird joyously welcomed as heralding spring in most European countries was the cuckoo. In the United Kingdom, the cuckoo's first calls were traditionally reported in the Times newspaper. As this event was so eagerly anticipated, many superstitious beliefs evolved around hearing the cuckoo's first calls, the most important being that a wish was immediately to be made when hearing its first call to ensure prosperity for the year ahead and to turn any coins in one's pocket.

On the other hand the disappearance of various birds in autumn incited disquiet amongst people and aroused speculation. In Europe, it probably gave rise to the belief dating back to antiquity that a cuckoo turned into a hawk in winter, thereby explaining the disappearance of this bird during the cold season. Alternately, some birds were thought to visit the land of the dead, probably related to knowing that winter's bleakness and nature's death were now imminent.

As messengers of the gods, birds were perceived as being wiser than humankind and holding secret knowledge. Hence, the courtship and other social displays of certain birds awakened in early societies the notion that they were engaging in some magical ceremony. It was, therefore, common to copy the birds' rituals, believing them to promote fertility and to encourage the onset of seasonal rains. North American

Indians and the Indians of Central America imitated bird behaviour in their rainmaking ceremonies. Similarly, in ancient Crete and in Japan, a crane dance was believed to produce rains; and in Yugoslavia, it was customary for boys to perform fertility dances, imitating a cock, during spring ceremonies.

Another factor that has influenced the folklore and superstition surrounding birds is their colouring. The cock's red crown inspired tales that the cock was responsible for removing the nails from Christ's Cross; the robin's red breast is reputed to have originated from Christ's blood when the bird pulled thorns from His crown; black, being linked with the devil and sorcery, connected black birds such as the crow or the raven with evil forces; whereas pure white birds were traditionally regarded as uncanny, awakening fear, because they were viewed as portents of death.

Our feathered friends are still popularly referred to in many common phrases. We speak of 'a bird in the hand being worth two in the bush', meaning that possession is better than expectation; we mention that 'birds of a feather flock together', in other words, that those with a similar mindset and taste form close associations; and we prefer to 'kill two birds with one stone', implying that it is advantageous to effect two objectives with only one outlay of effort and trouble.

The Cock – Favourite of the Gods

The central role the cock plays in folklore and myths worldwide is because of its loud crowing, its proud strutting, its aggressiveness, and its sexual ardour. Pliny the Elder, in his Natural History, praises the virtues of this bird in the highest terms: 'They have a knowledge of the stars and mark out each three-hour interval during the day with song, go to sleep at sunset, and in the fourth watch of the night, recall us to our duties and toil. They prevent the sunrise from creeping up on us unnoticed and announce the arrival of the day with song'.[3]

In all cultures, malevolent forces and the appearance of spirits were considered particularly active at night, hence, they were known as the powers of darkness. Therefore, the cock's crowing at dawn, heralding daybreak, was seen as a welcome indication that these forces had been dispelled. Eventually, the belief arose that the bird was effective in exorcising evil, frightening away devils, warding off ghosts, and scaring away dangerous animals.

Early Christians divided the night into four watches called the evening, midnight, cock crowing, and morning watch. It was tradition among common people – when class distinction in society was unquestionably accepted – to believe that, at cockcrow, all demons, spirits, and witches, abounding during the darkness of night, disappeared. This is why in country villages, where the way of life required an early start to the day's labours, inhabitants cheerfully went to work at cockcrow. Shakespeare reiterates this belief in Hamlet when the ghost of Hamlet's father suddenly disappears at cockcrow: 'It faded on the crowing of the cock. [...] And then they say no spirit can walk abroad, [...] no fairy takes, nor witch has power to charm'.[4]

The proud fearless strutting of the cock made him the symbol of dauntless courage, the protector of the weak, especially women and children. Not only did the bird hail the rising sun, but he also possessed a crimson comb that symbolised the fiery-pointed beams of the sun. Therefore, the cock was regarded as doubly sacred to the sun. Linked with the rising sun, the cock's image in ancient times assured protection from the sun-god, whereas the cock's crowing was seen as a hymn of praise to this deity. This is why in mythologies around the world, the cock performed the function of trumpeter to sun deities of practically all nations.

With the expansion of the Persian Empire, the sacred standing of the cock spread to Greece, where it was dedicated to the sun-god Apollo. In Scandinavian mythology, the function of the vigilant golden cock Vithafmir, also known as Gullinkambi or 'goldcomb', sitting on the ash tree Yggdrasil, was to guard against all evil. The Chinese believe that it is the cock's function to awaken the golden sun, which dispels darkness and disperses the evil spirits of the night. According to Islamic legend, a giant cock occupies the first heaven. When it ceases to crow, the Day of Judgment will be at hand.

To Christians, the cock's crowing represented alertness to temptation and vigilance to the devil's wiles. This is why cocks were placed on church towers – the vanes atop steeples made in the form of a cock reminding the faithful to be watchful. It was once firmly believed that on the Day of Judgment, all cockerels, even those made of wood and iron, would crow to wake the dead and the living.

Throughout the ages, in most cultures, the cock has been a chief sacrificial creature, its blood also used in magical rites and for casting spells. The Romans believed the bird to be especially favoured by the gods, hence, not only suitable for sacrifice, but also for divination. Pliny the Elder tells us that 'cocks hold very great power over the government of the world, being thanks to their entrails and innards, as acceptable to the gods as the most costly victims'.[5] In ancient Mexico, these birds were sacrificed to the sun. Similarly, cocks were sacrificed by the Arabs and are still used in various magic rituals among African and Pacific Island tribes. As guardians against all evil entities, these birds were buried under the foundations of buildings, dykes, and bridges in Europe, replacing the original human sacrifices offered to the appropriate deities.

In European countries, the black cock was eyed with great superstition and fear. It was generally thought to be linked to evil forces, which is why its blood was extensively used for magical incantations and sacrifice to the devil. Demons and the souls of the damned were believed to inhabit black cocks, and most witches in England and on the Continent were believed to have such a bird besides the traditional black cat. It is interesting to note that the association of black with evil forces is specifically Christian, as the colour was regarded as sacred by many pagan peoples. In Africa for instance, black was a revered colour and sacrifices to the moon-goddess always constituted black animals. Similarly, in Greek lore, black was one of the three most sacred colours, dedicated to the moon-goddess.

Curiously, the blood of cocks is not only linked to sacrifice and magic, but was also used in folk remedies to heal the sick. In Europe, a possible connection of the cock with the healing arts might be explained through its association with Apollo, who in Greek mythology was connected with the healing arts. However, this does not clarify why the bird was generally used in so many cultures, that is, Asian, African, and European countries, for the same purpose. In Ceylon, it was traditional for a cock to be dedicated to a sick person and to be sacrificed when that person recovered. In certain areas of Germany, it was customary to bury the head, heart, and right foot of a black cock under the threshold of dwellings, to keep illness and other evil influences at bay. A cure for epilepsy used in many European countries was to bury a cock under the house. To ensure a cure for other ailments and diseases, it was often thought sufficient, simply to rub a live cock over the affected body parts. Alternately, a black cock was buried alive with some hair or nail parings belonging to the patient needing a cure. At the heart of this universal superstition lies the belief that illness could be transferred to the earth or to another being.

In Europe, the various crowing habits of the cock led to many curious beliefs. For example, the cock's crowing at an unusual hour, especially after dark, was seen as an omen of death; the crowing of a cock heard at the moment of someone's departure or the birth of a child was also considered a bad omen; however, if a cock and a hen were seen sitting together on St. Valentine's morning, this was regarded as a sure sign that someone in the household would be getting married soon. No doubt such superstitions in modern times are labelled as mere 'cock and bull' stories – from the English word concocted and the Danish word bullen, meaning 'exaggerated'!

The Wise, Healing Serpent

From the beginning of time, on every continent on Earth, the serpent has been worshipped as well as reverently feared, and serpent mythology is arguably the most widespread known to humankind. Myths and legends from steaming Africa and Asia to the icy waters of northern Europe to outback Australia include tales of great serpents, dragons, and monster reptiles. Traditionally, these were regarded as the keepers of esoteric knowledge, revered as the guardians of temples and treasures and closely linked to the earth's waters.

In Indian, Egyptian, Cambodian, Sri Lankan, Central and South American, as well as African myth and legend, the serpent is symbolic of deity, eternity, and wisdom. As an emblem of eternity, the so-called

Ouroboros serpent is depicted forming a circle with its body, holding its tail in its mouth.

The serpent's connection with wisdom is found not only in ancient myths and legends worldwide, but also in the New Testament: 'Behold, I send you forth as sheep in the midst of wolves: be ye therefore wise as serpents, and harmless as doves'.[6] Similarly, the biblical account of Genesis states that '...the serpent was the shrewdest of all the wild beasts'.[7]

As a symbol of deity, the serpent is universally connected to the gods and goddesses of various cultures. The serpent is an attribute to the Sumerian goddess Ishtar, and the Cretan goddess Ariadne is depicted as wreathed in snakes or holding a serpent in each hand. On the altars of ancient Greeks and Romans, the snake was frequently represented as a protective entity. Hence, in the temple of Athena on the Parthenon in Athens, caged serpents were kept as divine presences, revered as the guardian spirits of the temple. Athena herself bears a serpent on her shield and is often identified with this creature of the gods.

The association of the serpent with the Earth's waters – underground water sources, springs, rivers, and lakes – is universal. Dwelling in the Earth, frequenting springs, marshes, and other water streams, the serpent was seen as gliding with a motion of waves. The Egyptian and the Mayan hieroglyph for water was a zigzag or wavy line representing the ripple of a wave. This universal, prehistoric sign has ever since represented 'water' or 'spirit'. Among the Mayans, the wavy hieroglyph for water terminated with the head of a snake, relating to the similarity of undulating water and a moving serpent. For this reason, they named the sea Canah, meaning 'Great and Powerful Serpent'. Another example is the anaconda, the giant serpent of South America. This word is made up of anak, meaning 'giant' and onda, meaning 'waves', thereby again connecting the serpent to the Earth's waters.

In Africa, 'early representations of serpent or dragon energies were symbolised by a spiral – the coiled serpent of the primordial waters known as kundalini – or by a zigzag line which represented a serpent in motion, the earth currents, the ripple of flowing water, life itself'.[8] In this context, it is interesting to note that the reptilian lizard or serpent men of Australian Aboriginal myth are called kondili. Symbolically, serpents were also used to invoke the powerful magnetic energies of the Earth, which is why they are found engraved and painted on sacred objects and rocks worldwide.

In Hindu mythology, the serpent represents the creative force. Early imagery of the god Vishnu shows him reclining on the Cosmic Serpent, which is in turn resting on the Cosmic Waters. In Celtic tradition, the serpent is connected with healing waters. In Nordic mythology, the Midgard serpent circles the world, representing the all-embracing ocean. In Central and South American myth, the creator god and the god of resurrection is the feathered serpent of the Aztecs' Quetztalcoatl or Kulkulcan, as the Maya call him. Chinese myth hardly distinguishes the serpent from the dragon. Both are symbolic of water's fertilising power. In Africa, the serpent is similarly linked with water, where snakes herald the wet season and the resulting rebirth of nature. Rainmaking ceremonies amongst African tribes, North American Indians, Melanesian tribes, and Australian Aborigines include traditional snake dances, whereas the myths and legends of these peoples depict the serpent as a rainbow or sky-hero.

The Rainbow Serpent is one of the most powerful mythological figures for all Aboriginal people throughout Australia. As in mythologies around the world, it is linked with watercourses, waterholes, and rock pools and thought to bring rain. The Aboriginal word Ngaljod or Nagal amongst certain Aboriginal tribes in western Arnhem Land strongly reminds us of Naga, the Indian serpent lord, or Nagual, the name of the Mexican serpent spirit guardian. Interestingly, Nák is the Egyptian serpent god with human arms and legs, and Nidhogg is the Norse serpent at the base of the World Ash. In Chinese myth, Nukua is the serpent goddess who formed the first people. The same root for serpent seems to pervade the African languages. In the Bantu languages of Sotho and Tswana, a serpent is called noga; in Xhosa and Zulu, it is nyoka.

A belief existed in India about a variety of snake known as the shesh nag. When the snake reached the legendary age of a thousand years, a precious stone was thought to form in its head. This stone, when applied to an affected body part, had the power to render the poison from any reptile harmless. This belief possibly permeated to Europe or originated there independently, because the fantastic tales about a legendary stone emanating from a snake took on various forms on that continent. The stone was thought to be a precious stone embedded in the head of a snake, one that the snake spat out, or alternatively, a stone magically fashioned by many snakes.

Similar tales are also found in Africa, where Xhosa folklore tells of a monster serpent believed to inhabit a gorge in the Drakensberg Mountains. In ages past, young maidens were regularly sacrificed to this monster, which was adorned with an enormous diamond in its forehead, just above the eyes. Furthermore, the African Basotho still believe that malicious snakes with a brilliant light shining from their heads inhabit deep pools and rivers in Lesotho.[9] The story of precious stones shed from the heads of serpents and dragons is also found in China, where the dragon's head is always supposed to contain some or other precious stone. Chinese works of art also often depict dragons with pearls in their mouths.

From ancient times, the serpent was credited with the power to incarnate the souls of the dead. As such incarnations could include the souls of ancestors, snakes seeking refuge in dwellings were never killed, but treated with reverence and respect. For example, any snake entering an African homestead was traditionally regarded as an ancestor returning with a message or demand. Similarly, the early Hebrews believed that all snakes entering a house were disembodied spirits. Pet snakes kept in Greece, Crete, and Rome were always treated with great veneration. This tradition is also found in northern and western European countries, where snakes were respected in households. In Germany, Norway, and Denmark, it was customary for families to have their own so-called house snake, both as a rat-catcher and as a guardian house spirit – made all the easier, because snakes in these countries were harmless creatures. Many cultures share the tradition that snakes have a guardian or protective influence. Therefore, tattoos often took the form of snakes, and in European countries, a dead snake's skin hung above the hearth was believed to protect the household and ensure good luck.

Snakes have been linked with the healing arts for thousands of years. The importance and effectiveness of the snake in healing remedies and cures is strengthened by the Old Testament account: 'And Moses made a serpent of brass, and put it upon a pole, and it came to pass that if a serpent had bitten any man, when he beheld the serpent of brass he lived'.[10] In ancient Greece and Rome, respectively, the snake was sacred to Asklépios or Aesculapius, the god of medicine and healing. In this context, we are reminded of the Greek snake symbol, the caduceus, still in constant use and recognised internationally as the symbol of medicine. Interestingly, the intertwined snakes of the caduceus mimic the intertwining of snakes during the mating ritual, a common symbol used to depict the DNA helix.

In western European countries, snakes were considered essential in medical cures and constituted a profitable trade item throughout the Middle Ages until the nineteenth century. Using snakes for healing purposes was so popular that snakes were brought to Paris in their thousands, tied together in bundles of twelve. When the French Academy of Sciences tried to ban the import of poisonous snakes in 1820, physicians requested that an exception be made with vipers, as they were thought vital to effect certain cures.[11] Generally, snakes were dried and pulverised or boiled. The fat gleaned from this process was made into a salve or oil. Snake powder ingested or salve used as a cream was believed efficacious in curing countless ailments and diseases ranging from arthritis, eye problems, cancer, epilepsy, stomach, kidney, and intestinal problems to boils, skin lesions, toothache, and nerve complaints. The eating of snake flesh, only affordable to very wealthy ladies, was also even thought to have anti-aging effects – a curious notion indeed!

Such examples of the varying pseudo-medicinal uses of once widely used snake products serve to explain the popular phrase of 'selling snake-oil', derogatory for bogus, fraudulent, and ineffective medication sold as a cure-all.

The Magical, Mythical Cat

Although cats are considered the most magical of animals, traditions vary whether they are viewed as fortunate or unfortunate omens. Cat lore, especially concerning the black cat, is complicated and all superstitions concerning the colour of cats depended on where one lived. In the United States and some European countries, such as Germany, Spain, and Belgium, the black cat was considered very unlucky, whereas the white cat was considered a favourable omen. If, however, a black cat should follow someone on the street, come walking towards a person, or come voluntarily into a home, this was considered a sign of good fortune to come, even in countries where the black cat was generally seen as unlucky.

In Britain, almost the only nation to do so, black cats were considered lucky omens, but white cats were viewed with great distrust. Perhaps the most famous superstition concerning cats is that of a black cat crossing one's path. This was believed to portend good luck, and for many years, it was fashionable at society weddings in London to have a black cat purposefully walking across the bride's path. If popular legend is believed, Charles I (1600–1649) owned a black cat, which was closely guarded, as he had a suspicious dread of losing the animal. When the cat eventually died, he is reputed to have said: 'My luck is gone'. A prediction, which came about the following day when he was arrested and later executed.[12]

In the ancient world, cats were invested with an aura of holiness. The ancient Egyptians regarded cats as the guardians of the Underworld and accorded divine status to these animals. Cats were sacred to the Egyptian Goddess Isis and her daughter Bast, a cat-headed goddess worshipped at Bubastis. [13] Cats were also popular household pets in ancient Egypt, as the Greek historian Herodotus, renowned as the Father of History relates: 'What happens when a house catches fire is most extraordinary: nobody takes the least trouble to put it out, for it is only the cats that matter: everyone stands in a row, a little distance from his neighbour trying to protect the cats, who nevertheless slip through the line, or jump over it and hurl themselves into the fire. This causes the Egyptians deep distress. All the inmates of a house where a cat has died a natural death shave their eyebrows...'.[14] If the pet cat died, its corpse was often taken to Bubastis, where it was embalmed and buried with much ceremony. Well-preserved ancient Egyptian cat mummies, as well as the mummies of mice – possibly intended as food for the cats – have been found in great numbers.

The ancient Greeks identified the cat with Artemis, to whom this animal was sacred, as well as with the goddess Hecate. Through Hecate, queen of the spirits of the dead, the cat became linked with the Underworld in Greek mythology. Cats were Hecate's favourite creatures, and she extended special treatment to them.

The Romans believed cats were sacred to the goddess Diana – associated with the moon, virginity, and hunting. Diana was known to assume the shape of a cat on various occasions. In ancient Rome, the cat was a symbol of freedom and the goddess of liberty was depicted with a cat at her feet—it is well known that no animal is as opposed to restraint as the cat.

Similar to ancient Egyptian, Greek, and Roman mythology, the cat also held sacred status in northern Europe. In Norse mythology, the cat was an attribute of Freyja, goddess of love, marriage, and the dead, whose chariot was pulled by black cats. To feed stray cats was believed to win Freyja's favour, bringing good fortune and prosperity to all so charitably inclined.

Although the cat was highly esteemed in the ancient world, Christianity connected the animal specifically to witchcraft and Satan, turning the cat into a witch's familiar. Derived from the Latin term famulus, meaning servant, 'familiars' were believed to be demons in human or animal form, feeding on witches' blood and doing everything according to their bidding. It was generally accepted that the witch could take on the shape of these familiars. Witches have always been linked to the belief in the power of transformation. The cat, the raven, the wolf, the hare and the sow were the favourite animals, whose shape witches and those possessed of the evil eye were thought to assume. In days gone by many people would show a reluctance to discuss family matters in the presence of a cat, just in case it was a witch's familiar or a witch in disguise. Therefore, a cat was never to be left alone with an infant, as this could result in the child being bewitched. It was also thought that the cat would creep into the cradle to suck the breath from the infant.

Specific characteristics, peculiar to cats served to link them to witchcraft. Evil forces were traditionally believed to be active at night, which was corroborated by the nocturnal character of the cat.

Additionally it's oddly independent behaviour, eyes contracting and dilating ominously in the dark and its eerie, almost human-like cries in the stillness of night reinforced the notion of the cat's connection with evil. As cats prowled through the night, seeing in the dark, they became a symbol of intuition, linked with supernatural, mediumistic powers. Together with the colour black, reminiscent of the forces of darkness, all the above-mentioned factors compounded in Christian Europe, to connect black cats with witches and evil spirits. As a result, large numbers of unfortunate cats suffered abominable treatment and were burnt alive during the Middle Ages, because of their imagined connection with witchcraft.

The modern superstition that a cat has nine lives derives from the belief that it was permitted for a witch to take on the body of a cat nine times only. After seven years a cat was thought to turn into a witch. Often cats were marked with crosses to prevent them from turning into witches, or they were given another name, only known to select family members, in the belief that a witch could not take on the cat's body if she did not know its name.

A magical skill generally attributed to cats was their ability to forecast the weather. In Europe, it was thought that when cats were seen to wash their ears or eat grass, rain could be expected; when they scampered wildly, high winds were bound to come up; when they sat with their backs to the fire or sneezed, it meant upcoming frost and storms; and to wash a cat most certainly brought on rain. A similar superstition is found in Indonesia, where it was believed that to pour water over a cat's back produced rain. In the past, European seamen firmly believed that cats brought luck to a ship, holding the conviction that a cat was invaluable when a ship was becalmed, as the animal could raise a good wind by simply being placed under a pot on deck. To throw any cat overboard was considered unthinkable, as this would most certainly raise a storm.

The cat, its blood and hair, was for hundreds of years credited with curative powers for various ailments. During the Middle Ages, right through to the nineteenth century, bizarre concoctions from the feline's blood and hair were especially used to cure shingles and whooping cough. Folk remedies against whooping cough traditionally consisted of chopping up nine tail hairs of a black cat, soaking them in water, and then drinking the infusion. During the seventeenth century, it was common in Europe to boil a whole cat in olive oil, as this was thought to be an excellent wound dressing. The boiled skin on its own was also used to relieve toothache. The cat's tail was especially considered effective in many remedies, which accounted for the fact that the tails were often simply cut off! A popular remedy for various eye diseases was to stroke or rub a black cat's tail over the eyelid three or nine times – whether the animal's body was still attached while this procedure was carried out remains unclear. If drawn over the eyes, a cat's tail was believed to remove sties. However, if sickness and disease resisted all the mentioned conventional forms of treatment, a last customary option was simply to transfer all ailments to the family cat by dousing the unsuspecting animal with the patient's washing water or urine and then noisily chasing it from the house – with or without the tail attached.

In the past, on board ship, a different kind of cat's tail, known as cat-o'-nine-tails, was respectfully feared and avoided by all sailors. This constituted a whip, initially with three, then six, and lastly nine lashes with several knots tied into each lash to inflict maximum pain. It was used for punishing offenders and briefly called 'the cat'.

The Rose — Funeral Flower and Symbol of Silence

The word rose comes from the Latin term rosa which is expressive of red colour. Therefore, etymology would make the rose a red flower par excellence, yet there are anomalies such as the white rose, the yellow rose, and we even speak of a red rose.

Because of the universal popularity of this favourite blossom, all countries have variations on rose myths, tales, and legends. However, it might be said that this beautiful flower universally symbolises the heavenly Spirit of the Highest. In Greek mythology, Cupid spilt nectar on Olympus, roses springing forth where the nectar touched the ground. Greek legend tells us that Aphrodite, while hastening to her wounded lover Adonis, trod on a white rosebush. The thorns tore her feet, and her sacred blood dyed the white rose forever red. Aphrodite then presented the rose to her son Eros, the god of love. Similarly, in Roman mythology, the rose sprang from blood spurting from Venus' foot while she was pursuing Adonis. Hence, the rose became Venus' symbol, representations showing the goddess of love crowned with roses. Both Eros – which in English and French happens to be an anagram of 'rose' – the Greek god of love, and Hymen, the Greek god of marriage, are often represented crowned with rose wreaths. It is, therefore, easy to understand why the rose became symbolic of love and beauty.

The Romans cultivated roses on a large scale, using them to strew on banquet hall floors, to fill cushions, to decorate their gods' shrines and their heroes' monuments, to make wine and perfume, and to garland those honoured in Roman society. In Islamic belief, roses sprang up from the ground wherever the perspiration from Mohammed's brow dripped. In Hindu myth, Lakshmi was born of a rose, and it is said by the Brahmins that the Almighty has his permanent abode in the heart of a silver rose. The Persian word for rose is gul, meaning the 'Mighty God'.

Common to many myths is the belief that the rose stemmed from spilt blood. According to Christian tradition, the flower's red colour originated from the fact that the Crown of Thorns worn by Christ was made of rose briars. Another legend holds that the red rose sprang from the extinguished branches heaped around a virgin martyr at Bethlehem.

The ancient Greeks and the Romans attached great value to the rose as a funeral flower, especially planting it on lover's graves. In Austria, Germany, and Switzerland, cemeteries are still often referred to as rose gardens because of this flower's significance for the dead. In England and on the Continent, white roses were traditionally planted on a virgin's tomb, whereas red roses were considered appropriate for the grave of any person distinguished for goodness and benevolence. (See Chapter VI, Flowers and Trees for the Dead).

Regarding the various superstitions attached to it, the rose is one of the most ominously significant of all flowers. If a rose shed its petals, this was believed to be a portent of death, especially when someone was wearing or carrying the flower. In a similar vein, roses blooming out of season were once looked on with misgiving as this foretold misfortune in the year ahead. In Germany, a white rosebush 'putting out' unexpectedly was believed to be a sign of death in the nearest house and to dream of a white rose or withered roses was thought to prognosticate death.

The rose as a symbol of silence, confidentiality, and secrecy is indicated by the Latin phrase sub rosa, 'under the rose'. The 'rosette' still often found gracing the ceilings of older homes is a remnant of this symbol. As an emblem of secrecy, roses also decorated the ceilings of council chambers and banquet halls to remind everyone that what was spoken there was confidential or sub rosa, even if it happened to be sub vino, in other words, 'under the influence of wine'. As a symbol of silence, carved roses were also commonly placed over confessionals in churches. The origin of the phrase sub rosa is probably to be found in Greek myth, relating that Eros, the god of love, gave a rose to Harpocrates, the god of silence, to induce him to keep the amours of Aphrodite a secret. However, some maintain that the true origin of the saying sub rosa comes from the perpetual plotting and counter-plotting between the Houses of York and Lancaster during the War of the Roses (1455–1485). Supporters of the House of Lancaster habitually wore a red rose, and those of the House of York, a white rose in their caps. When an important matter was communicated by either party to a friend in the same quarter, it was said to be 'under the rose', in other words, to be kept secret.

After the War of the Roses, the flower became one of the foremost heraldic emblems. This war, lasting for thirty years, ended with the establishment of the House of Tudor on the English throne. Therefore, the Rose of Tudor, represented as a white rose on a red one, is the flower emblem of England today.

From the common practice during the Middle Ages of naming collections of verse after bunches of flowers – hence anthology, from the Greek word for 'flower' – comes the rosary. From the Latin term rosarium, meaning 'rose garden', the rosary is a beadroll used by Roman Catholics for keeping count of their repetitions of certain prayers. The term was probably encouraged by the symbolic association of roses with the Virgin Mary, the red and white Mystical Rose appearing early in the Christian period as an emblem of the Virgin. Others maintain that the word 'rosary' is derived from fact that the first chaplets being made of rosewood.

Because the rose is a symbol of love, lovers attach importance to the flower's colour. Red roses are symbolic of passion, whereas white roses stand for pure love and yellow roses for infidelity.

Royal Fleur-de-Lis

Native to southern Europe and the Mediterranean region, the iris has been considered a symbol of power and strength throughout the ages. This multi-coloured flower was named after Iris, the Greek goddess of the beautiful many-shaded rainbow. One duty of the goddess Iris was to lead the souls of dead women to the Elysian Fields, which is why this flower was often planted specifically on women's graves. Throughout the centuries, the iris was placed on the sceptres of kings and rulers because the three large petals of the flower symbolise faith, wisdom, and valour.

The popular French term fleur-de-lis refers to a stylised flower design, common to all eras and many cultures. Ornamentation resembling this symbol is found on Mesopotamian cylinders and in ancient Egyptian art and depicted on Mycenean pottery, on coins from ancient Gaul, and in Indonesian and Japanese designs. It is also represented in heraldic emblems, appearing on many European coats of arms and flags.

The fleur-de-lis is particularly linked with the French monarchy. The term fleur-de-lis is a corruption of Fleur-de-Löys, and Löys is how French kings, from King Louis I in the ninth century right up to King Louis XII in the sixteenth century, signed their names. The Fleur-de-Löys was the common purple iris, and not the white lily, as the fleur-de-lis has falsely been referred to in the past. According to historic tradition, when Louis VII, King of France (1121–1180) was setting out on his crusade to the Holy Land, he chose the purple iris as his heraldic emblem. From then onwards, the flower became known as the Flower of Louis, or the Fleur-de-Löys, which in later times degenerated to fleur-de-lis. But not until the reign of Charles IV (1294–1328) did the iris officially adorn all banners of France.

However, the iris featured in French historical lore long before the thirteenth century. Legend has it that when King Clovis I of the Franks defeated the Alemanni in 496 CE in the Battle of Tolbiac, his victorious soldiers crowned themselves with hundreds of irises blooming near the battlefield.

Touch Wood

At the dawn of history, Europe was covered with immense primeval forests that stretched for thousands of kilometres. Pliny the Elder tells us in his work, Natural History, that on the northern European continent, Germanic tribes travelled through forests for months without ever reaching a clearing.[15] Excavations have revealed that the Po Valley of modern Italy was once covered with extensive forests of elms, chestnuts, and especially oaks. Similarly, in antiquity, the Greek peninsula was clothed in dense forests from sea to sea. The British Isles were just as densely forested, with trees covering the whole south-eastern portion of the island and the west coast. Therefore, it is hardly surprising that tree-worship, uniform in its rites and celebrations in all European cultures, has played such a significant part in religious history. Jane Philpot expounds on this subject in her well-known book, The Sacred Tree: 'The worship of the tree was not only the earliest form of divine ritual, but was the last to disappear before the spread of Christianity; it existed long before the erection of temples and statues to the gods, flourished side by side with them and persisted long after they had disappeared'.[16]

In forested countries, one of the most favoured seats of the gods was perceived to be in trees, their mysterious growth thought to be determined by the supernatural forces housed within. In these regions, the life of all humans depended largely on trees for survival. Trees supplied shelter, shade, and fuel; houses were built of wood; timber provided warmth during the long European winters, and the fruits from various trees yielded nourishment not only for livestock, but also humans.

Because some trees live for hundreds of years, seemingly dying every winter and being mysteriously reborn in spring, they were thought to harbour supernatural powers. Adding to their mystery was that trees were observed as spanning the three layers of the cosmos, their roots set firmly in the Underworld, their trunks in the world of mortals, and their canopies reaching into the heavenly world of the skies, the abode of the gods. Possibly the best known European example of this is the Scandinavian World Ash Tree, Yggdrasil, of the Eddas, the wondrous verses capturing the myths and legends of the North. Like the Sephirothal Tree of the Kabbalists and the Asvatha Tree of the Hindus, the mighty Yggdrasil has three roots reaching out into three different worlds. One root reaches up to the land of the gods, where they gather daily beneath its branches to hold their council meetings; the middle root goes to the land of the Frost giants; the third root extends to the Underworld, where Nidhogg the giant serpent gnaws at it, while an inexhaustible spring bubbles through the ages.

The symbol of the majestically spreading tree features in mythologies worldwide and is an emblem for the cosmos, youth, life, immortality, and wisdom. Hence, there are Cosmic Trees, Trees of Life, Trees of Immortality, Trees of Knowledge, Trees of Youth, Trees of Speech, and Wishing Trees, represented in differing cultures and their myths. Trees came to express everything religious and sacred to humankind. Therefore, myths describing a quest for youth or immortality were about sacred trees with magic fruit or leaves, growing in a distant land, guarded by dragons, snakes, or griffins. In antiquity, such monsters were emblems of wisdom rather than of cunning and had to be confronted by the hero for him to reach his goal successfully.

In the past, tree-worship was based on the notion that the world at large was animate. This meant that everything in nature possessed a soul and was therefore accorded the necessary reverence and respect. There was a time in Britain and on the Continent when it was a punishable offence to chop down a tree. All trees were regarded as sheltering tree-spirits, which were offended and inclined to be vengeful if their abode was harmed in any way. It was believed that should a man chop a large branch off a tree, he would later lose a limb. Every tree was thought to feel any injuries, so when an oak was being felled '...it gives a kind of shriek or groan, that may be heard a mile off, as if it were the genius of the oake lamenting'.[17]

When a paddy of rice was in bloom, the Javanese regarded it as pregnant, and no noise was made near the field lest they spoil the crop. In the African Congo, calabashes of liquid were placed at the foot of certain trees for them to drink. In India, shrubs and trees were formally married, and in Germany, peasants used to tie fruit trees together, thus marrying them in the hope that they would bear fruit. The medicine men of African tribes profess to have heard the cry of pain emitted by trees cut down. This might not be as far-fetched as it seems. In his book, The Secret Life of Plants, Peter Tompkins describes experiments conducted in the U.S. and Russia that confirm that plants and trees emit sounds; inaudible to us but which might be registered by specially designed sensitive electronic instruments.[18]

Amongst Christians, the mournful tree, which gave its wood for the Cross of Calvary, has always been a disputed question and has caused many curious legends about various trees. Foremost amongst the trees with this dubious distinction are the aspen, the poplar, the oak, the mistletoe, and the elder – all trees revered as sacred during pagan times. Hence, there are legends explaining the shivering of the aspen leaf and the trembling of the poplar. Apparently, the oak was the only tree that did not split itself in half to avoid being desecrated when the Jews were looking for wood to build the Cross. This is why many woodcutters tended to avoid the oak, as they regarded it as an accursed tree.

The once sacred mistletoe, which now exists as a parasite, was not spared either. Legend has it that it existed as a fine, tall forest tree before the Crucifixion, its present condition being a lasting monument to the disgrace it incurred through its ignominious use. The elder tree was similarly singled out. Although the elder does not naturally grow in Palestine, the legend arose that its wood was used to make the Cross of Calvary on which Christ was crucified. This would explain the widespread antipathy to using elder twigs for firewood. In the past, all firewood was carefully checked for elder pieces, as it was considered dangerous by the superstitious to burn elder wood, known widely as 'wicked wood', because of its association with the Cross. It is, however, possible that the elder's unlucky reputation long predates Christianity and that the awesome respect accorded this tree has its roots in old pagan beliefs of northern Europe. To this day, it is said in Denmark that a being called the 'elder-mother' protects the tree so that it is not safe to damage it in any way.

Another universal belief regarding trees is that they are bound up with humanity's health and lives. For hundreds of years, it was customary in Europe to plant trees at the birth of a child, whose life and well being was then forever thought connected with the growth and health of the tree – if the tree died, the person it represented would also die. In northern European countries, children were still passed through cleft trees to cure various ailments as late as the early 1900s. Among the Maori, the power of making women fertile was once ascribed to trees, and barren women were directed to embrace trees to alleviate their shortcoming. Slav women hung an undergarment on a tree bearing plenty of fruit so that through contagious magic they themselves would be made fruitful. The power of easing delivery during childbirth was ascribed to certain trees, known as 'birthing trees'. Hence, in Sweden and other European countries, women in labour clasped ash or elm trees to ensure an easy delivery.

Those who, in modern times, still touch wood or knock on it for luck unknowingly do so because of ancient tree-worship. There is only a difference in degree between worshipping a tree and touching wood in the vague belief that to perform this action will ward off some calamity. Concerning magic, this action can be defined as defensive magic, as the wood is animated only with the imaginary power of warding off evil and cannot attract good luck. The expression 'touch wood' is generally uttered when we desire a wish to come true, seek protection for future health and prosperity, or wish to counter the threat of evil. It is firmly anchored in superstition and well-known in many cultures, although the origins of this superstition are unclear. Some believe that it stems from the time when many Christian churches treasured relics of the true Cross, which offered protection from misfortune when touched by the devout.

Another explanation for the term stems from old-time sanctuary. When a hunted fugitive touched a church door, it was considered sacrilege for any pursuer to apprehend the runaway, as the Cross depicted on the church door was believed to give protective sanctuary. The most likely origin of the superstition, however, is that it is a relic of prehistoric times when beneficent tree-spirits and tree-gods who dwelt in trees were worshipped. Certain trees were identified with certain deities. For example, the oak tree was dedicated to the Greek god

Zeus; the ash was sacred to the Norse god Odin; whereas the sycamore was dedicated to the Egyptian deity Hathor. Therefore, touching or knocking on the sacred tree's trunk requested protection and assistance from the sylvan deity residing within that tree.

Usually, the gesture of touching wood was adhered to when it was feared that certain utterances tempted fate. Particularly after boasting of one's exemption from misfortune or after having expressed satisfaction over one's own health or fortune, the phrase 'touch wood' was, and still is, habitually added, accompanied by a distinct rapping on anything made of wood. Originally, it was considered essential that wood be touched with the right hand – never the left – to gain protection and ward off any impending evil. With the passage of time, however, the superstition was gradually modified, and in modern times, it is considered adequate to simply utter the expression 'touch wood' while demonstrably tapping one's forehead.

The Thunder Tree

Known in England, as Monarchs of the Forest and venerated throughout Europe for their strength, durability, and hardness, oak trees were traditionally planted on the boundaries of lands. The survival of this custom is evident in the so-called Gospel Oaks of many English parishes.

In the mythological beliefs of many ancient cultures, the oak was the first tree to be created and humans sprang from it. In antiquity, the oak was sacred to the Hebrew people because Abraham reputedly received Jehovah's angel under its branches. The ancient Greeks dedicated the oak to Zeus because his Oracle in Dodona was located in a grove of oaks. Here, all oracles were delivered from the tops of the oak trees, priests interpreting the rustling of the oak leaves in the wind as the voice of Zeus. The Romans consecrated the oak to Jupiter because it had sheltered him at his birth, and originally, the image of Jupiter was represented solely by a natural oak tree.

To the Celtic priesthood known as the Druids, found in Britain, France, and Ireland, the oak represented the Celestial Tree and was considered a principal object of worship. All Druidic ceremonies reputedly included the oak and its parasite, the mistletoe. The Druids worshipped in holy oak groves, their midsummer festival characterised by the gathering of the sacred mistletoe from oak trees, and solely, the friction of oak wood kindled the midsummer need-fires. Pliny the Elder erroneously derived the name Druid from the Greek term drus, meaning 'oak'. He did not know, however, that the Celtic word for oak was very similar, namely daur. Therefore, druid was a Celtic word describing the 'priest of the oak'. The oak was also the sacred tree of the pagan deity Dagda, the creator of the ancient Irish Gaels, whereas the Germanic tribes similarly ranked the oak first among their holy trees.

The cult of the oak tree became universal throughout Europe in prehistoric times. It was observed that the oak tree was struck by lightning far more frequently than any other tree. Therefore, it was widely deduced that the oak must surely be the dwelling place of the god of thunder. In Scandinavia, the oak was sacred to Thor, the god of thunder, and further south, to Donar, his Teutonic counterpart. For this reason, the oak was known as the 'thunder tree' and a Sussex rhyme intones: 'Beware the oak; it draws the stroke'. However, in time, the incorrect lore developed that the oak ensured safety from lightning strikes, and around Europe, oak branches were traditionally kept in houses in the belief that this protected against lightning.

As sacred to Thor, the oak was seen to be under his immediate protection. Hence, it was considered sacrilege to mutilate this tree in any way, and with Thor's tree standing in every hamlet, it must have provided a great sense of security to all. An unwritten law among Germanic and Celtic tribes was that oak trees were not to be felled, and that bad luck would follow anyone who chopped down such a tree. It was this very belief that the Anglo-Saxon missionary Boniface (circa 680–754) tapped into when he used the sacred status of the oak tree amongst Germanic tribes to win thousands of converts to Christianity. He accomplished this by publicly chopping down Donar's Oak – known as Thor's Oak in Scandinavian countries. By this act, he assured all people watching that their god, believed to be residing in the sacred tree, did not have the power to avenge the destruction of his abode and that the Christian God was the far more powerful – his ploy was convincing, as it earned him the title 'Apostle of the Germans'.

Oaks and their leaves were also believed to have powerful protective powers against witchcraft and magic. The Venerable Bede (circa 673–735), Anglo-Saxon scholar and historian, recorded how the heathen King Ethelbert forced the proselytising St. Augustine – sent by Pope Gregory I to convert the Anglo-Saxons to Christianity – to preach to him under an oak tree rather than indoors. This was done so that the sacred oak could protect the fearful Ethelbert from any spell the unfamiliar Christian missionary might cast on him.

The choice of oak-leaf clusters as a military decoration hails back to the ancient Romans. According to Pliny the Elder, a wreath of oak leaves, called the Civic Crown, was given to any Roman who saved a fellow citizen in battle.[19] Similarly, soldiers who had performed feats of bravery or selflessness were honoured with the presentation of an oak-leaf crown. After battle, it was customary for Roman soldiers to place wreaths of oak and myrtle on their swords, and the ancient Greeks awarded a crown of oak leaves to the victors at the Pythian Games, held in honour of Apollo – next in importance to the Olympic Games in Greece.

The oak's qualities of endurance and resilience made the timber from these trees ideal for shipbuilding, and records show that, on average, about 3,500 full-grown oak trees were used in the construction of a three-decker battleship.[20]

IX

NUMBERS, METALS AND PRECIOUS STONES

Counting is older than writing and probably dates to prehistoric times. Numbers seem to be deeply impressed in our collective subconscious, explaining why our dreams often refer to age, dates, and other aspects of the numerical. This might also explain why children start to count before they recognise letters. Numbers are at the root of letters and, in many cultures, the letters of the alphabet have a numerical value. This lends itself to magical computations and connections, especially when concerned with the divine and the names of ancient deities.

Odd Numbers

People put great faith in lucky numbers, while avoiding those considered ill-omened. A belief in the occult importance of numbers is deep-rooted and widespread. In a tradition inherited from the Greeks and Romans, scholars of Renaissance Europe endowed numbers with magical significance. Certain numbers, particularly odd single figures such as the numbers three, seven, and nine, throughout the ages, have always been considered imbued with mystical properties. In the ancient world, odd numbers were thought to bring good fortune. This was reiterated by the Roman poet Virgil who observed that 'odd numbers delight the gods',[1] whereas Pliny the Elder wondered why odd numbers were thought effectual for every purpose. Hence, he poses the question: 'Why do we believe that in everything, odd numbers are more powerful?'[2] In The Merry Wives of Windsor, Shakespeare also refers to the belief that odd numbers are lucky: 'This is the third time; I hope good luck lies in odd numbers. [...] They say there is divinity in odd numbers....'.[3]

However, even numbers, with some notable exceptions such as the number forty, were always considered nondescript. Because they could easily be divided and, therefore, diminished in their value, no special significance was attached to them.

The Curative Value of Three, Seven, and Nine

In folk medicine, much attention has been paid to lucky numbers. For a remedy to prove efficacious, it was thought that it had to be administered according to certain numerical rules. Similarly, countless spells dictated that, to be effective, certain words and actions should be repeated a certain number of times. The efficacy of numbers in medicinal cures goes back thousands of years and was hardly confined to one locality.

Universally, the prescribed numerical values for spells and cures were three, seven, or nine, and countless examples exist. For instance, the Babylonians believed that seven knots tied three times on a three-fold cord wound around the head cured a headache. To protect their infants from evil influences, Egyptian mothers suspended a cord with seven knots around their baby's neck. At various healing wells and springs around Europe, those afflicted with skin ailments were plunged under the water three times and carried nine times around the well or spring to effect a cure. As a preventive act, spitting had to be done three times. In Devonshire it was believed that all poultices should be made of seven types of herbs, and three rushes taken from a running stream and passed through the mouth of an infant were a sure cure for thrush. In Brandenburg, a cure for dizziness was to run naked three times through a field of flax. A Sussex cure for ague, a type of malarial fever, was to eat three sage leaves on an empty stomach nine mornings in a row, whereas in Cuba, a safeguard against jaundice was to wear three cloves of garlic around the neck for three days. In Thuringia, to eat three daisies ensured freedom from toothache, and in Cornwall, burns and scalds were treated with nine bramble leaves applied to the affected parts.

In the past, it was customary in many parts of Europe to whirl lighted candles and an open Bible around a baby three times to keep evil forces at bay. During baptism, a child was dipped in water three times; three circuits of the communion table had to be completed by sufferers of rheumatism, while nine knots tied in a piece of wool were recommended as a cure for a sprained ankle. Many thousand such 'cures' are known in popular folk medicine.

Everything Comes in Threes

Three, a complete and mystical number, is given in the scriptures as an exact number, whereas other numbers simply denote the meaning of many or few or very many, as we today speak of dozens.

The Greek philosopher Pythagoras (circa 580–500 BCE) taught that three was the perfect number as it indicates beginning, middle, and end. This explains why the three-sided triangle, symbolic of deity, is found as a potent magico-religious emblem worldwide. Because of the sanctity linked with this emblem, it was thought to keep evil forces at bay. The ancient Greeks and Romans observed the number three in their sacred rites. When sacrifices were offered up to the gods, the altar was sprinkled three times with a laurel dipped in holy water; frankincense was taken from the censer with three fingers and sprinkled three times.

Much of humankind's existence is founded on a threefold basis: life consists of past, present, and future, having a beginning, middle, and end; humans comprise of body, mind, and spirit; the world consists of earth, sea, and air; nature embraces the animal, vegetable, and mineral kingdom; the three Christian graces are faith, hope and love; and the three cardinal colours are blue, red, and yellow.

In classical mythology, Hecate had threefold power, Jove's symbol was the triple thunderbolt, Neptune's emblem was the sea trident,

Pluto had a three-headed dog, and there were three Fates, three Furies, three Graces, and three Harpies.

Two equilateral triangles, one imposed on the other, form the hexagram used in European magic to master spirits and to banish evil. The hexagram is a well-known magical sign found in almost every part of the world. Persian Zoroastrian tradition used this symbol to depict the forces of good and evil battling for supremacy. The term 'hexagram' is derived from hex, the Greek term for 'six'. The hexagram has been the subject of many misconceptions, and various explanations exist about its symbolism. The triangle pointing upwards was believed by some to represent the forces of light and goodness, whereas the triangle pointing downwards stood for evil and darkness opposing the powers of light. To others, it represented the hermetic principle of 'as above, so below' and symbolised the male principle (the triangle pointing up) and the female principle (the triangle pointing down). It was referred to in early times as the Seal of Solomon and has erroneously become known as the 'Star of David'. However, the hexagram is not an indigenous symbol of Judaism and does not seem to have become distinctly identified with Jewry until after the seventeenth century. It was only formally adopted as an emblem by the first Zionist Congress in 1897 and was much later incorporated into Israel's flag.

The deep-rooted traditional unity of the number three led to the firm belief that all good and bad things happen in threes. Therefore, 'never two, but three', is an adage most people have heard of. Accidents were believed to come in threes, especially breakages around the home. Deliberately smashing two relatively worthless items after the first breakage was suggested to protect more prized items from damage. Similarly, deaths were believed to come in threes. Magic formulas had to be repeated three times to be effective, and practically all magic and curative rituals had to be performed in threes or multiples of three.

Now, we continue to give 'three cheers' to success, speak of a 'third time lucky', and intone that 'all things thrive at thrice', implying that to be successful the third time means to flourish ever after.

Seven — The Vehicle of Life

In all religions and amongst all nations of antiquity, seven was regarded as a sacred number. Plutarch, in discussing the symbolism of this number, says: 'And what need is there to talk about the others when the seven, sacred to Apollo, will alone exhaust the whole day, should one attempt to enumerate all its properties'.[4]

According to Jewish interpretation of biblical texts, there are seven Spirits of God,[5] and generally throughout the Scriptures prophetic times are denoted in sevens.[6] The great significance of the number is explained by some in lunar terms as representing the four phases of the moon's cycle, which lasts for seven days. However, the most common explanation for the mystique surrounding the number is that the ancient Babylonians and Egyptians recognised seven planets, including the sun and the moon. The ancients regarded the planets as divine, still reflected in some of the names of the seven days of the week: Saturday dedicated to Saturn, Sunday to the sun-god, Monday to the moon-god, Tuesday to Tuisto or Tiw,[7] Wednesday to Wotan or Woden, Thursday to Thor, and Friday to Freyja or Frigg. Another point of distinction is that the number seven has the added attribute of being indivisible and, hence, unrelated to any other number in the sequence of one to ten, adding to its perceived supernatural quality.

The association of seven with the spirit of God seems universal. Christians speak of the 'sevenfold gifts of the septiform spirit', the Christian Church has seven sacraments, and there are seven divisions in the Lord's Prayer. In Hebrew religious ritual and custom, the Biblical menorah has seven branches, the three great Jewish feasts lasted seven days, whereas seven weeks separated the first Jewish feast from the second, and Levitical purifications lasted for seven days.

The prominence of the number seven is evident in all the ancient traditions. The Assyrian Tree of Life has seven branches; Ormuz, the Persian supreme God of Light, was said to sit at the head of a hierarchy of seven Holy Immortals; the ancient Egyptians expressed the name of the Supreme Being by a word consisting of seven vowels; the cave of Mithras had seven doors; the Vedas describe the Hindu god Indra with seven rays bedecking his brow and seven great rivers flowing from him;

Brahmins speak of seven prophetic rings, on each of which the name of a planet was engraved; the Hindu god Agni is represented with seven arms; in ancient Japanese lore, there are seven gods of luck; Muslims believe in seven heavens of which the seventh is the holiest. The list of examples goes on and on.

Similarly, seven is a number mentioned repeatedly in the Old Testament, linked with countless occurrences, and the Hebrew word 'to swear' means literally 'to come under the influence of seven things'. Therefore, seven ewe lambs figure in the oath Abraham makes to Abimelech;[8] Aaron is consecrated for seven days;[9] atonement at the altar of the Lord lasts seven days;[10] sin offerings are to be made for seven days;[11] after touching a dead man, one is unclean for seven days;[12] for seven days, the Lord had 'smitten the river' punishing the Egyptians.[13] Again, the list might continue endlessly, but enough examples have been shown to verify the number seven as sacred in ancient religions.

The Pythagoreans called the number seven the vehicle of human life: there are seven days in the week, seven planets, seven phases of the moon, seven metals, seven ages of man, seven notes, seven virtues, seven graces, and seven deadly sins. In Greek mythology, the number was sacred to the God Apollo; there were seven Argive heroes who made war on Thebes, which had seven gates; the flute that the god Pan played had seven pipes; the lyre touched by Apollo had seven strings.

The number's holiness led to its expression of symbolic perfection and completeness. This, however, is not to be taken literally, which is why we speak of the 'seven wonders of the world' when, in reality, there were many more, and why we still speak of the 'seven seas' and say we are in 'seventh heaven' when describing pure bliss.

Seven also features in superstitious beliefs. For example, every seven years, our body is believed to change its physiological make-up. This notion probably gave way to the myth of the 'seven-year itch', said to tempt adults, who have been in the same relationship for seven years, to find a new partner. The idea also forms the basis for the belief that to break a mirror incurs seven years of bad luck – because it takes seven years for the body to renew itself, hence seven years for the bad luck incurred, when breaking a mirror, to wear off. Parents with unruly children used to console themselves with the thought that everything would change after the child reached the age of seven. The seventh child in a family was believed to possess second sight and always be lucky, whereas the seventh son of a seventh son was purported to have the gift of healing and, therefore, would make a good doctor. On a more sinister note, a German superstition contends that when seven girls in a row are born of a marriage, then one of them is sure to be a werewolf [14] – a comforting thought indeed.

Unlucky Thirteen

All numbers over twelve were regarded as insignificant, with the exception of the number thirteen and forty. One of the reasons why thirteen has been regarded as an unlucky number throughout the ages may be that it is one number more than twelve, which is universally regarded as a number of completeness. As the number thirteen crosses the unity of the number twelve it assumed the connotation of dangerously exceeding the 'proper limits' and hence of starting on a new and uncertain course.

The number thirteen's ill-omened associations in superstition are universal and the number has been regarded as fraught with misfortune and ill luck since antiquity. The prejudice against this number is of obscure origin and already existed in ancient Greek and Roman times. For example, the Romans considered it unlucky for thirteen people to be in a room together. In pre-Christian civilisations, as far apart as India and Italy, the number thirteen was considered a bad omen.

Christian religious circles ascribe the origin of all ominous beliefs related to the number thirteen, to the Last Supper, attended by Christ and the twelve disciples. But this does not account for the dislike the ancient Greeks, Romans and other cultures had towards the number long before the spread of Christianity. The thirteenth day of the month has for centuries held ominous associations, but when the thirteenth day of the month also falls on a Friday the negative omens linked with both concepts are compounded. (See Chapter IV – Unlucky Friday the 13th)

In modern times, the fear of the number thirteen, known as 'tridecaphobia' is probably still the most common of all superstitions and is still prevalent. A dinner party with thirteen guests is inadvisable; furthermore the number is often avoided on office doors and by some hotels and airlines. There are even buildings without a thirteenth floor, the numbers instead jumping from twelve to fourteen.

When we speak of a baker's dozen, we mean thirteen of something. The term is believed to be derived from a custom, dating from the Middle Ages, of baking an extra loaf of bread with each batch of twelve. The extra loaf was meant to compensate for any shrinkage and consequent loss in mass.

Sacred Forty

The number forty was sacred amongst most nations of antiquity and is significant in Jewish, Christian, and Islamic tradition. The ancient Babylonians noted that the Pleiades, a revered constellation of stars in Taurus, disappeared for forty days with the seasonal rains. This might have contributed to the reverence with which the number was regarded, although it seems likely that the number was used simply to represent a rough calculation of large units, reflecting a lot or many, much like in modern times we might speak of dozens.

The number forty keeps coming up in the scriptures, expressing a period of probation or trial. Amongst the countless times the number forty is mentioned in the Old and New Testaments are the following examples: Moses went up to the mountain and spent forty days and forty nights there with the Lord;[15] Moses and the Israelites wandered in the desert for forty years before finding the promised land;[16] Elijah fasted for forty days and forty nights;[17] the rain was on the Earth for forty days;[18] after forty days, Noah sent out a raven from the ark;[19] the search for the land of Canaan took forty years;[20] the children of Israel were delivered into the hands of the Philistines for forty years;[21] many kings were reputed to have ruled for forty years, among them Eli,[22] David,[23] Solomon, and Gideon.[24] The punishment of criminals in biblical times was limited to forty strokes.[25] Jesus spent forty days and nights in the desert, tempted by Satan.[26] Forty days was the period from Jesus' resurrection until his ascension into heaven. The list goes on and on.

According to Creationism in Catholic theology, it was believed in medieval times that God created the soul forty days after conception of boys and eighty days after conception of girls. The foetal cycle or period of human gestation, from conception to birth, is forty weeks long. The number forty has also been retained on the Christian calendar. For instance, Halloween is celebrated forty days after the autumn equinox in the Northern Hemisphere. Similarly, the festival of Candlemas on February 2 falls forty days after Christmas, and Lent consists of forty days preceding Easter. In Europe, it was customary for a woman to be 'churched' forty days after childbirth before she could resume all her normal duties, as women were traditionally looked upon as unclean until forty days after confinement.

In Muslim culture, the dead are mourned for forty days, and Mohammed is believed to have been forty years old when he received the revelation delivered by the angel Gabriel.

The number forty is still echoed in the word 'quarantine', from the Italian term quaranta, which carries the same meaning. Sailors were usually kept in isolation for this period, observing the early tradition of the magic figure forty, presumably in the belief that the magical significance of this number protected them and dispelled any evil in the form of diseases clinging to them.

In modern times, the expression 'to catch forty winks', meaning a short sleep is still in use, and a popular maxim is that 'life begins at forty'.

Magical Iron

To the ancient Greeks and Romans and to medieval alchemists, all metals and minerals seemed alive and vibrant. They were perceived as growing in the Earth's bowels and were thought endowed with procreative and other magic powers. Traditionally, the seven planets of old were linked with the seven known metals of antiquity, and each metal was thought to develop in the Earth under its planet's influence.

Created from the holy flame of fire, iron has always been regarded as the most magical, supernaturally potent metal. The major technological breakthrough that iron represented to our ancestors cannot be underestimated. As bronze weapons had proved ineffective against invading tribes' swords, the forging of iron made a huge impact on ancient people's minds. Iron proved to be the magic agent of transmutation that enhanced the quality of life from brutish to civilised. The first iron known to humans, having descended from heaven as meteors further elevated this metal's reputation to extraordinary status. Early humans must have seen meteors, coming from outer space, as fiery, heavenly missiles. They must have seemed like divine gifts from the gods, whose abode was thought to be in the heavens. The ancient Egyptians called iron 'metal from the sky', and the Aztecs named it 'gift from heaven'. According to Egyptian tradition, it was at the ancient, holy city of Edfu, dedicated to the god Horus, that Horus established a foundry of 'divine iron'. The earliest known iron tools date from circa 3000 BCE, but not until the 2nd millennium BCE were weapons forged from iron, the Hittites leading in this industry.

Several factors contributed to the mystique causing various magic practices and taboos traditionally associated with iron: first, the inexplicable fall of meteorites from heaven, traditionally considered the abode of the gods; second, the magnetic properties of this metal; and third, the impressive process of smelting and forging. The change from solid to liquid state and back again, controlled in casting, must have been seen as an extraordinary feat – the blacksmith in effect tamed and controlled the hardest metal then known. Therefore, throughout history, those associated with the craft of metallurgy have been connected to the magical and the mystical. As knowledge empowers, the mysteries of metalworking were kept as closely guarded secrets in antiquity – secret knowledge in turn has since time immemorial been shrouded in sanctity. Presumably, the craft lore of smiths and metallurgists was transmitted by creed and example and was only divulged to initiate members of the community, smiths keeping their profession's secrets to themselves. Therefore, blacksmiths were regarded as very important craftsmen, credited with special powers in all societies.

The magical associations connected with the blacksmith also extended to the tools he used, and in many countries, these implements were venerated. In African countries, where smiths were feared because of their supposed powers of sorcery, the hammer was revered because it forged agricultural tools. Many African tribes similarly esteemed the bellows, and oaths could be sworn before the hammer and anvil.

In England, there is a tradition that eloping couples may be married by the blacksmith of Gretna Greene, just over the border in Scotland. The application of this custom, a by-product of Scottish law, stems from a time when every blacksmith performed a magico-religious role within the community, because he worked with the magic metal iron and was the master of fire, considered sacred throughout the ages. In Europe, communities traditionally gave blacksmiths tributes of corn and donations of food. This was a mark of the special esteem in which the craft was held and done because a blacksmith's task was perceived as superseding that of growing food. Hence, any slaughtered animal's head was always given to the local blacksmith.

Since the beginning of the Iron Age, the blacksmith's fire and the glowing red-hot iron have evoked countless tales of mysterious magic and enchantment. Smiths, dwarfs, and other real or legendary metalworkers are described in many peoples' myths. In the Roman classical world, Vulcan, the son of Jupiter and Juno, was the god of fire and metalworking. The traditional father of British blacksmiths, Wayland Smith, is an anglicised version of the Norse Volund and the Anglo-Saxon Wieland. In Scandinavian countries, Volund, appearing as a dwarf or troll was a renowned metalworker with supernatural powers, who fashioned magical swords and suits of armour keeping the wearer safe from any harm. Similarly, the Celtic smith, Goibhniu, was noted for his magic healing brew and his skill in producing invincible weapons.

Myths and legends from various countries abound with magic swords, reputed to never rust or blunt, to cut through stone and iron, to never miss a stroke, and always keep the wearer safe. Usually, dwarves forged these wondrous weapons in their underground domains. Arguably, the most famous magic swords appear in Arthurian Legend, namely the 'Sword in the Stone' and the famed 'Excalibur'. One of Christianity's most famous metalworkers was St. Dunstan, tenth-century English monk and church reformer, patron saint of goldsmiths, jewellers, and blacksmiths. In the latter part of his life, he became Abbot at Glastonbury and, eventually, the Archbishop of Canterbury.

Universally, using iron for religious purposes on sacred occasions was once considered taboo. Whether amongst Hottentots, the inhabitants of the African Gold Coast, Jews, Greeks, Druids, Indians, or any other cultures, superstitions regarding the use of iron for religious purposes stay the same. Moses commanded the Israelites not to use any iron tool in the construction of holy places, as God had instructed Moses: 'If thou wilt make me an altar of stone, thou shalt not build it of hewn stone: for if thou lift up thy tool upon it, thou hast polluted it'.[27] Solomon had similarly ordered that no iron tools should be used to cut and dress the many massive stone blocks from which the outer walls and the courtyard of the Temple were built: 'The house, when it was in building, was built of stone made ready before it was brought thither: so that there was neither hammer, nor axe, nor any tool of iron heard in the house while it was in building'.[28] Instead, Solomon had provided the masons with an ancient device dating from Moses' time. This device was called a shamir or 'the stone that splits rocks'. It could cut the toughest of materials, even the hardest of diamonds, without using any friction or heat, while working totally without noise.[29] With the Temple's destruction, the shamir vanished.[30] In the ancient Greek temples, no iron tools were permitted, and the taboo regarding iron also extended to Roman and Sabine priests, who were not under any circumstances to be shaved with iron, but only with bronze razors or shears.

Beliefs and superstitions surrounding this metal are charged with ambivalence. On the one hand, iron was regarded with fear and disfavour and disallowed in the rites and rituals of all major religions, which might in part be because of references made to iron in the Old Testament.[31] However, iron was also held in awe and respect, believed endowed with the power to ward off all evil, through the notion that the gods gave iron to humankind – any such gift had to be loathsome to all evil entities. The fact that this metal was considered so obnoxious to supernatural forces gave rise to it being used as a charm in banning and repelling all unwanted influences. Evidence of this custom is found universally, throughout the ages, from ancient Egypt, Greece, and Rome to Scotland, India, Burma, Germany, and Morocco.

The dislike of all ghosts, spirits, witches, and demons for iron was thought so great that they would not approach anything or anyone protected by the metal, which also explains the protective power ascribed to the horseshoe. Already, the ancient Egyptians believed in the shielding powers of 'the metal from the sky' referring to it in the Pyramid Texts of King Unas. Amulets of meteoric iron were found in Tutankamen's tomb to safeguard the sarcophagus from evil. The Romans associated iron's protective powers with the war god Mars. The metal was also sacred to the Norse God Tyr and was used by the Scandinavians to repel unwanted influences. In India, iron's shielding powers were also well-known and widespread, this metal being used in certain funeral rites to guard the living and the dead.

Throughout Europe, iron objects were believed to counteract the influence of witchcraft, fairies, and every kind of evil. Evil spirits were blinded, hence, warded off by the brightness of shiny, new iron. Because old, rusted iron had no such effect, allowing spirits to take up residence wherever they pleased, all rust had to be meticulously removed from iron objects. As witches and all evil entities were thought unable to cross over iron, anything made from this metal – a knife, a nail, or a pair of scissors placed just inside the door, under the doormat, or buried near the front gate – would keep them away. A sword or some other piece of cold iron was laid in an expectant mother's bed or a piece of iron sewn into a child's clothes, at least until baptism, to prevent fairies spiriting away mother and child.

Knives and other cutting instruments, which in the past were all made of iron, were especially used extensively as protective agents against witchcraft, fairies, and thieving goblins. For this reason, it was advisable to place a knife in an infant's cradle to ensure a modicum of safety. However, such cutting instruments were also linked with bad luck and, therefore, handled with caution. It was considered unlucky to receive or present a knife, scissors, or any other sharp, cutting instrument as a gift, as these were thought likely to 'sever' the friendship and 'cut' love and good fortune; the dropping of a knife meant death or disaster, which could only be warded off by waving the knife around one's head three times; to lay one's knife and fork crosswise was thought to bring about crosses and misfortune; and to stir food with a knife was believed to 'stir up strife'. In many parts of Europe, the use of iron tools was still popular in the second half of the twentieth century to ward off evil, and on November 18, 1968, the London Observer noted: 'It is still common practise to keep scissors under the doormat to ward off witches and evil spirits'.

Iron was also highly regarded for its perceived curative powers. Pliny the Elder mentions this specifically: 'Iron is employed in medicine.... Water in which iron has been plunged at a white heat is useful as a potion, in many diseases.... Rust, too, is classed among the remedial substances ... usually obtained by scraping old nails.... It has the effect of uniting wounds....'.[32] Pliny also gives specific instructions on the gathering of medicinal herbs. They were never to be touched by iron or risk contamination and render them ineffectual for healing purposes.[33] In northern European countries, an iron ring worn on the fourth finger was considered effective against rheumatism and arthritis, whereas a piece of iron in the bedroom was believed to ward off nightmares and regenerate the body's ability to reject illness.

Supernatural Silver

Alchemists referred to silver as Luna and ascribed to it the symbol of the crescent-shaped moon. In ancient times, this metal was sacred to the Egyptian lunar goddess Isis and to the Greek and Roman goddess Diana. From the earliest times, silver has been used to fashion images of goddesses, and silver bells were especially considered powerful evocative agents to summon protection from the Mother Goddesses of all cultures.

Silver has always been associated with psychic and intuitive abilities, especially when its ruling influence, the moon, is full. Because of its lunar connection, silver was believed to possess supernatural powers and is linked with occult practices. Therefore, silver cups were often used by the ancients for divination, as in the Biblical story of Joseph and his brothers.[34]

The metal was also thought resistant and invulnerable to enchantment, its powers unable to be deflected by magical means. Therefore, it was believed that only a silver bullet from a firearm would kill witches, werewolves and vampires. In modern times, the metaphor of a 'silver bullet' is generally used to describe an easy solution to a prevailing problem by some or other new technology.

Because of its unassailability, silver has traditionally been considered a lucky metal, one of the most potent precious metals, with powerful protective qualities. Hence, when laying the foundation or corner stone of a building, the first sod of earth was traditionally dug with a silver spade. Similarly, due to its shielding, as well as luck-bringing properties, silver cups or spoons, or anything made from silver, were and are still given as christening presents and brides would sew a silver coin into their dress for good luck, or the groom wore one in his shoe, whereas silver coins were carefully set aside to ensure continuing prosperity, for 'luck-money' should always be silver. In northern European countries, it was customary while bowing to a new moon, to turn over a silver coin in the pocket, to ensure good fortune and prosperity for the next cycle of the moon. Silver coins were also often buried under the threshold of houses to ensure luck for all who resided within, while boat-builders would hide a silver coin under the mast of a vessel for the same purpose.

To make the sign of the cross with a piece of silver was considered especially protective. Therefore, it was customary to cross the fortune teller's hand with silver – to have one's fortune told meant tapping into supernatural forces, and silver protected from any possible harm incurred from these forces.

Divine Mythical Gold

This glowing metal has fascinated humankind since the beginning of civilisation. The ancient Egyptians identified gold with the sun-god Ra, believed to be born every morning as a calf in the east, then to rise in the sky and turn into a bull, only to change into liquid gold as he died in the setting sun. Gold, 'the divine element', was the natural choice for humankind to glorify its gods. Like the gods themselves, it seemed immortal and incorruptible and was the symbol of power, wealth, and status. To the pharaohs, who believed themselves descendants of the gods, it was a reminder of their own divinity and an assurance of their celestial existence in the hereafter. Like the Egyptians, the Incas also associated gold with the sun. The sun was the ancestor of the Inca kings, and their metal, representing nobility, was gold. According to Inca creation myth, life originated from three eggs that dropped from the heavens. One egg was gold, from which emerged male nobility; one was silver from which came noble women; and one was copper, which produced the common people.

Throughout the ages, attitudes towards this metal have been marked by ambivalence. When Solomon built the Temple in Jerusalem, its lavish gold embellishments glorified Yahweh.[35] But after the Exodus from Egypt during the epic years of wandering, gold proved a bane for the Israelites. While Moses was on Mount Sinai, the Israelites forced Aaron to fashion gods from gold to lead them in their wanderings. From all the gold in their possession, Aaron fashioned the golden calf, which Moses later destroyed: 'And he took the calf which they had made and burnt it in the fire, and ground it to powder and strewed it upon the water and made the children of Israel drink of it'.[36] In penance for their sin of idolatry, the Israelites were forced to drink the gold.

Gold has always been regarded as the highest and most sophisticated metal. In the myths and folk tales of all cultures, the lure of gold abounds and is the ultimate prize. In Greek myth, the Golden Fleece was taken from its dragon guardian by Jason and the Argonauts. The fleece had been that of a winged ram, sacrificed to Zeus by Phryxos and immortalised in the heavens as the constellation of Aries. In Greek legend, the apples of the Hesperides, the Golden Fruit of Life, hung temptingly from its tree on the Island of the Blessed, yet Hercules was hard put to pull the apples away. Many are also the recurring stories of cities of gold, such as the fabled El Dorado, where unbounded wealth prevails.

Gold was also associated with the white-berried mistletoe, parasite of the oak tree. The mistletoe, revered by the Celtic Druids, was known as the 'golden bough' and, with a golden sickle, played an important part in Druidic religious ritual. The association between gold and the mistletoe can similarly be found in folk traditions of the Germanic peoples, as they believed that anyone finding a sprig of mistletoe on Midsummer Eve would find a buried crock of gold, whereas in Sweden, anyone using the mistletoe as a divining rod was assured of finding treasure. This association was also found in Russia, where it was believed that one would find treasure by throwing mistletoe in the air and digging on the spot on which it landed.

In countless myths and legends, gold symbolises greed, corruption, temptation, and treason, as in the tale of King Midas, whose touch turned everything into gold. Midas, king of Phrygia, requested the god Bacchus to turn everything he touched to gold. His request was granted, but when even his food turned to gold, he begged to be released from this dubious blessing. Divine penance constituted a pilgrimage to the River Pactolus to wash away his sin of avarice. The king obeyed, and from that day, according to legend, the waters of the Pactolus ran gold.

Throughout the ages, gold has been the symbol of power and prestige. There are many examples: The Mogul conquerors ruling Russia during the ninth and tenth centuries were dubbed the Golden Horde. During the fourteenth century, the Golden Bull was an edict issued by the Holy Roman Emperor Charles IV (1316–1378) to fix the process of electing German emperors. An order of knighthood instituted in 1429 by Philip III the Duke of Burgundy was titled the Golden Fleece. In a similar vein, an award for valour in the papal service, inaugurated in the sixteenth century by Pope Gregory XIII, was named the Order of the Golden Spur. For centuries, popes honoured monarchs and religious rulers for special distinction with the exquisitely crafted Golden Rose, created by master jewellers. The Colonel of Life-Guards, who walks before the British sovereign at all processions, bears the title of Golden Stick, and the age of innocence at the beginning of time is known as the Golden Age.

It is interesting to note the many presumed curative and protective powers attached to this metal. Gold was once considered the Elixir of Life and idealised as a divine antidote to disease and death. Therefore gold was especially popular with sailors, who maintained that wearing a gold earring in one ear would protect them from blindness and drowning. In medieval times, nothing seems to have possessed such admirable healing qualities as the drinking of gold powder, Aurum Potabile or 'Solar Oil'. Especially, when liquid gold was mixed with 'Lunar Oil' or silver, it was believed to cure most diseases. A gold coin kept in one's mouth when in contact with persons suspected of having the dreaded plague was thought to be protective. Similarly, some water first poured over a gold coin and then given to a patient to drink was thought to cure various ailments. Gold beads worn around the neck were commonly used to cure throat ailments and warts; fistulas and ulcers were believed to disappear when rubbed with gold, particularly a gold wedding ring. Similarly, there was no better remedy to cure a sty than by rubbing it daily with the gold wedding ring, a superstition still around in the 1980s.[37]

Clear as Crystal — Precious Stones

Many literary works on gemstones have originated from various ancient and medieval authors. A famous text on the history of gemstones, the Cysianides, came from the ancient Alexandrian School of Greece. Furthermore, Pliny the Elder expounds on the history and the effective medicinal uses of various gems. However, the most renowned and most copied early text on gemstones is The History of Jewels by the twelfth-century medieval philosopher and alchemist Albertus Magnus.

Many gems are included in myths, legends, religious beliefs, and rituals from around the world. Especially gem-laden trees seem universal. Babylonian legends tell of trees that instead of fruit are laden with precious stones. The ancient Sumerian Gilgamesh Epic describes a most splendid tree bearing precious stones for fruits and crystal branches. Hindu mythology also describes such a tree, known as the Kalpa Tree, a glowing mass of precious stones, pearls, and beautiful emeralds hanging from its boughs, with corals and rubies representing the fruit, the foliage made of zircon, the roots of sapphire, and the base of diamonds. Hindu legend also tells of a huge container made of the purest crystal, the creation of the god Maya, encrusted with pearls and precious stones. Although it contained no fluids, its transparency created the illusion of being filled with fresh clear water so that all approaching it were tempted to plunge into its depths. Some Christian legends about the Holy Grail portray this sacred receptacle as fashioned from pure amethyst, whereas the visions of the prophet Ezekiel compare the throne of Jehovah to a magnificent sapphire.[38] In the visions of John of Patmos, the Glory of God is similarly compared to multicoloured gemstones.[39]

Besides universal gem-trees and receptacles, descriptions of wonderful gem-cities are also found in various religious texts. In the Book of Revelations, the New Jerusalem is described as built of precious gems.[40] In the Hindu Puranas, the divine Krishna takes up abode in the wonderful gem-city of Devârakâ, which was decked in pearls, rubies, diamonds, and other precious stones. Another such gem-city is described in Greek literature, known as the City of the Islands of the Blessed. Made of gold, it has walls fashioned from emerald, temples formed of beryl, and altars of amethyst. Similarly, in Islamic legend, the various heavens are composed of different precious stones.

Since ancient times, precious and semi-precious stones have been credited for their supernatural powers. Many such gems were believed to glow magically in the dark, symbolising hope and endurance. Rabbinical tradition describes a stone that Noah placed in the Ark as providing brightness when the Flood obscured the sun and moon. Another Hebrew legend relates that Abraham presented the six sons his wife Hagar bore to him with enormous precious stones, their brightness exceeding that of the sun, the stones able to light the way during times of darkness and gloom.[41]

A curious quality ascribed to precious gems in the past was their perceived ability to produce progeny. This strange idea, which survived until well after the Middle Ages, was first related by Theophrastus (372–circa 287 BCE), the earliest Greek writer on the subject of precious stones. An account dating to the sixteenth century relates that diamonds owned by a noblewoman of the House of Luxemburg regularly produced offspring.[42] A popular idea during the Middle Ages was that male and female diamonds grew together if nourished by the dew from heaven. This notion related to the belief that certain stones had supernatural indwelling powers.

Occult and mystic forces were attributed to the various beautiful stones that captured and played with rays of light, emitting a spectrum of magnificent colours. Benevolent or evil spirits were believed to dwell in such stones, therefore, the popular seventeenth-century notion that angels often entered precious stones to protect humankind. The supernatural powers considered inherent in gemstones could be lost if the stones were handled or gazed on by someone evil.

Throughout the ages, specific stones have been attributed special powers. Gemstones were credited with inspiring creativity, love, and passion. Some stones became known especially for their luck-bringing qualities, whereas others over the centuries acquired a reputation of ill luck. The precious violet amethyst is still traditionally linked with Episcopal eminence. Blue gems such as the lapis lazuli and the sapphire were looked on as symbols of chastity and, therefore, considered appropriate for those of ecclesiastical rank. The emerald and the turquoise were used in rites to incite love and passion; the sapphire was believed to sharpen the intellect; the emerald strengthened memory; and the amethyst was thought to promote temperance and sobriety. Both opals and pearls have always been considered unlucky, whereas sparkling diamonds are still known as 'a girl's best friend'.

Gemstones were often selected for their symbolic value. The diamond stood for unyielding durability, the pearl for purity, the ruby for the administration of justice, whereas the topaz was an emblem for nobility and regal splendour. In the past florid gems were an important status symbol for the aristocracy and laws were actually in place, ensuring that only the privileged class wore gemstones, thereby preserving a visible division of social rank.

Throughout history, amongst most civilisations, the use of gemstones as amulets and charms is evident. The virtues believed inherent in precious stones were believed to gain added potency when the gems were engraved with sacred or symbolic symbols. Amulets containing gemstones such as jasper, lapis lazuli, purple amethyst, red coral, green jade, and orange carnelian, have been found in Egyptian tombs dating back thousands of years. The ancient Egyptians placed the forms of scarabs and various animals carved from or containing these precious stones on their mummies to protect the dead from evil influences in the afterlife. Such amulets were invariably inscribed with the names of gods, pharaohs, priests, and other personages to add to their protective powers. The Egyptians used specific stones for particular amulets. For example, heart amulets were mostly fashioned from carnelian, and eyes were mainly fashioned from lapis lazuli, turquoise, and jade. Worn as amulets, gemstones were believed to prevent many diseases. The ruby was used to ward off plague and pestilence; jade amulets were reputed to protect from kidney complaints; the onyx prevented attacks of epilepsy; the topaz staved off inflammation; whereas jasper was worn to ward off fevers.

In the past, gems were also humanised and attributed with exercising moral judgement. Therefore, it was believed that certain stones were influenced by the mental and moral states, as well as the general health condition of the wearer. In sickness, approaching death, unfaithfulness, or perjury, the lustre of precious stones was thought to dim and their bright colours darken. Any stone, if perfect to look at, was seen as the source of all blessings, whereas a gem lacking in lustre was sure to bring misfortune to its owner.

Beautiful gems, rare and costly, have always been prized, not only for their aesthetic effect, but also their therapeutic value. Throughout history, precious stones have been used for healing, either placed into wounds or ground up as medicines and elixirs. Many of the remedies were prized because their rarity added mystery and intrigue. It was also believed that gems lying as seeds deep in the earth had been nurtured through moisture and heat generated from the heavens above, hence they were profoundly influenced by the movements of the stars.

Belief in the curative powers of gemstones dates to ancient Babylon and Egypt but was once universal among all those to whom gems were known. The Ebers Papyrus, the most profound and voluminous record of ancient Egyptian medicine, dated circa 1500 BCE, offers various prescriptions containing gemstones and minerals. For instance, lapis lazuli was recommended as an ingredient in eye salves because of astringent substances purported to be contained in the stone, and the iron oxide, haematite, was used for preventing and treating haemorrhages and inflammations. Now, of course, we find it curious and difficult to understand how such seemingly ineffectual remedies could once have been used and firmly believed in. The curative properties long attributed to precious stones, although thought to be greatly enhanced by inscriptions and designs, were ultimately determined by their colour, according to the laws of sympathetic magic. Accordingly, the therapeutic effects of gemstones were often related to a fanciful analogy between the stone's colour and the character of the malady to be treated.

According to the principle similia similibus curantur, 'like cures like', all red or reddish stones, whose colour suggested blood, such as the ruby, garnet, carnelian, and bloodstone, were thought to be valuable remedies in curing blood disorders. These red gems were used to stem blood flow and believed to confer invulnerability from wounds. Furthermore, red stones were thought to aid the circulation, treat inflammatory diseases, and exercise a calming influence, removing anger and discord. However, it was thought that red stones used as weapons inflicted severer wounds than normal weapons. In 1892, the rebellious Hanzas used bullets made from red stone during their hostilities with British troops on the Kashmir frontier, believing that such bullets inflicted deadlier wounds than leaden bullets.

In much the same way, yellow stones were indicated in curing all liver dysfunctions, especially jaundice. Yellow amber crushed and mixed with oil was recommended as a salve to cure skin infections, whereas green and milky stones were regarded as most beneficial for treating the eyes, which is why the opal was used to treat weak eyesight – green most probably suggested through the beneficial influence this colour exerts on the eyes.

Although most ancient lore surrounding gemstones has been lost with the passing of time, we constantly use the names of precious and semi-precious stones as adjectives. We speak of emerald meadows, turquoise skies, sapphire eyes, sapphire seas, ruby lips, ruby wine, pearly skin, pearly teeth, coral lips, amber hair, and diamond eyes.

Natal or Birthstones

In ancient times, the entire mineral kingdom was intricately involved in a complex scheme of occult correspondences, endowing each stone with celestial values. All stones, even those not strictly speaking 'precious', were classified according to the planets, which in turn were thought to influence the various stones and all properties attributed to them. Priests and magicians further elaborated these properties.

Zodiacal stones are those gems believed to be mystically related to the various Zodiac signs. Whereas these signs constitute a twelvefold division of the year the same as the months, they, however, do not coincide with each month, but overlap each other. This naturally allowed for enlarging the selection of birthstones, while preserving the established order suitable for the relevant months, an order which dates to the Scriptures.

The origin of the belief that each month of the year is represented by a specific stone stems from the writings of Jewish historian Flavius Josephus (circa 37–100 CE) and the church father St. Jerome (circa 345–420 CE). Both men expounded on a perceived connection among the twelve stones found on the breastplate of the Jewish high priest, the twelve months of the year, and the twelve signs of the zodiac. Josephus stated that the twelve stones inlaid in the Jewish high priest's breastplate represented twelve virtues, among them wisdom, truth, justice, humility, peace, strength, faith, and victory, as well as symbolising the twelve months of the year and the twelve tribes of Israel.

Based on the writings of Flavius Josephus and St. Jerome, astrologers and magicians later evolved a complicated system of correspondences, relating and associating various gems, metals, colours, animals, and flowers to the planets and Zodiac signs. In assigning stones to different planets, their colour was especially considered important. Lengthy postulations about the symbolic significance of colours developed over time. For example, all colourless, white stones, such as rock crystal, quartz, and the pearl, known as the 'stone of the sea', were connected with the moon and, therefore, partook in the enigmatic characteristics ascribed to this heavenly body. Illuminating the night sky, when treacherous and maleficent spirits were thought to abound, the moon was regarded with ambivalence, seen on the one hand as menacing and on the other to have the power to drive off evil forces. As the colour white symbolised integrity, purity, friendship, and religion, all stones linked with the colour took on these characteristics. Each stone was not only related to a planet, but also, depending on its colour, with a day of the week. White stones, through their connection with the moon, were assigned to Mondays. Lists of gems associated with the various Zodiac signs differ, depending on period of origin and tradition. Another factor considered in the complexity of lore surrounding natal stones applies to the variety of Zodiacs pertaining to differing cultures: the Chaldean

Zodiac, Arabian Zodiac, Hindu Zodiac, Chinese Zodiac, and Islamic Zodiac – every one having specific gemstones ascribed to a particular month.

Although the connection between each stone and a specific month of the year had been expounded on in early antiquity, the wearing of natal stones only became popular as late as the eighteenth century. Before that, it was recommended to wear various stones, because many virtues, especially in a therapeutic context, were attributed to them all. Consequently, if affordable, it was customary for a person to acquire all twelve stones and to wear each during the respective month to which it was assigned. During that period, the stone was believed to exercise its talismanic and therapeutic effect to the fullest extent. It was not until much later that a mystic bond was perceived between the stone of the month and the person born in that month, leading to the assumption that each stone was endowed with the same virtues as the person born in that month, and it became customary to wear one's birthstone to ensure good fortune throughout life.

The most popular association and identity of astrological gemstones according to British and American birthstone charts is as follows:

January, Capricorn	the garnet, symbolising truth and constancy
February, Aquarius	the amethyst, symbolising sincerity and sobriety
March, Pisces	the bloodstone, alternately the aquamarine, symbolising courage and presence of mind.
April, Aries	the diamond, symbolising innocence and strength
May, Taurus	the emerald, symbolising success in love

June, Gemini	the pearl, symbolising purity and tears
July, Cancer	the ruby, symbolising courage and purity
August, Leo	the sardonyx, alternately, the peridot
September, Virgo	the sapphire, symbolising love
October, Libra	the opal, symbolising hope, alternately, the tourmaline
November, Scorpio	the topaz, symbolising fidelity
December, Sagittarius	the turquoise, symbolising prosperity, alternately, the lapis lazuli

The King of Gems

The diamond is the birthstone for April, its golden sparkling rays attributed to the sun, under whose influence it is with Jupiter. The 'King of Gems', also called adamas, the 'Adam of Gems', the diamond is the hardest substance known to humans, with a unique radiance. Although the word 'diamond' is said to have come from the Greek adamas, many authorities agree that when the word adamas is used, a stone other than the diamond is being referred to because the Greeks are not thought to have known the true diamond.

Suggested by the brilliant flashes of light emitted by the diamond, it is known in Sanskrit as indrajudha, 'Indra's weapon' or vajra, 'thunderbolt'. The Assyrian word for diamond is elmêshu, the word el meaning 'God'. This divine association is also found in the Hebrew word for diamond, which is yahālōm, and Yah or Yaw are Hebrew words for 'God', showing how highly the ancients prized diamonds.

Before the discovery of diamonds in Brazil and South Africa during the early part of the eighteenth century and later in many other parts of the world, all diamonds came from India. The marketing of diamonds in India goes back to about 3000 BCE. References in Roman literature about fabled diamonds date from the first century CE. Although diamonds have been mined in India for thousands of years, the rest of the world popularly believed diamonds came from The Valley of Diamonds, described in Pliny's Natural History. According to Pliny, the Valley of Diamonds was an unimaginably black pit that was so steep, no man could descend it and return. To retrieve the gemstones from the pit's floor, clever men threw chunks of meat down. Birds of prey would swoop down, pick up the meat, and with it, the diamonds stuck to it. Once they had dropped the meat into their nests, the clever men stole the diamonds. Many grisly, horrible variations of such tales persisted for centuries.

Most virtues ascribed to this sought-after gemstone are directly traceable either to its hardness or transparent purity. Because of its indestructibility, it has always been regarded as an emblem of eternity. Symbolically linked with love and innocence, the diamond is traditionally a love-bearing gift popularly used in engagement rings in America and parts of Europe. Traditionally, also a symbol of good luck, the diamond is believed to inspire courage in a man and pride in a woman. Diamonds, associated with wealth, power, and prestige, indicate success and security. Coloured diamonds, red and yellow, were in the past assigned only to royalty.

Many myths and legends concern the powers of diamonds to ward off evil and dangers. Because of its brilliance, this stone, like a continuous shining light, was thought to protect the wearer from evil. During the Middle Ages, alchemists asserted that diamonds could render the wearer invisible. According to widespread superstition, the protective powers of a diamond were lost if the stone was sold or bought – only when given as a gift did the spirit dwelling in this most precious gem not take offence. If the stone was given as a pledge of love or friendship, then its protective powers were believed to be greatly enhanced.

Because of its hardness, the diamond was used to cut other stones, giving origin to the idea that the gem was indestructible. This caused the firm conviction that anyone swallowing a diamond was doomed to die. It was believed from as early as the seventh century onwards that diamonds put into one's mouth fractured the teeth and if swallowed, ruptured the intestines, a falsity, however, proved because slaves who worked in diamond mines often swallowed the stones to conceal them, never suffering ill effects, the gems recovered naturally. Similarly, diamond dust, when taken internally, was widely believed to act as a dangerous poison.

In direct contradiction to the diamond being seen as highly toxic, one of its most noteworthy medicinal virtues was that it was widely considered an antidote to all poisons and believed to protect against pestilence and, most of all, the dreaded plague. During the Middle Ages, aristocrats wore diamonds specifically to ward off the Black Death engulfing Europe. This notion probably stems from the fact that the plague attacked the poorer classes first, whereas the rich, decked out in diamonds were spared to start with – an observation highlighting the squalid conditions of the poorer classes rather than the wearing of diamonds.

EPILOGUE

Human customs and mores change over time. Scientific thinking and continuing research, as well as instant communication and easy travel from one continent to another, have transformed life around the world. As a result our world has become 'smaller', and humankind has learnt to think globally, respecting and valuing cultural diversity and multi-culturalism and not merely 'tolerating' it, as in the past.

In most modern technology-progressive societies, the bondages of traditions and ancient ritual heritage are being been cast aside as inappropriate and out-dated, becoming lost in obscurity. The pursuit of a better understanding through improved education has in many cases eradicated deep-rooted prejudices and outmoded beliefs. Societies' long-held customs and traditions have changed or have been forgotten. However, remnants of our past remain, although not always understood or recognised.

The numerous chapters of this book have attempted to draw attention to the universality of cultural mores – thereby highlighting an underlying connection and concord of human traditions. The book has aimed to emphasise how, in spite of the accomplishments of modern thinking, vestiges of old-time customs, relics, emblems, and beliefs have survived, albeit some with different meanings, as proof of their endurance. Hopefully, the time when humankind's cultures cease to be a fascinating study in their wide diversity of 'strange' traditions is still a long way off.

BIBLIOGRAPHY

Abbot, Elisabeth. A History of Celibacy. New York: Scribner, 2000.

Anton, A. E. 'Handfasting in Scotland'. Scottish Historical Review 37, 124 (1958).

Bächtold-Stäubli, Hans. Handwörterbuch des Deutschen Aberglaubens. 10 vols. Berlin: de Gruyter Publishers, 1987.

Ball Philip, The Devil's Doctor – Paracelsus and the World of Renaissance, Magic and Science, Farrar, Straus and Giroux, New York 2006

Bar-Ilan, M. 'Witches in the Bible and in the Talmud.' Herbert W. Basser and Simcha Fishbane (eds.). Approaches to Ancient Judaism, New Series. Atlanta: Scholars Press, 1993.

Bartlett, Sarah. The World of Myths and Mythology. London: Blandford Publishers, 1998.

Bayley, Harold. The Lost Language of Symbolism. 2 vols. London: Bracken Books, 1996.

Berndt, Ronald M. and Catherine H. The First Australians. Sydney: Ure Smith Publications, 1952.

———— Arnhem Land—Its History and Its People. Melbourne: F.W. Cheshire, 1954.

————The World of the First Australians—Aboriginal Traditional Life Past and Present, Canberra: Aboriginal Studies Press, 1999.

Brand, John. Observations on Popular Antiquities. London: Charles Knight & Co., 1841.

Brasch, Rudolph. How Did It Begin? Victoria, AU: Longmans and Co, 1965.

———— Strange Customs. Victoria, AU: Fontana Books, 1976.

———— The Supernatural and You. New South Wales, AU: Cassell Publishers, 1976.

————There's a Reason for Everything. Victoria, AU: Fontana Books, 1982.

Brock, Peggy, ed. Women, Rites and Sites—Aboriginal Women's Cultural Knowledge. Sydney: Allen & Unwin, 1998.

Brooke, Christopher. The Medieval Idea of Marriage. Oxford: Oxford University Press, 1989.

Bryant, Page. Native American Mythology. London: Harper Collins, 1991.

Budge, Wallis, trans. The Egyptian Book of the Dead. New York: Dover Publications, [1895] 1967.

Bulfinch, Thomas. Bulfinch's Mythology. New York: Avenel Books, 1978.

Burkert, Walter. Creation of the Sacred. London: Harvard University Press, 1999.

Burne, Charlotte. The Handbook of Folklore. London: Random House, 1996.

Campbell, Joseph. The Masks of God—Primitive Mythology. New York: Penguin Books, 1987.

———— The Hero with a Thousand Faces. London: Fontana Press, 1993.

Caradeau, Jean-Luc. The Dictionary of Superstitions. London: Granada Publishing, 1985.

Cawte, John. Healers of Arnhem Land. Marleston, South Australia: J B Books, 1996.

Cawthorne, Nigel. The Curious Cures of Old England. London: Piatkus Books Ltd., 2005.

Charles, R. H., trans. Book of Enoch. Bristol: Longdun Press, 1997.

Chetwynd, Tom. Dictionary of Sacred Myth. London: Aquarian Press, 1986.

Christian, Paul. The History and Practice of Magic. Secaucus, NJ: Citadel Press, 1972.

Conger, Jean. The Velvet Paw—A History of Cats in Life, Mythology and Art. New York: Obolensky Inc., 1963.

Cooper, J. C., ed. Brewer's Myth and Legend. London: Cassell Publishers Ltd., 1992.

Cotterell, Arthur. The Encyclopedia of Mythology. London: Anness Publishing, 1996.

Cox, Marian. An Introduction to Folklore. London: Singing Tree Press, 1904.

Cramer, F. H. Astrology in Roman Law and Politics. London: Ares Publishers, 1954.

Cressy, David. Birth, Marriage and Death: Ritual Religion and Life Cycle in Tudor and Stuart England. Oxford: Oxford University Press, 1997.

Christie-Murray, David. A History of Heresy. Oxford: Oxford University Press, 1976.

De Buck, A. and Gardiner, A., eds. 'The Egyptian Coffin Texts', Oriental Institute Publications 34 (1935).

Dickens, Charles. Complete Works. Centennial Edition. Geneva: Heron Books, 1967.

Doane, T. Bible Myths and Their Parallels in Other Religions. New York: Somerby Publishers, 1882.

Dreyer, J. L. A History of the Planetary Systems from Thales to Kepler. New York: Cosimo, 2007.

Eason, Cassandra. Ancient Wisdom. London: Robinson Publishing, 1997.

Eliade, Mircea. Images and Symbols: Studies in Religious Symbolism. New Jersey: Princeton University Press, 1991.

Elkin A. P. The Australian Aborigines and How to Understand Them. Sydney: Angus and Robertson, 1974.

————Aboriginal Men of High Degree — Initiation and Sorcery in the World's Oldest Tradition. Vermont: Inner Traditions, 1977.

Ellis, Henry. Popular Antiquities: Vulgar Customs, Ceremonies and Superstitions, 2 vols. London: Knight & Co., 1841.

Elworthy, Frederick. The Evil Eye. New York: Bell Publishing Company, 1989.

Emrich, Duncan. The Folklore of Weddings and Marriage. New York: Heritage Press, 1970.

Eusebius. The History of the Church. G. A. Williamson, trans. London: Penguin Books, 1989.

Feather, Robert. The Copper Scroll Decoded. London: Harper Collins, 2000.

Frazer, James. The Golden Bough. New Jersey: Random House, 1981.

Friend, Hilderic. Flowers and Flower Lore. London: Swan Publishers, 1892.

Fuller, John Grant. The Day of St. Anthony's Fire. London: Hutchison Publishers, 1969.

Geddes. Guide to the Occult and Mysticism. New Lanark: Geddes and Grosset Ltd., 1996.

Ginzberg, Louis. Legends of the Jews, 6 vols. Philadelphia: Publication Society of America, 1909.

Goldberg, P. J. Women, Work and Life Cycle in a Medieval Economy. Oxford: Clarendon Press, 1992.

Goring, Rosemary. A Dictionary of Beliefs and Religions. Hertfordshire: Wordsworth Reference, Wordsworth Editions, 1992.

Graber, G. Sagen und Märchen aus Kärnten. Graz, 1944.

Graves, Kersey. The World's Sixteen Crucified Saviours. Illinois: Adventures Unlimited Press, 2001.

Gray, John. Near Eastern Mythology. London: Hamlyn Publishing Group, 1969.

Grimm, Jacob. Teutonic Mythology, 4 vols. London: George Bell and Sons, 1883.

Haining Peter. Superstitions. London: Treasure Press, 1979.

Hall, Angus. Mysterious Cults. London: Aldus Books, 1976.

Harney, W. E. Taboo. Sydney: Australasian Publishing Company, 1943.

Herodotus. The Histories. Aubrey de Selincourt, trans. London: Penguin Books, 1972.

Holroyd, Stuart. Magic, Words and Numbers. London: Aldus Books, 1975.

———— Minds without Boundaries. London: Aldus Books, 1976.

Ions, Veronica. Egyptian Mythology. Middlesex: Hamlyn House, 1968.

Isaacs, Jennifer. Australia's Living Heritage. Sydney: Lansdowne Press, 1984.

Jahoda, Gustav. The Psychology of Superstition. London: The Penguin Press, 1969.

Johnston, Susan. Aboriginal Civilisation. Brisbane: Methuen Australia, 1981.

Jung, Carl. Man and his Symbols. London: Aldus Books, 1964.

King, Francis. The Cosmic Influence. London: Aldus Books, 1976.

Kingston, Jeremy. Healing without Medicine. London: Aldus Books, 1976.

Knowlson, Sharper. Popular Superstitions and Customs. London: Random House, 1994.

Kunz, George. The Curious Lore of Precious Stones. New York: Dover Publications, 1971.

Laing, Lloyd. Anglo-Saxon England. London: Routledge and Kegan, 1979.

Larousse. Encyclopedia of Mythology, 12th ed. New York: Hamlyn Publishing Group, 1977.

Laymon, Charles, ed. The Interpreter's One-Volume Commentary on the Bible. New York: Abingdon Press, 1971.

Lehner, Ernst. Folklore and Symbolism of Flowers, Plants and Trees. New York: Tudor Publishing Company, 1960.

Lévi-Strauss, Claude. Anthropology and Myth. Oxford: Basil Blackwell, 1987.

Lewis, James. The Astrology Encyclopedia. Detroit: Visible Ink Press, 1994.

Lorie, Peter. Superstitions. New York: Simon and Schuster, 1992.

Mackenzie, Donald. Egyptian Myth and Legend. New York: Bell Publishing Co., 1978.

Matossian, Mary. Poisons of the Past: Moulds, Epidemics and History. New York: Yale University Press, 1991.

Mead, G. R. M. Thrice Greatest Hermes, 3 vols. London: John Watkins Publishing, 1964.

Meyer, Elard. Mythologie der Germanen. Strassburg: Karl Truebner Verlag, 1903.

Meyer, Marvin W. The Ancient Mysteries: A Sourcebook. San Francisco: Harper Collins, 1987.

Miles, Clement. Christmas in Ritual and Tradition—Christian and Pagan. New York: Frederick A. Stokes Company, 1912.

Mooney, James. 'The Ghost-Dance Religion and the Sioux Outbreak of 1890'. In Annual Report of the Bureau of American Ethnology 14, 2 (1896).

Moser, Dietz-Rüdiger. Glaube im Abseits—Beiträge zur Erforschung des Aberglaubens. Darmstadt: Wissenschaftliche Buchgesellschaft, 1992.

Mountford, Charles P. Ayers Rock – Its People, Their Beliefs and Their Art. Sydney: Angus and Robertson, 1965.

——— The Dreamtime – Australian Aboriginal Myths. Adelaide: Rigby Ltd., 1966.

——— Nomads of the Australian Desert. Adelaide: Rigby Ltd., 1976.

Müller, Klaus. Soul of Africa. Cologne: Könemann Verlagsgesellschaft, 1999.

Murray, Alexander. Who's Who in Mythology. London: Studio Editions, 1988.

Murray, Grace. Ancient Rites and Ceremonies. London: Random House, 1996.

Newall, Venetia. The Encyclopedia of Witchcraft and Magic. London: Hamlyn Publishing, 1974.

Nicholson, Irene. Mexican and Central American Mythology. London: Hamlyn Publishing, 1967.

Neusner Jacob, Frerichs Ernst, Mc Flesher Paul eds., Religion, Science and Magic: In Concert and In Conflict, Oxford: Oxford University Press, 1989.

Opie, Iona and Tatem, Moira. A Dictionary of Superstitions. New York: Oxford Press, 1989.

Pachter Henry, Paracelsus: Magic into Science, New York: Henry Schuman Publishing, 1951.

Philpot, J. The Sacred Tree — The Tree in Religion and Myth. London: Macmillan & Co., 1897.

Pickering, David. Dictionary of Superstitions. London: Cassell Publishers, 1995.

Picknett, Lynn and Prince, Clive. The Templar Revelation. London: Corgi Books, 1998.

Pliny the Elder. The Natural History of Pliny, 6 vols. J. Bostock, trans. London: Henry G. Bohn, 1855.

Pliny the Elder. Natural History — A Selection. J. F. Healy, trans. London: Penguin Books, 1991.

Porteous, Alexander. Forest Folklore. London: Unwin Ltd., 1928.

Radford, Edwin. Encyclopaedia of Superstitions. New York: The Philosophical Library, 1949.

Read, Carveath. Man and his Superstitions. London: Random House, 1995.

Reed, A. W. Aboriginal Place Names, NSW, AU: Reed Books Pty Ltd, 1970.

——— An Illustrated Encyclopedia of Aboriginal Life. NSW, AU: J W Books, 1982.

——— Aboriginal Myths, Legends and Fables. NSW, AU: Heinemann, 1993.

——— Aboriginal Stories. Chatsworth, NSW, AU: Reed Books, 1994.

Reid, Howard. In Search of the Immortals. London: Headline Publishing, 1999.

Roland, Paul. Revelations: The Wisdom of the Ages. London: Carlton Books, 1995.

Scott, George Ryley. Customs of Sex and Marriage. London: Senate Publishing, 1995.

Searle, Mark and Stevenson, Kenneth. Documents of the Marriage Liturgy. Collegeville, MN: Liturgical Press, 1992.

Shakespeare, William. Complete Works. London: Rex Library Co., 1974.

Sitchin, Zecharia. The Lost Realms. New York: Avon Books, 1990.

Stanner, W. E. 'Modes of address and reference in the northwest of the northern territory', Oceania 7, 3 (1937).

Sullivan, Brenda. Africa through the Mists of Time. Johannesburg: Covos Day Books, 2001.

Tacitus. Germania. Stuttgart: Reclam, 1975.

Taplin, G. ed. The Folklore, Manners, Customs and Languages of the South Australian Aborigines. Adelaide: Government Press, 1879.

Thiselton-Dyer, Thomas. The Folklore of Plants. London: Singing Tree Press, 1889.

Thompson, Charles. The Hand of Destiny. New York: Bell Publishing Company, 1989.

Thule. Isländische Sagas. Köln: Eugen Dietrichs Verlag, 1978.

Tompkins, Peter. The Secret Life of Plants. New York: Avon Books, 1973.

Trevor-Roper, Hugh. The European Witch-Craze. London: Harper Torchbooks, 1968.

Urlin, Ethel. A Short History of Marriage, Marriage Rites, Customs and Folklore in Many Countries and All Ages. Detroit: Singing Tree Press, 1969.

Vandenberg, Phillip. The Mystery of the Oracles. New York: Macmillan Publishing, 1982.

Vermes, Geza. Scripture and Tradition in Judaism. Leiden: Penguin Books, 1973.

―――― The Dead Sea Scrolls in English. London: Penguin Books, 1990.

Verrill, Hyatt. Strange Customs, Manners and Beliefs. Great Britain: Page & Co., 1946.

Von Eschenbach, Wolfram. 'Parzival'. Wilhelm Stapel, trans. München: Müller Verlag, 1973.

Ward. Seal Cylinders of Western Asia. Washington, DC: Carnegie Institute Publication, 1910.

Waring, Philippa. The Dictionary of Omens and Superstitions. London: Treasure Press, 1978.

Watts, Alan W. Myth and Ritual in Christianity. Boston: Beacon Press, 1968.

White, Andrew Dickson. A History of the Warfare of Science with Theology in Christendom, vol. 1 New York: Appleton and Company, 1898.

White, Suzanne. The New Astrology. London: Pan Books, 1986.

Yearsley, Macleod. The Folklore of Fairy-Tale. London: Watts & Co., 1924.

INDEX

NOTES

Chapter I

1   Ezekiel 13:19.
2   Who later became George IV.
3   Venetia Newall, The Encyclopedia of Witchcraft and Magic (London: Hamlyn Publishing, 1974), 103.
4   John Cawte, Healers of Arnhem Land (Marleston South Australia: J & B Books, 1996): 61.
5   Nigel Cawthorne, The Curious Cures of Old England (London: Piatkus Books Ltd., 2005),29
6   August 1993, 30.
7   Pliny the Elder, The Natural History of Pliny, 6 Vols. translated by J. Bostock, London 1855, XXVIII v. 277
8   Opie Iona and Tatem Moira, A Dictionary of Superstitions, Oxford Press, New York 1989, p.359
9   Cawthorne Nigel, The Curious Cures of Old England, Piatkus Books Ltd., London 2005, p. 45.
10 Pliny the Elder, Natural History - A Selection, translated by J.F. Healy, Penguin Books, London 1991, Vol. XXVIII, v. 7, p. 252.
11 In the greater district of Manchester, United Kingdom.
12 Cawthorne Nigel 2005, p. 101.
13 Pliny 1991, Vol. XXVIII, v. 49, p. 256.
14 Cawthorne Nigel 2005, p. 88.
15 ibid. p. 85.
16 Derived from: 'scape' an obsolete word for 'escape' and 'goote' meaning 'goat'. This goat was conceived as embodying the spirit of Azazel, the fallen angel perpetually bound and chained in the wilderness.
17 Leviticus 16:8, 21-22.
18 Herodotus, The Histories, translated by Aubrey de Selincourt, Penguin Books, London 1972, p. 100.
19 Frazer James, The Golden Bough, Random House, New Jersey 1981, p. 212.
20 Müller Klaus, Soul of Africa, Könemann Verlagsgesellschaft, Cologne 1999, p. 61.
21 Cawthorne Nigel 2005, p. 36.
22 ibid. p. 37.
23 Farmers Weekly 9. Nov. 1973, Page 93.
24 Cawte John 1996, p. 89.
25 Murray Grace, Ancient Rites and Ceremonies, Random House, London 1996, p. 15.
26 Budge Wallis, The Egyptian Book of the Dead, Egyptian Text Transliteration and

Translation, Dover Publications, New York 1967, p. 198.

27   Feather Robert, The Copper Scroll Decoded, Harper Collins, London, 2000, p. 61.
28   Exodus 3:14.
29   Pliny 1991, XXVIII, v. 18, p. 253.
30   Taplin G. (editor), The Folklore, Manners, Customs and Languages of the South Australian Aborigines, Government Press, Adelaide 1879, p. 28.
31   Budge Wallis 1967, p. 198.
32   Pliny 1991, Vol.VII, v. 37, p.81.
33   Sullivan Brenda, Africa through the Mists of Time, Covos Day Books, Johannesburg 2002, p. 12.
34   Mooney James, The Ghost-Dance Religion and the Sioux Outbreak of 1890, In: Annual Report of the Bureau of American Ethnology, XIV, 2, Washington 1896, p. 721.
35   Cawte John 1996, p. 43.
36   This is clearly indicated in A Permeability of Boundaries? New approaches to the Archaeology of Art, Religion and Folklore, a paper published by Dinah Eastop in 2001.

Chapter II

1.   Pliny 1991, Vol. XXVIII, v. 19, p. 253.
2.   2 Ibid., vol. 30, v. 5–6, 269.
3.   Ibid., vol. 28, v. 13, 252.
4.   Pliny the Elder, The Natural History of Pliny, 6 vols., vol. 30, v. 22, J. Bostock, trans. (London: Henry G. Bohn, 1855).
5.   Herodotus, The Histories, Aubrey de Selincourt, trans. (London: Penguin Books, 1972), 170.
6.   Book of Proverbs 23:6.
7.   Frederick Elworthy, The Evil Eye, Bell (New York: Publishing Company, 1989), 219.
8.   Pliny the Elder, The Natural History of Pliny, 6 vols., vol. 25, v. 67, J. Bostock, trans. (London: Henry G. Bohn, 1855).
9.   Jacob Grimm, Teutonic Mythology, vol. 4 (London: George Bell and Sons, 1883), 1812.
10.   Edwin Radford, Encyclopaedia of Superstitions (New York: The Philosophical Library, 1949), 159.
11.   Edwin Radford, Encyclopaedia of Superstitions (New York: The Philosophical Library, 1949), 99.
12.   Frederick Elworthy, The Evil Eye, Bell (New York: Publishing Company, 1989), 185.
13.   Book of Ruth 4:7.
14.   Joshua 5:15.
15.   Deuteronomy 25:9.
16.   Howard Reid, In Search of the Immortals (London: Headline Publishing, 1999), 242–243.
17.   Matthew 5:13.
18.   Formally in 753 BCE by the legendary ruler Romulus.
19.   Numbers 18:19 and II Chronicles 13:5.
20.   Jacob Grimm, Teutonic Mythology, vol. 4 (London: George Bell and Sons, 1883), 1784.
21.   Iona Opie and Tatem Moira, A Dictionary of Superstitions (New York: Oxford Press, 1989),341.
22.   Jacob Grimm, Teutonic Mythology, vol. 4 (London: George Bell and Sons, 1883), 1800.
23.   Harold Bayley, The Lost Language of Symbolism (London: Bracken Books, 1996), 129, 126.
24.   Nigel Cawthorne, The Curious Cures of Old England (London: Piatkus Books Ltd., 2005),98.

25. Brenda Sullivan, Africa through the Mists of Time (Johannesburg: Covos Day Books, 2002), 68.
26. Iona Opie and Tatem Moira, A Dictionary of Superstitions (New York: Oxford Press, 1989), 79.
27. William Shakespeare, Henry IV, Part II, Act I, Scene I, in Complete Works (London: Rex Library Co., 1974).

Chapter III

1. Exodus 7:11.
2. Daniel 2:2.
3. Micah 3:5.
4. 4 Deuteronomy 18:10-12.
5. Exodus 22:18.
6. I Samuel 28:7.
7. ibid.
8. II Kings 9:22.
9. Nahum 3:4.
10. Galatians 3:1
11. Acts of the Apostles 8: 9-11; Galatians 5:20.
12. Circa ninth to fifteenth century.
13. David Christie-Murray, A History of Heresy (Oxford: Oxford University Press, 1976), 109.
14. Wolf's bane is also known as aconite.
15. Linda Caporael. 'Ergotism: The Satan Loosed in Salem?' In: Science, Vol 192, April 1976.
16. Matossian, Mary. Poisons of the Past: Moulds, Epidemics and History. New York: Yale University Press, 1991.
17. Venetia Newall, The Encyclopedia of Witchcraft and Magic (London: Hamlyn Publishing, 1974),174.
18. Venetia Newall, The Encyclopedia of Witchcraft and Magic (London: Hamlyn Publishing, 1974),179.
19. Elisabeth Abbot, A History of Celibacy (New York: Scribner, 2000), 54.
20. Ibid.,49.
21. Ibid., 66.
22. Philip Ball. The Devil's Doctor – Paracelsus and the World of Renaissance, Magic and Science, Farrar, Straus and Giroux, New York 2006, 312.
23. William Shakespeare, Macbeth, Act IV, Scene I, in Complete Works (London: Rex Library Co., 1974).
24. Venetia Newall, The Encyclopedia of Witchcraft and Magic (London: Hamlyn Publishing, 1974), 47.
25. Ibid., 46.
26. 8William Shakespeare, Merry Wives of Windsor, Act III, Scene II, in Complete Works (London: Rex Library Co., 1974).
27. Matthew 25:32–41.
28. Psalm 132:17 and Jeremiah 48:25.

Chapter IV

1. Herodotus, The Histories, Aubrey de Selincourt, trans. (London: Penguin Books, 1972), 114.
2. Walter Burkert, Creation of the Sacred (London: Harvard University Press, 1999), 159.
3. Howard Reid, In Search of the Immortals (London: Headline Publishing, 1999), 90.
4. A reverence for cauldrons and chalices seems to be universal. Cauldrons and chalices, as holders of liquids in a confined space, represented miniature ponds and wells. Used to transfer nourishment in the form of food and drink, as well as for ritual practices, the powers of these containers could be heightened by fashioning them from precious metals.
5. Howard Reid, In Search of the Immortals (London: Headline Publishing, 1999), 90.
6. Phillip Vandenberg, The Mystery of the Oracles (New York: Macmillan Publishing, 1982), 226.
7. The most famous of the numerous oracles throughout the ancient world were the Oracle of Apollo at Delphi, the Oracle of Zeus in Dodona, the Oracle of Amun at the Oasis of Siwah in Egypt (consulted by Alexander the Great), the Oracle of Jupiter in Crete, the Oracle of Minerva in Mycenea, the Oracle of Venus at Paphos in Cyprus, the Oracle of Aesculapius at Epidaurus, and the Oracles of Claros and Didyma in modern-day Turkey.
8. Phillip Vandenberg, The Mystery of the Oracles (New York: Macmillan Publishing, 1982), 134.
9. Tacitus, Annals, 2.54.
10. Brenda Sullivan, Africa through the Mists of Time (Johannesburg: Covos Day Books, 2002), 198.
11. Pliny the Elder, Natural History — A Selection, vol. 36, v. 193, J. F. Healy, trans. (London: Penguin Books, 1991), 362.
12. Dante, Paradiso, Canto XXI.
13. Book of Judges 8:21.
14. William Shakespeare, Othello, Act V, Scene II, in Complete Works (London: Rex Library Co., 1974).
15. Shakespeare alludes to this particular superstition in Richard II: Act II, Scene IV.
16. Arabic ka'bah, meaning a square house.
17. Wolfram von Eschenbach, Parzival, Wilhelm Stapel, trans. (München: Müller Verlag, 1973), 241.
18. Circa 673–735 CE.
19. Andrew Dickson, White. A History of the Warfare of Science with Theology in Christendom, vol. 1 (New York: Appleton and Company, 1898),381.
20. J. L. Dreyer, A History of the Planetary Systems from Thales to Kepler (New York: Cosimo, 2007), 12–13.
21. Phillip Vandenberg, The Mystery of the Oracles (New York: Macmillan Publishing, 1982), 223.
22. William Shakespeare, Othello, Act V, Scene II, in Complete Works (London: Rex Library Co., 1974).
23. William Shakespeare, King John, Act III, Scene III, in Complete Works (London: Rex Library Co., 1974).
24. Papyrus No. 10184.
25. Dietz-Rüdiger Moser, Glaube im Abseits—Beiträge zur Erforschung des Aberglaubens (Darmstadt: Wissenschaftliche Buchgesellschaft, 1992), 155.

Chapter V

1. In ancient times, the ancient Greeks dated everything from the Olympic Register, a traditional list of victors in the Olympic Games starting in 776 BCE. The Romans, on the other hand, originally counted time from the founding of their city in 754 BCE. Now, there remain various religiously based calendars that are different from the Gregorian calendar. Hence, diverse groups celebrate New Year on differing dates. As Eastern Orthodox Churches (Romanian and Greek Orthodox excluded) continue to use the Julian calendar, which is currently thirteen days later than the Gregorian calendar, their New Year celebrations take place on January 14. The Islamic world celebrates New Year on the first day of the first month in the Islamic calendar—calculated from July 16, 622 CE, the date of the Hegira, when Mohammed led his followers from Mecca to Medina to escape assassination. The Hindu calendar is based on the start of the Saka Era 78 CE. Hindus observe the joyful festival of Divali, ushering in the New Year on October 19, historically commemorating the coronation of Lord Rama as king of Ayodhya. The Jewish moon-based calendar is based on the belief that the universe was created in 3761 BCE. The Jewish New Year celebration called Rosh Hashanah takes place on the first and second days of Tishri, the seventh month of the Jewish year. The Buddhist year starts in 596 BCE in early December with the celebration of the enlightenment of Buddha.
2. Jeremiah 44:19.
3. The Days of the Dead.
4. Luke 2:8.
5. G. R. M. Mead, Thrice Greatest Hermes, vol. 3 (London: John Watkins Publishing, 1964), 99.
6. Harold Bayley, The Lost Language of Symbolism, vol. 1 (London: Bracken Books, 1996), 145.
7. Emperor Constantine, realising the potential value of a unifying state religion, at first flirted with the idea that the supreme god should be Sol and, therefore, had coins issued depicting this deity and had Sol declared as patron of his dynasty. However, it soon became obvious to him that the Christian Church had a structure and hierarchy that was far superior to the pagan faith, which is why he decided to promote the Christian religion for his own purposes, although he only embraced the faith on his deathbed, when he chose to be baptised. An example of how different religions coexisted during the early centuries of Christianity is a mosaic from the mausuleum of the Julii underneath St. Peter's in Rome. Jesus is depicted as Sol Invictus, driving the horses of the sun-god's chariot.
8. Marvin, Meyer, The Ancient Mysteries: A Sourcebook (Harper Collins: San Francisco, 1987), 8.
9. Myrna, in modern-day Turkey.
10. Clement Miles, Christmas in Ritual and Tradition—Christian and Pagan (New York: Frederick A. Stokes Company, 1912), 268.
11. William Shakespeare, Titus Andronicus, Act II, Scene III, in Complete Works (London: Rex Library Co., 1974).

Chapter VI

1. Joseph Campbell, The Masks of God — Primitive Mythology (New York: Penguin Books, 1987), 117.
2. Sain from old English segnian, to sign with the cross.
3. Cassandra Eason, Ancient Wisdom (London: Robinson Publishing, 1997), 192.
4. William Shakespeare, Henry VIII, Act V, Scene II, in Complete Works (London: Rex Library Co., 1974).
5. A. E. Anton, Handfasting in Scotland' Scottish Historical Review, vol. 37, no. 124 (1958): 91.
6. George Ryley Scott, Customs of Sex and Marriage (London: Senate Publishing, 1995), 68.
7. I Kings 11:1–3; II Samuel 16:15.
8. Mark Searle & Kenneth Stevenson, Documents of the Marriage Liturgy (Collegeville, MN: Liturgical Press, 1992),14.
9. A. E. Anton, 'Handfasting in Scotland,' Scottish Historical Review, vol. 37, no. 124 (1958): 99.
10. Christopher Brooke, The Medieval Idea of Marriage (Oxford: Oxford University Press, 1989), 250.
11. Geoffrey, Chaucer. The Wife of Bath. In: The Canterbury Tales, Prologue, (Penguin Classics 1975)Line 460.
12. Grace Murray, Ancient Rites and Ceremonies (London: Random House, 1996), 39.
13. In: William D'Avenant's stage play The Rivals (1664)
14. Pliny the Elder, Natural History — A Selection, vol. 33, v. 32, J. F. Healy, trans. (London: Penguin Books, 1991).
15. Genesis 38:18.
16. Edwin Radford, Encyclopaedia of Superstitions (New York: The Philosophical Library, 1949), 254.
17. Charles Dickens, David Copperfield in Complete Works, Centennial Edition, vol 2. (Geneva: Heron Books), 10.
18. John Cawte, Healers of Arnhem Land (Marleston, South Australia: J & B Books, 1996): 44.
19. Edwin Radford, Encyclopaedia of Superstitions (New York: The Philosophical Library, 1949), 43.
20. Shakespeare refers to it in Richard II, Act II, Scene I.
21. Shakespeare, Richard III, Act III, Scene IV.
22. Genesis 49:1, 33.
23. Leviticus 19:27–28; Deuteronomy 14:1.
24. Pliny the Elder, Natural History — A Selection, vol. 28, v. 22, J. F. Healy, trans. (London: Penguin Books, 1991).
25. Wallis Budge, trans., The Egyptian Book of the Dead, Egyptian Text Transliteration and Translation (New York: Dover Publications, [1836] 1967), xcii.
26. Venetia Newall, The Encyclopedia of Witchcraft and Magic (London: Hamlyn Publishing, 1974), 52.
27. Numbers 19: 11-12
28. Iona Opie and Tatem Moira, A Dictionary of Superstitions (New York: Oxford Press, 1989), 341.
29. Deuteronomy 28:26.
30. Isaiah 26:19.
31. Hilderic Friend, Flowers and Flower Lore (London: Swan Publishers, 1892), 566.

32. Pliny the Elder, Natural History — A Selection, vol. 16, v. 50, J. F. Healy, trans. (London: Penguin Books, 1991).
33. Shakespeare, Richard II, Act III, Scene II.

Chapter VII

1. Mafart B., Pelletier J., Fixot M., Post-mortem Ablation of the Heart: A Medieval Funerary Practice, In: International Journal of Osteo-Archaeology Vol. 14, 2004, pp. 67-73.
2. Hans Bächtold-Stäubli, Handwörterbuch des Deutschen Aberglaubens, vol. 3 (Berlin: de Gruyter Publishers, 1987), 1799.
3. Mafart B., Pelletier J., Fixot M., Post-mortem Ablation of the Heart: A Medieval Funerary Practice, In: International Journal of Osteo-Archaeology Vol. 14, 2004, pp. 67-73.
4. Hans Bächtold-Stäubli, Handwörterbuch des Deutschen Aberglaubens, vol. 3 (Berlin: de Gruyter Publishers, 1987), 1801.
5. Wallis Budge, trans., The Egyptian Book of the Dead, Egyptian Text Transliteration and Translation (New York: Dover Publications, [1836] 1967), lxvii.
6. Ibid., 115.
7. Ibid., 117.
8. Pliny the Elder, The Natural History of Pliny, 6 vols., vol. 28, v. 67, J. Bostock, trans. (London: Henry G. Bohn, 1855), 391.
9. Ibid., 69.
10. Numbers 14:9.
11. In modern society, the word taboo has come to mean the prohibition of something by social convention, a breach in social etiquette or custom. Originally, however, a taboo implied sacredness and supernatural character. A Polynesian word, taboo refers to a prohibition against touching, taking, or using something because of the sanctity with which it is charged. It means much more than caution, respect, or reverence and is normally used in approaching something sacred. The object or person is believed imbued with a mystic essence, which is considered infectious and dangerous. Priests and priest-chiefs in native societies, believed to have descended from the gods, were often considered taboo.
12. Job 7:1, 2.
13. Exodus 24:6–8.
14. Pliny the Elder, Natural History — A Selection, vol. 26, v. 8, J. F. Healy, trans. (London: Penguin Books, 1991), 245.
15. Hans Bächtold-Stäubli, Handwörterbuch des Deutschen Aberglaubens, vol. 1 (Berlin: de Gruyter Publishers, 1987), 1437.
16. Iona Opie and Tatem Moira, A Dictionary of Superstitions (New York: Oxford Press, 1989), 189.
17. Jacob Grimm, Teutonic Mythology, vol. 4 (London: George Bell and Sons, 1883), 1824.
18. Leviticus 7:26–27; Deuteronomy 12:16, 12:23.
19. William Shakespeare, Richard III, Act I, Scene II, in Complete Works (London: Rex Library Co., 1974), 585.
20. Edwin Radford, Encyclopaedia of Superstitions (New York: The Philosophical Library, 1949), 189.
21. Leviticus 12:2–5.
22. Jacob Grimm, Teutonic Mythology, vol. 4 (London: George Bell and Sons, 1883), 1778:35.
23. Pliny the Elder, Natural History — A Selection, vol. 28, v. 38, J. F. Healy, trans. (London: Penguin Books, 1991), 255.
24. Brenda Sullivan, Africa through the Mists of Time (Johannesburg: Covos Day Books,

2002), 136.

25. Pliny the Elder, The Natural History of Pliny, 6 vols., vol. 28, v. 88, J. Bostock, trans. (London: Henry G. Bohn, 1855).
26. Mark 7:32–34.
27. Brenda Sullivan, Africa through the Mists of Time (Johannesburg: Covos Day Books, 2002), 151.
28. James Frazer, The Golden Bough (New Jersey: Random House, 1981), 123.
29. I Samuel 10:19–21.
30. Judges 20:9–10.
31. Luke 1:8–10.
32. John 19:24.
33. Jacob Grimm, Teutonic Mythology, vol. 4 (London: George Bell and Sons, 1883), 1785.
34. Ibid., 1824.
35. Corinthians I 11:14.
36. Judges 16:19.
37. Tacitus, Germania (Reclam: Stuttgart, 1975), 45.
38. Pliny the Elder, Natural History — A Selection, vol. 8, v. 184, J. F. Healy, trans. (London: Penguin Books, 1991), 123.
39. Jeremiah 48:37, 38.
40. Job 1:20.
41. James, Frazer, The Golden Bough (New Jersey: Random House, 1981), 197.
42. John Cawte, Healers of Arnhem Land (Marleston, South Australia: J & B Books, 1996): 24.
43. Jacob Grimm, Teutonic Mythology, vol. 4 (London: George Bell and Sons, 1883), 1822.
44. Iona Opie and Tatem Moira, A Dictionary of Superstitions (New York: Oxford Press, 1989), 325.

Chapter VIII

1. William Shakespeare, Venus and Adonis in Complete Works (London: Rex Library Co., 1974), 1046.
2. William Shakespeare, Macbeth, Act II, Scene II in Complete Works (London: Rex Library Co., 1974), 828.
3. Pliny the Elder, Natural History — A Selection, vol. 10, v. 46, J. F. Healy, trans. (London: Penguin Books, 1991), 143.
4. William Shakespeare, Hamlet,, Act I, Scene II in Complete Works (London: Rex Library Co., 1974), 848.
5. Pliny the Elder, Natural History — A Selection, vol. 10, v. 49, J. F. Healy, trans. (London: Penguin Books, 1991), 144.
6. Matthew 10:16.
7. Genesis 3:1.
8. Brenda Sullivan, Africa through the Mists of Time (Johannesburg: Covos Day Books, 2002), 193.
9. Ibid., 199.
10. Numbers 21:9.
11. Hans Bächtold-Stäubli, Handwörterbuch des Deutschen Aberglaubens, vol. 7 (Berlin: de Gruyter Publishers, 1987), 1165.
12. Venetia Newall, The Encyclopedia of Witchcraft and Magic (London: Hamlyn Publishing, 1974), 48.

13. Modern Tell Basta.
14. Herodotus, The Histories, Aubrey de Selincourt, trans. (London: Penguin Books, 1972), 110.
15. Pliny the Elder, Natural History — A Selection, vol. 16, v. 5, J. F. Healy, trans. (London: Penguin Books, 1991), 206.
16. J. Philpot, The Sacred Tree—The Tree in Religion and Myth (London: Macmillan & Co., 1897), 21.
17. James Frazer, The Golden Bough (New Jersey: Random House, 1981), 61.
18. Peter Tompkins, The Secret Life of Plants (New York: Avon Books, 1973), 77.
19. Pliny the Elder, Natural History — A Selection, vol. 16, v. 7, J. F. Healy, trans. (London: Penguin Books, 1991), 207.
20. J. C. Cooper, ed. Brewer's Myth and Legend (London: Cassell Publishers Ltd., 1992), 201.

Chapter IX

1. Virgil. Eclogues VIII, 75.
2. Pliny the Elder, Natural History — A Selection, vol. 28, v. 22, 23, J. F. Healy, trans. (London: Penguin Books, 1991), 254.
3. William Shakespeare, The Merry Wives of Windsor, Act V, Scene I in Complete Works (London: Rex Library Co., 1974), 75.
4. Stuart Holroyd, Magic, Words and Numbers (London: Aldus Books, 1975), 37.
5. Revelation 3:1, 4:5, 5:6.
6. Genesis 41:29, 41:30, Leviticus 25:8, Ezekiel 39:9
7. A Germanic deity identified with Mars.
8. Genesis 21:28.
9. Exodus 29:35.
10. Ibid., 29:37.
11. Ezekiel 43:25.
12. Numbers 19:11.
13. Exodus 7:25.
14. Jacob Grimm, Teutonic Mythology, vol. 4 (London: George Bell and Sons, 1883), 1826.
15. Exodus 24:18.
16. Numbers 8:13.
17. I Kings 19: 8.
18. Genesis 7:4.
19. Ibid., 8:6.
20. Numbers 13:25.
21. Judges 13:1.
22. I Samuel 4:18.
23. I Kings 2:11.
24. Ibid., 11:42; Judges 8:28.
25. Deuteronomy 25:3.
26. Matthew 4:2.
27. Exodus 20:25.
28. I Kings 6:7.
29. Louis Ginzberg, Legends of the Jews, vol. 1 (Philadelphia: Publication Society of America, 1909), 34.
30. Ibid., 334.

31.   Exodus 20:25; I Kings 6:7.

32.   Pliny the Elder, The Natural History of Pliny, 6 vols., vol. 34, v. 201–211, J. Bostock, trans. (London: Henry G. Bohn, 1855).

33.   Ibid., v. 41–42.

34.   Genesis 44:5.

35.   I Kings 6:20–7:51.

36.   Exodus 32:19.

37.   Iona Opie and Tatem Moira, A Dictionary of Superstitions (New York: Oxford Press, 1989), 175.

38.   Ezekiel 1:26.

39.   Revelations 21:11.

40.   Ibid., 21:18–21.

41.   Louis Ginzberg, Legends of the Jews, vol. 1 (Philadelphia: Publication Society of America, 1909), 162

42.   Louis Ginzberg, Legends of the Jews, vol. 1 (Philadelphia: Publication Society of America, 1909), 208

Also from

CRUX
PUBLISHING

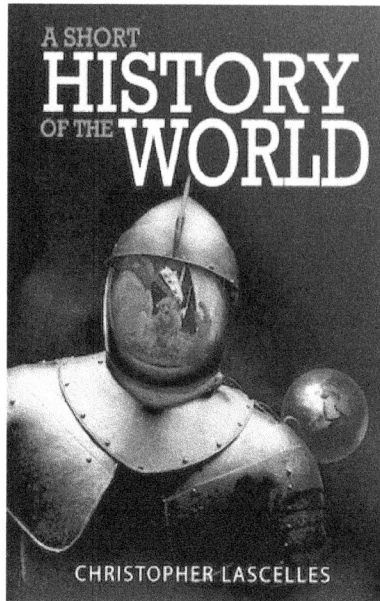

A Short History of the World
by Christopher Lascelles

'A clearly written, remarkably comprehensive guide to the greatest story on Earth - man's journey from the earliest times to the modern day. Highly recommended.'

DAN JONES, author of *The Plantagenets: The Kings Who Made England*

A Short History of the World is a short and easy-to-read history book that relates the history of our world from the Big Bang to the present day. It assumes no prior knowledge of past events and 36 maps have been especially drawn to give the reader a better understanding of where events occurred.

The book's purpose is not to come up with any ground-breaking new historical theories. Instead it aims to give a broad overview of the key events so that non-historians will feel less embarrassed about their lack of historical knowledge when discussing the past. The result is a history book that is reassuringly epic in scope but refreshingly short in length – an excellent place to start to bring your knowledge of world history up to scratch!